TYPOGRAPHY

THE BEST WORK FROM THE WEB

Jeff Carlson | Toby Malina | Glenn Fleishman

ROCKPORT PUBLISHERS

Copyright ©1999 by Rockport Publishers, Inc.

Rockport Publishers, Inc.

First published in the United States of America by:
Rockport Publishers, Inc.
33 Commercial Street
Gloucester, Massachusetts 01930-5089
Telephone: (978) 282-9590
Facsimile: (978) 283-2742

Distributed to the book trade and art trade in the
United States by:
North Light Books, an imprint of
F & W Publications
1507 Dana Avenue
Cincinnati, Ohio 45207
Telephone: (800) 289-0963

Other Distribution by:
Rockport Publishers, Inc.
Gloucester, Massachusetts 01930-5089

ISBN 1-56496-517-1

10 9 8 7 6 5 4 3 2

Designer: The Design Company
Cover Image: Disappearing, Inc., p. 57

Printed in China

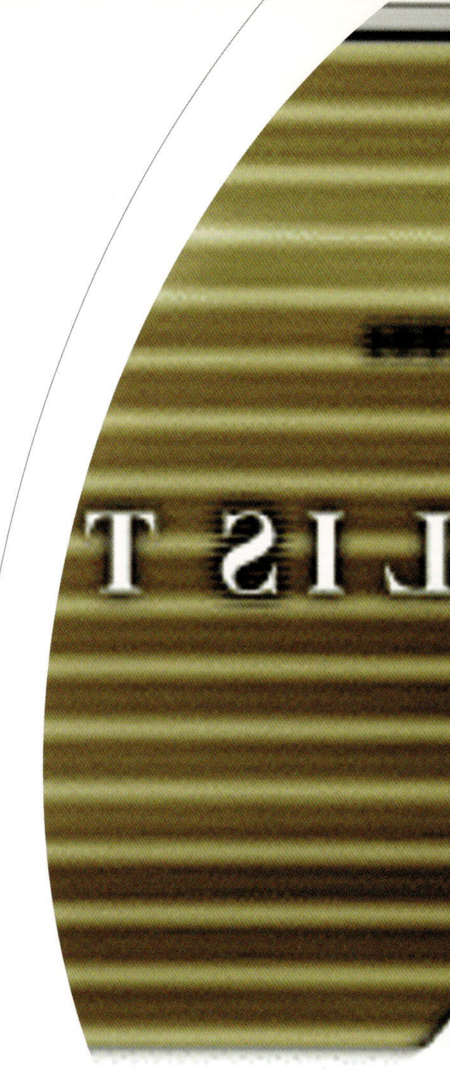

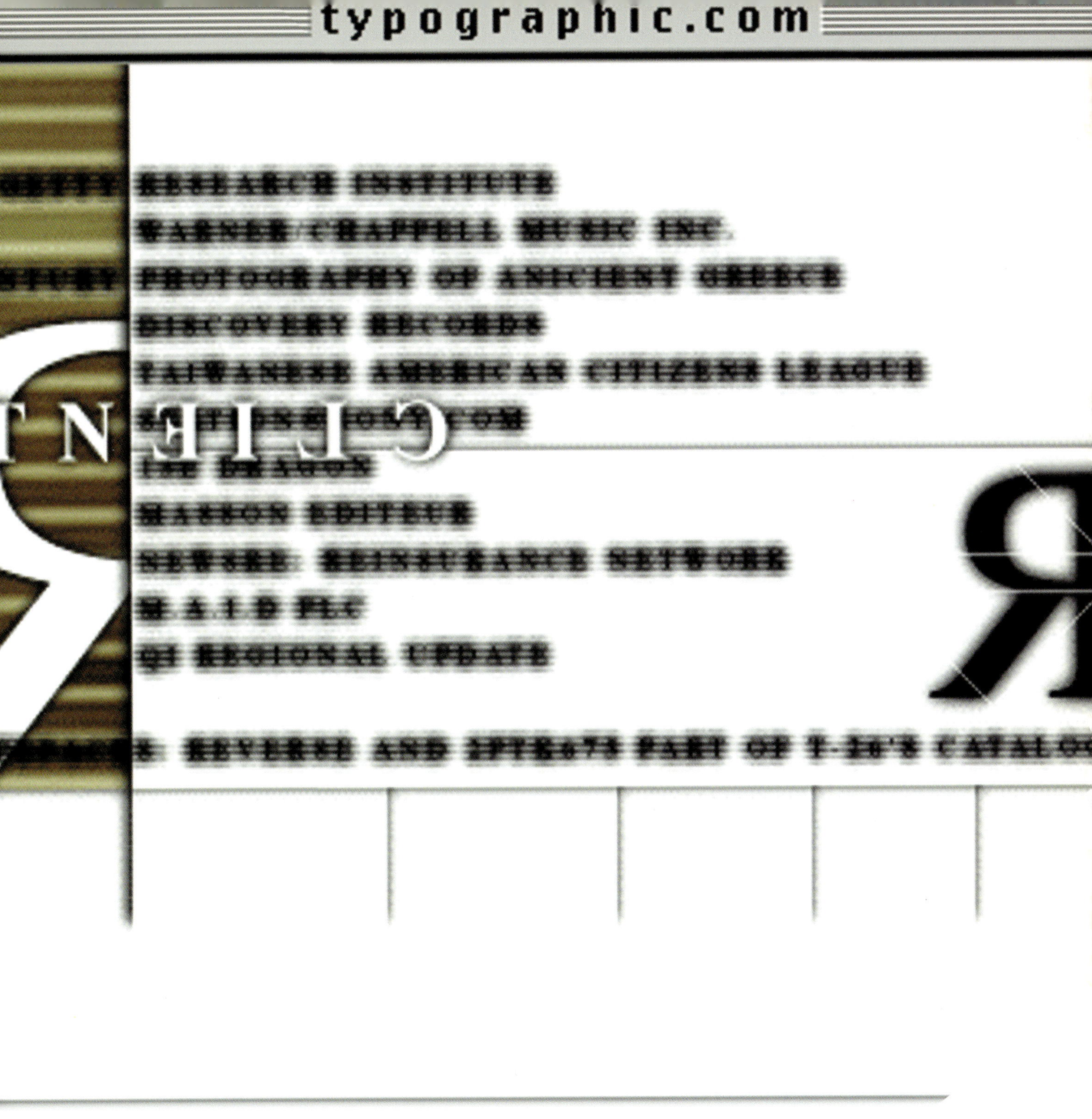
CLIENT
R

Introduction

It took a while to convince typographers that electronic publishing was a good idea. The amount of control that a designer could exercise over the spacing, kerning, and leading of type was poor, at best, during the first years of desktop publishing.

But with maturity came precision. Each new revision of QuarkXPress or Aldus-cum-Macromedia FreeHand brought with it finer controls, better options, and a greater sense that you could really make type do whatever you wanted it to.

Then along came the World Wide Web, and years of progress appeared to be thrown out the window. Fortunately, it was a temporary setback.

As with desktop publishing, it took some time to regain balance, and four years after the real introduction of the graphical World Wide Web, typography has reasserted itself in the design process.

The examples you'll find in this book are drawn from sites we found that had gone beyond simply creating images out of printed pages. Each site draws some advantage from or is designed for the Web, and takes into account the special requirements needed to render or display type in a small, scrollable, and live window.

Some sites actively fight legibility with a purpose: ironically enough, typographic.com is one of them; but others also push the aesthetic line, but not so far that we're repelled.

The competing innovations incorporated in Cascading Style Sheets (CSS), OpenType, and TrueDoc haven't yet trickled down to every designer or every user. Most sites that use type well have worked either with rendered type—type turned into an image—or have used a few standard font adjustments (like increasing or decreasing size with the <FONT SIZE=X> tag) to achieve more variety.

There's a lot of ingenuity in these pages from designers who have had to struggle to meet their own standards for typography in a limiting medium. However, the future promises to offer as much flexibility as desktop publishing now affords.

“ There’s a lot
of ingenuity in
these pages from
designers who
have had to
struggle to
meet their own
standards for
typography in
a limiting medium.
However, the future
promises to offer as
much flexibility as
desktop publishing
now affords. ”

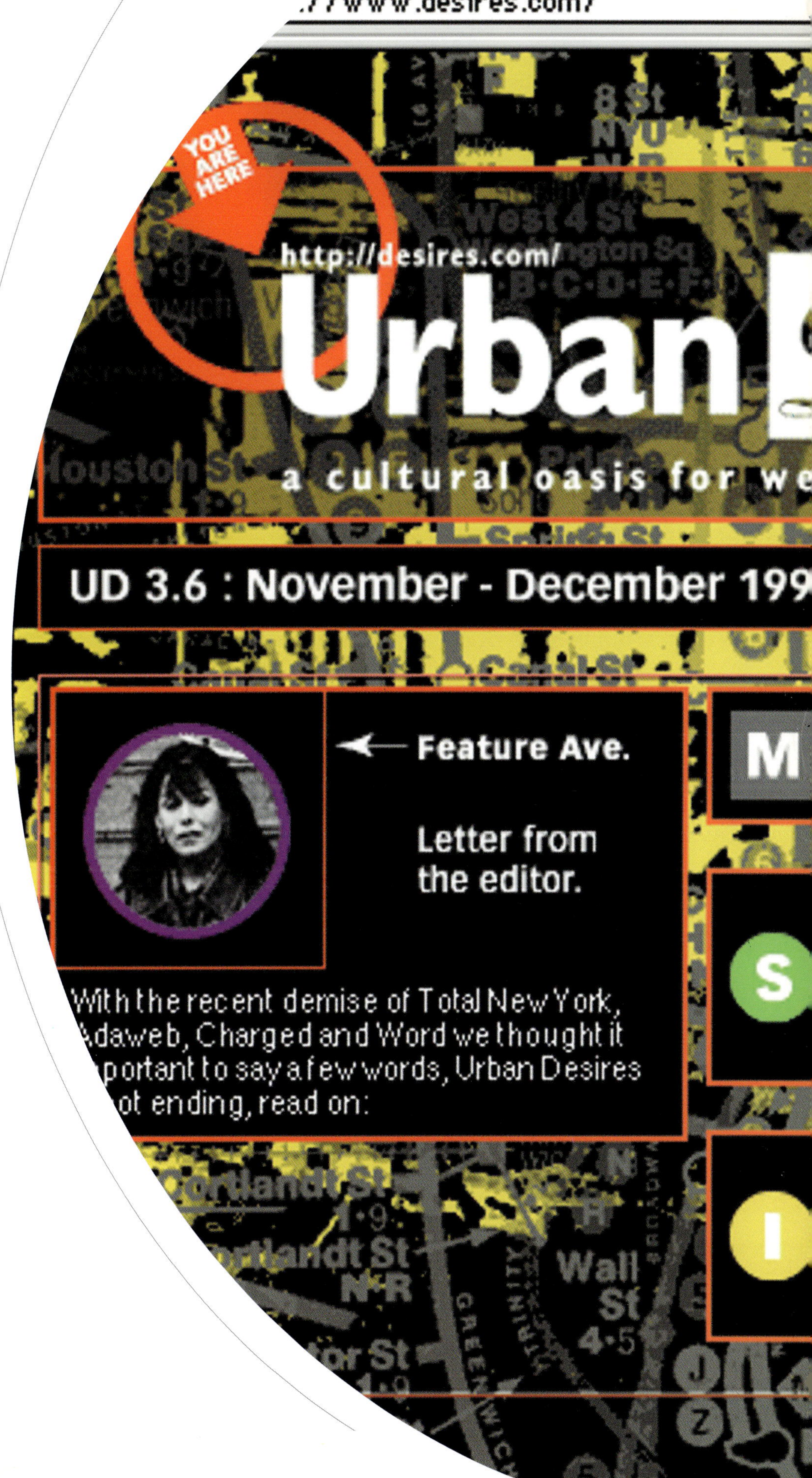

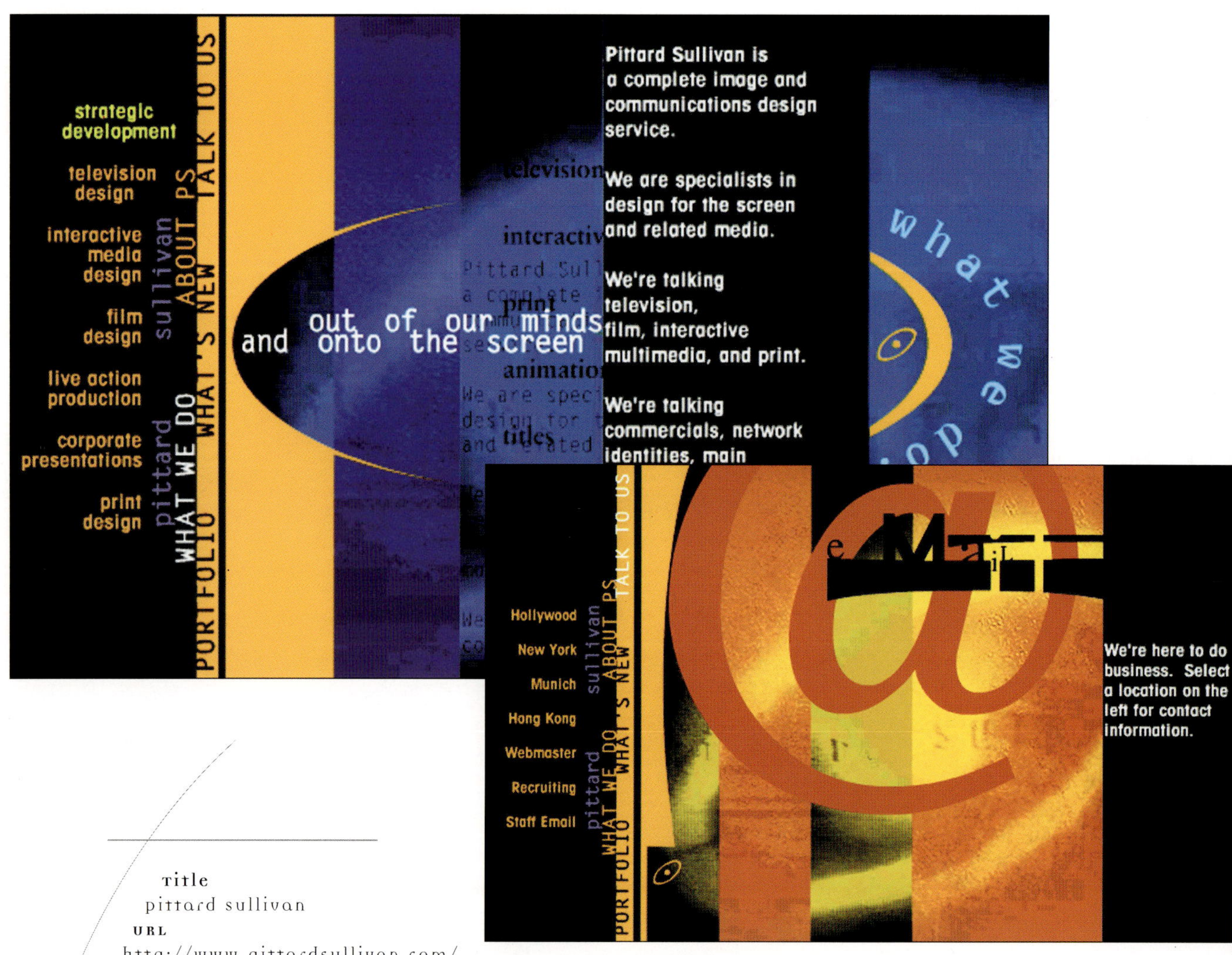

Title
pittard sullivan
URL
http://www.pittardsullivan.com/
Design Firm
pittard sullivan
Designers
Aaron King, Soo Chyun, Ron Romero
Programmers
Bryan Keeling, Marvin Price

It's impossible to ignore the typography on these pages. Using primarily sans-serif fonts, text is the basis for the site's navigation and graphic elements, which are made interactive with the use of JavaScript rollovers and Shockwave Flash technology.

The gothic font chosen for Goblin's name isn't unexpected, but creating the appearance of being cast in metal makes the title of this page decidedly modern. In the navigation bar, raised metallic-looking letters seem to be set behind rounded glass, giving the site a professional feel without resorting to Photoshop filter excesses.

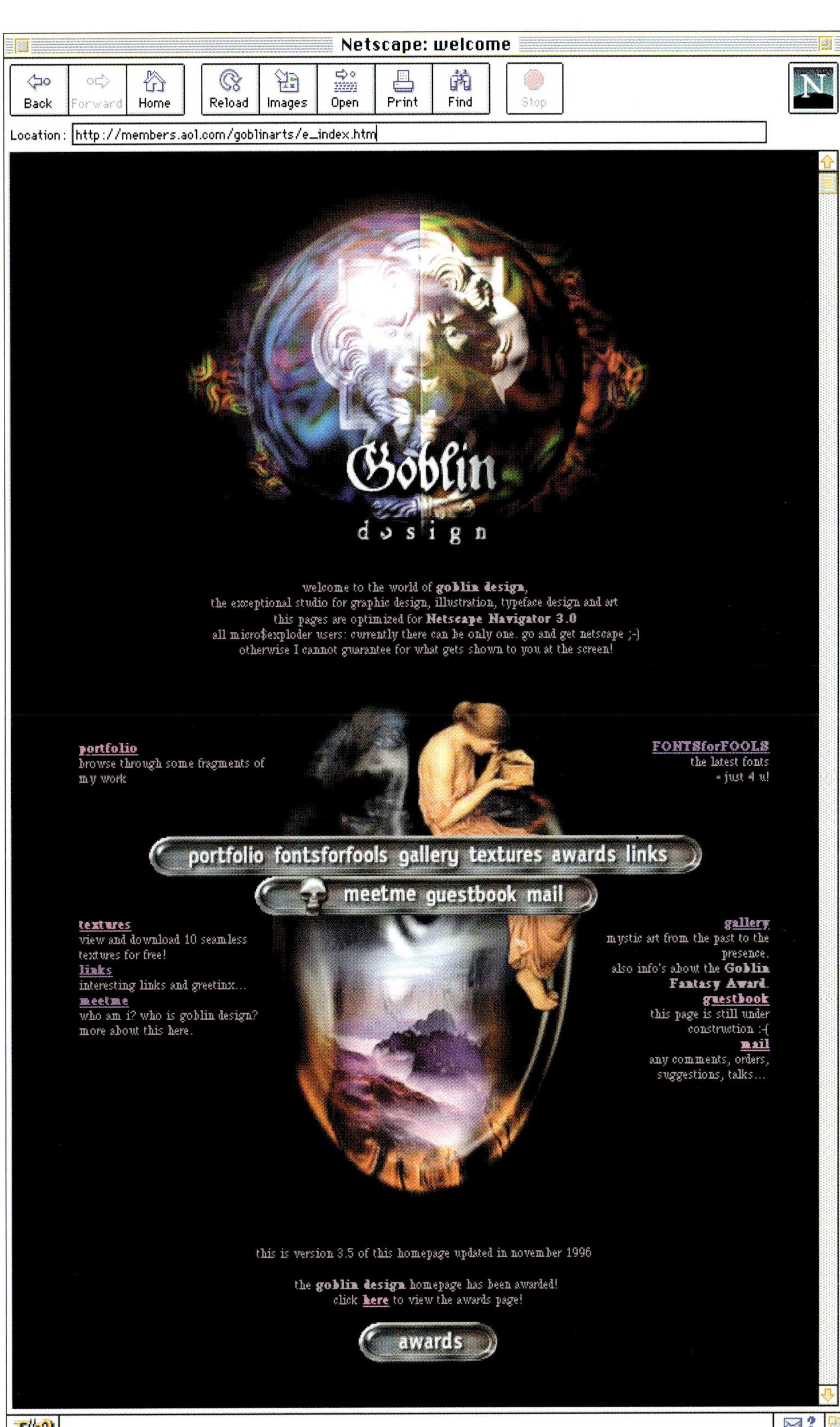

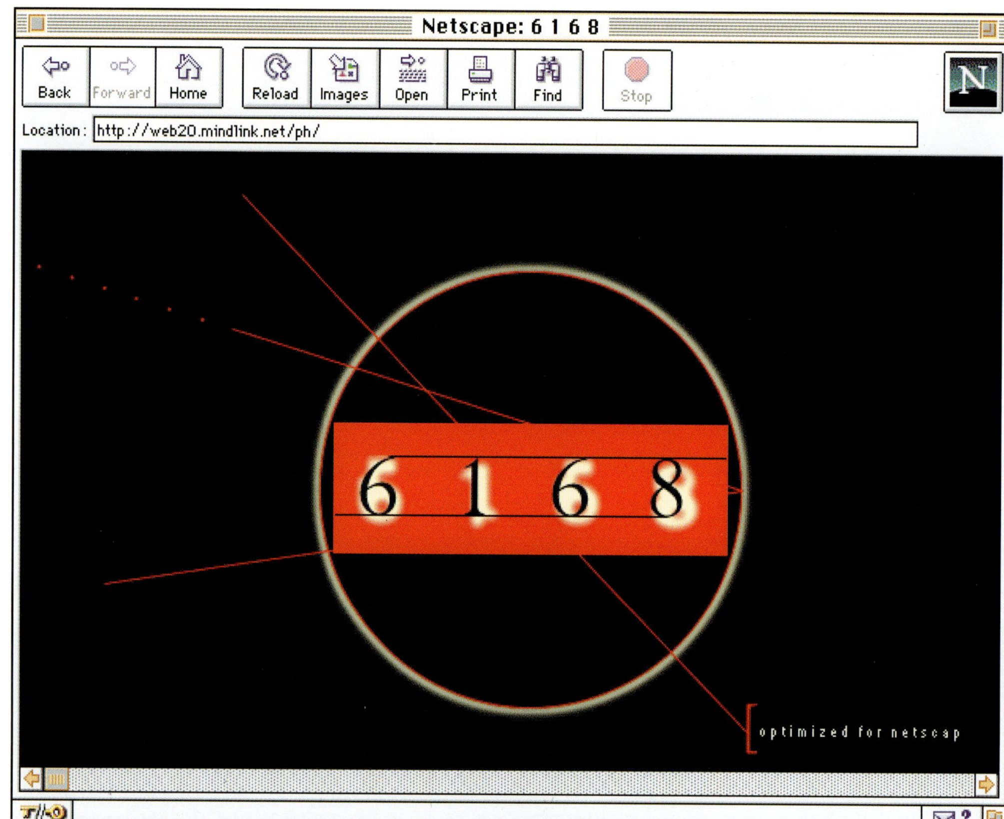

title
6168
URL
http://www.6168.org/
design firm
MCO Digital
productions
designers
peter horvath,
sharon matarazzo

Most Web typography involves creating graphics of text in a variety of fonts, so it's refreshing to find a site that focuses its design on plain old browser-generated text. Expanded letterspacing and extra leading add atmosphere to the 6168 art exhibit. The surprise here, however, is that the same plain text blocks are actually animated GIFs!

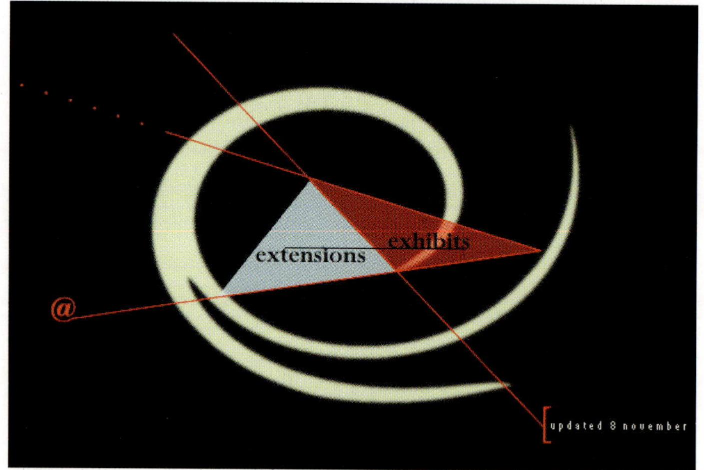

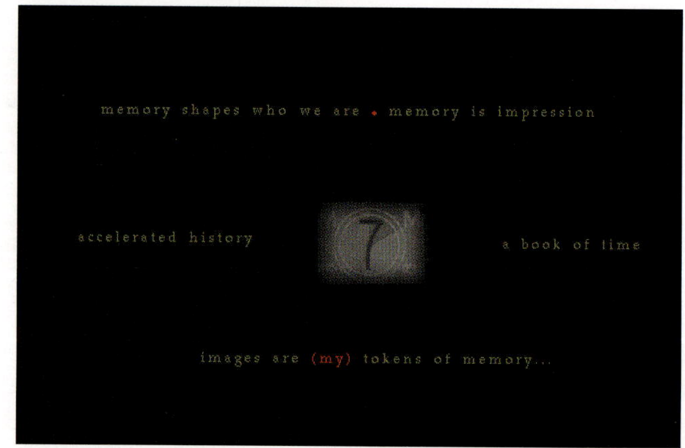

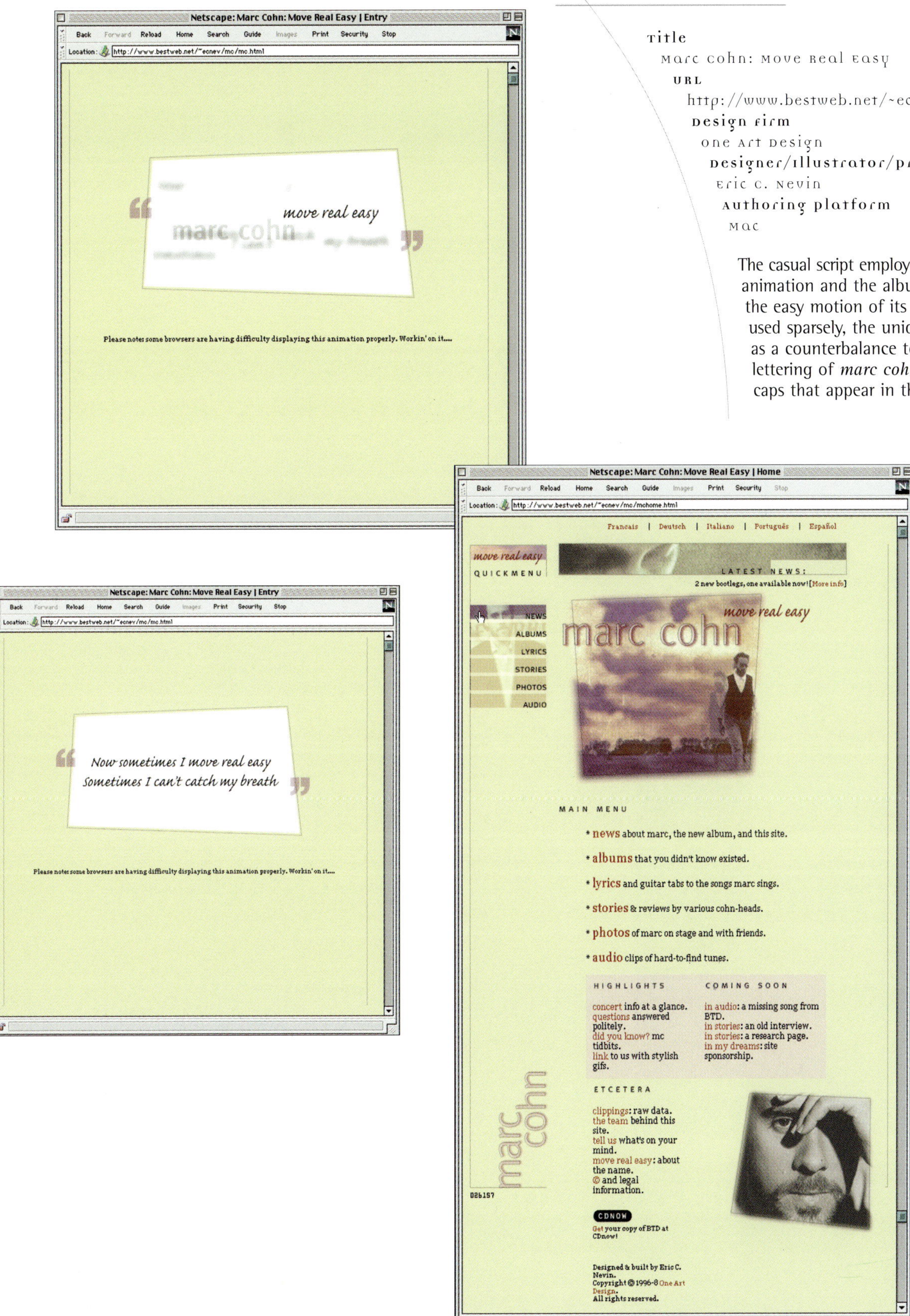

The casual script employed on the opening animation and the album title reflects the easy motion of its subject matter; used sparsely, the unique typeface works as a counterbalance to the loose, open lettering of *marc cohn* and the formal caps that appear in the navigation.

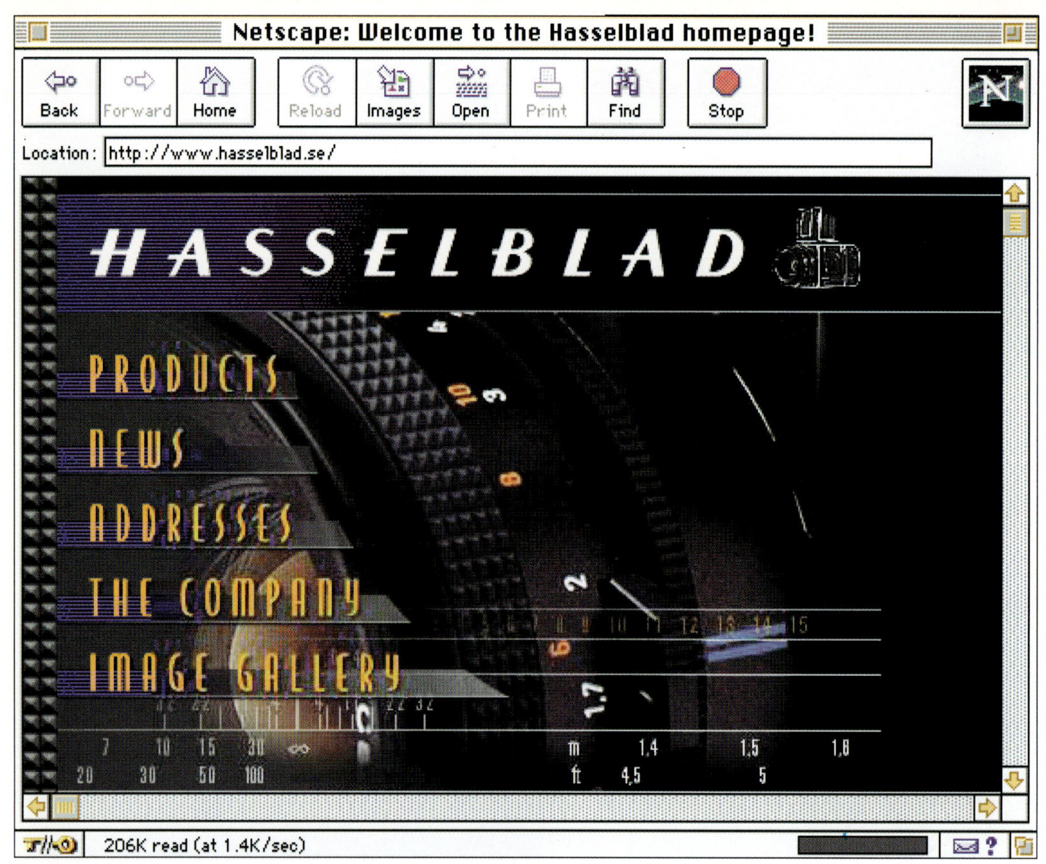

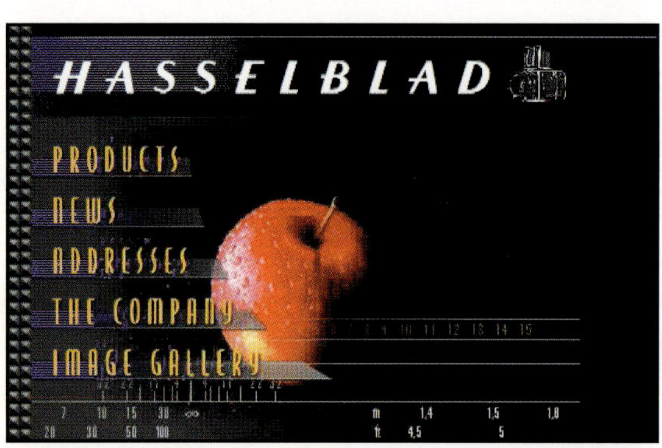

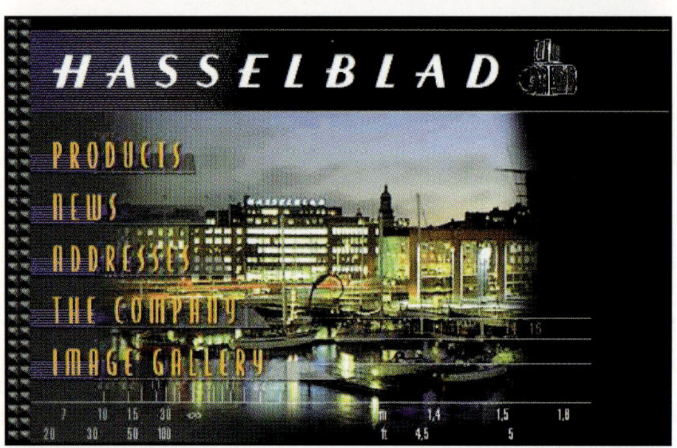

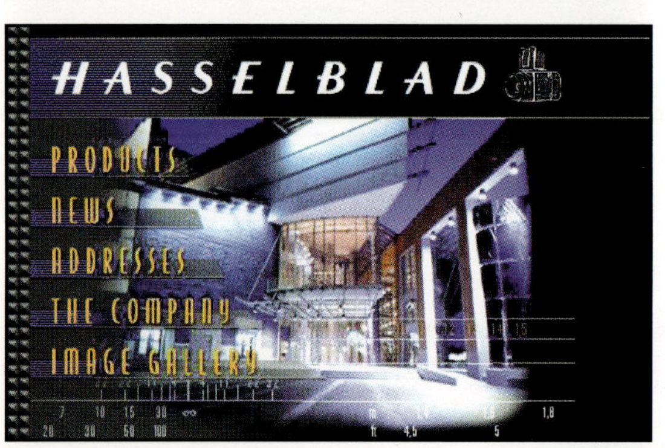

TITLE
Hasselblad
URL
http://www.hasselblad.se/
DESIGN FIRM
Adera Digital Media AB
DESIGNERS
Jaanus Heeringson, Ola Carlberg
ILLUSTRATORS
Jaanus Heeringson, Laszlo Nagy
PHOTOGRAPHERS
Jens Karlsson, Victor Hasselblad AB
PROGRAMMERS
Jaanus Heeringson, Ola Carlbert,
Thomas Friberg

Beautiful photos are required for Hasselblad, a leading manufacturer of photographic equipment, which presents the challenge of where to place navigational text. Rather than relegate the text to the side, the designers used a bold, narrow typeface that stands out from the images underneath.

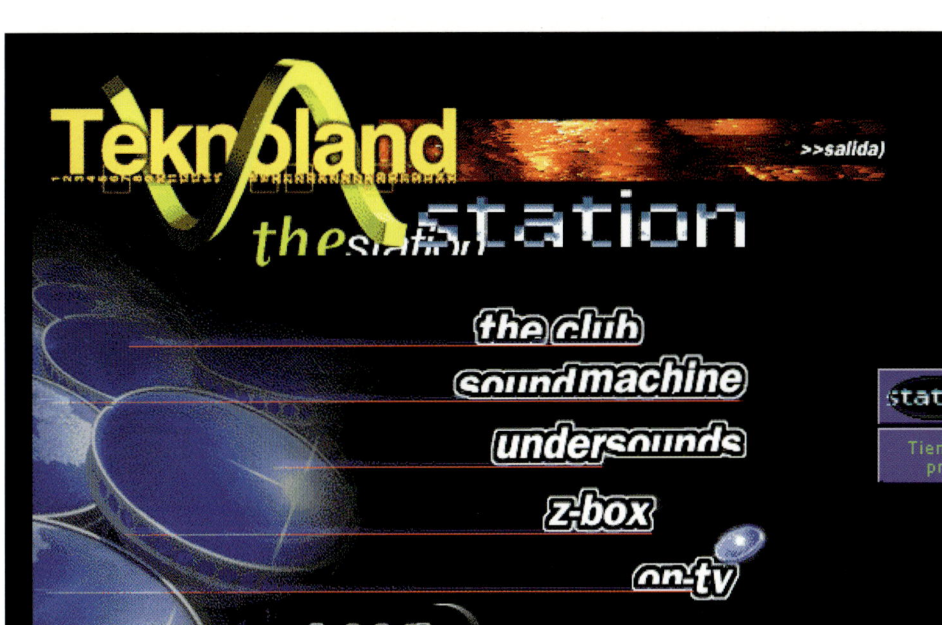

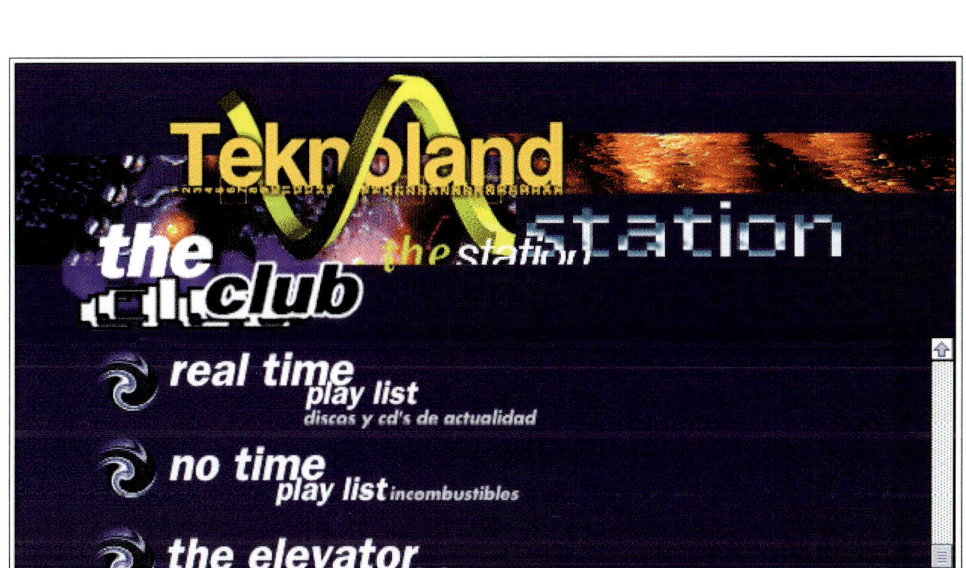

TITLE
teknoland
URL
http://www.teknoland.
es/arte/fura/
DESIGN FIRM
teknoland
ART DIRECTOR
david l. cantolla
DESIGNER
joe luis garcia
PROGRAMMERS
colman lopez, jesus suarez
AUTHORING
nestor matas, michael mangicotti
AUTHORING PLATFORM
mac, pc

To emphasize the eclectic nature of La Fura dels Baus, an artistic performance company, the Teknoland designers have taken standard sans-serif type and assembled it at various sizes without regard for baselines. After dirtying-up the letters a bit, the resulting text is simultaneously descriptive and contextually expressive.

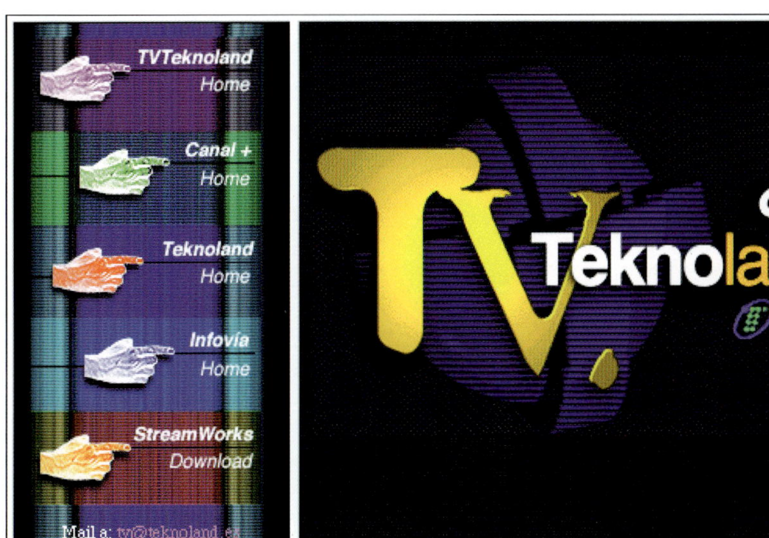

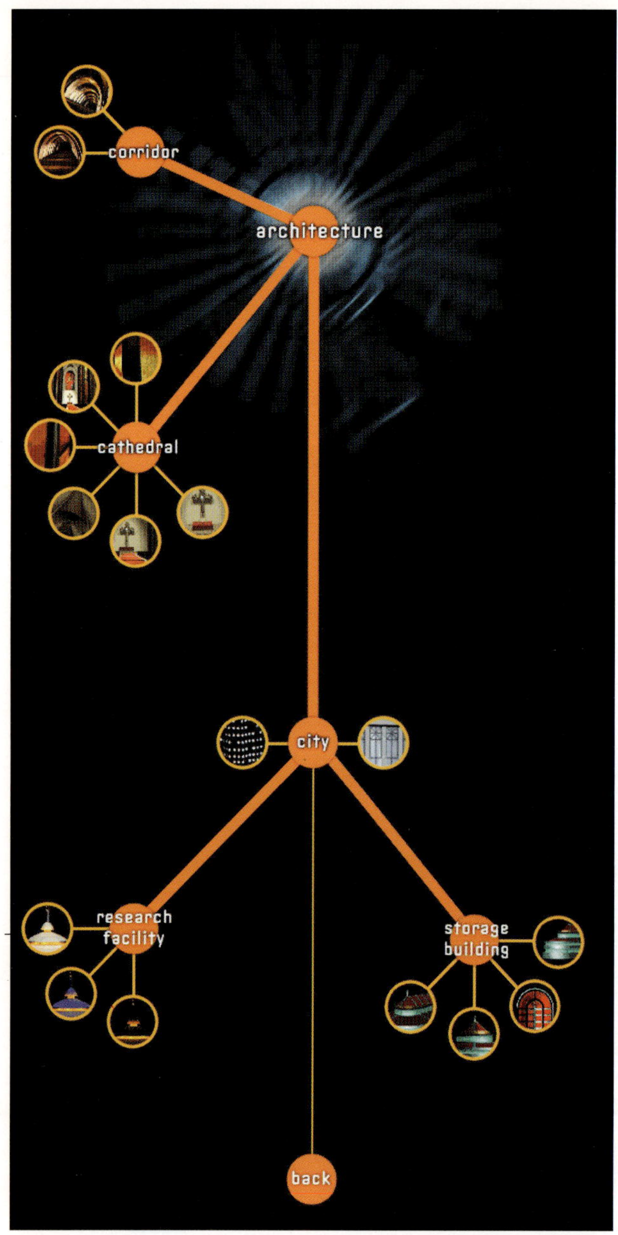

TITLE
Kjetil Vatne Graphics + Design

URL
http://www.prodat.no/personer/kjetil_vatne/

DESIGN FIRM
Kjetil Vatne Graphics + Design

DESIGNER
Kjetil Vatne

The rounded sans-serif face used here possesses enough weight to justify its use as navigational titles, while softening the edge of the pages' bold colors. Expanding the table of contents title past the point of visibility suggests that a single screen can't hold everything the viewer is about to see.

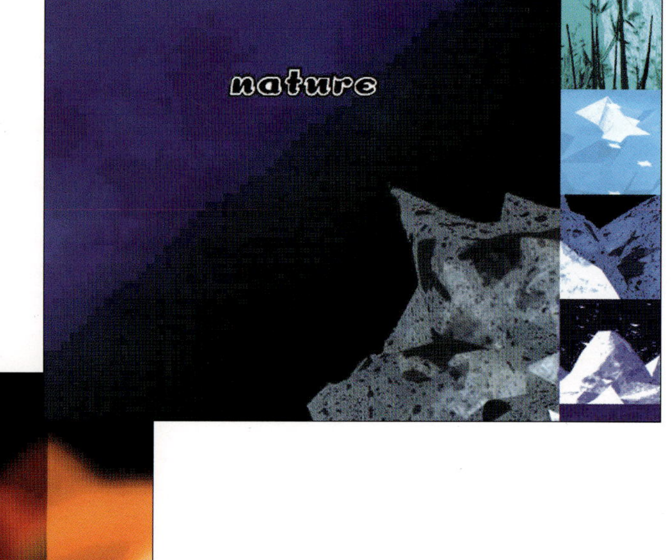

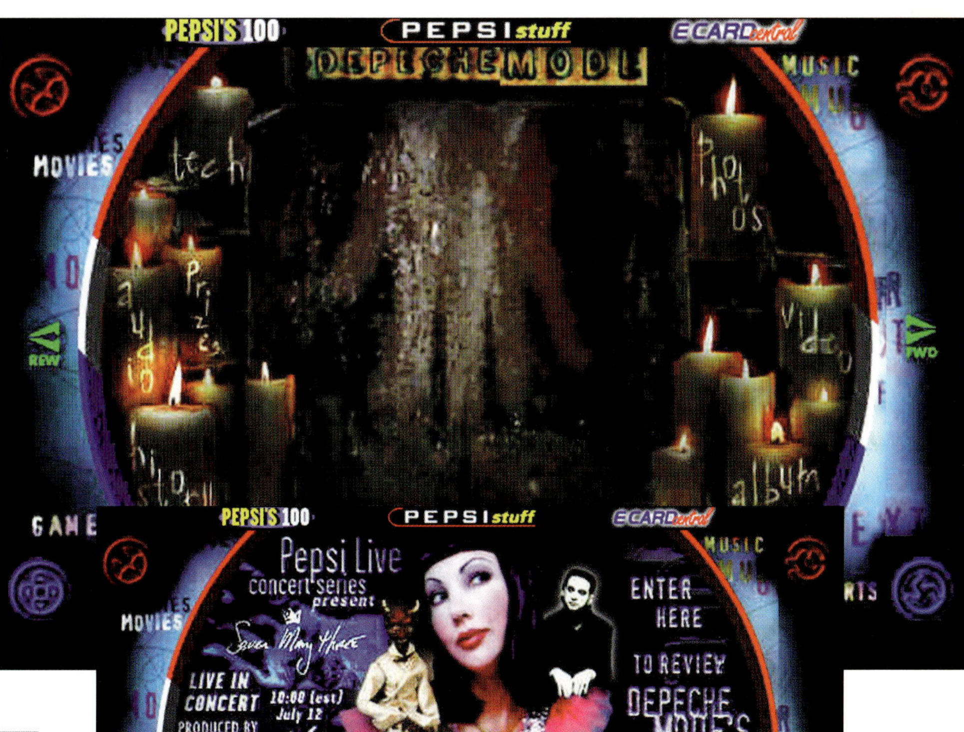

title
pepsi world
url
http://www.pepsi.com/
design firm
DDB interactive
designers
chris hess, frances ko,
mike gonzales, tricia elliot
photographer
jill green
programmers
thomas jeffry, shelley shay,
sal torneo

Pepsi wants to show the diversity of its world, and here you'll find the gamut of typographic styles and layouts. That does not necessarily mean a mess of overturned alphabet soup; the carved letters in candle wax of the Depeche Mode screen proves that effective typography does not have to come from a keyboard.

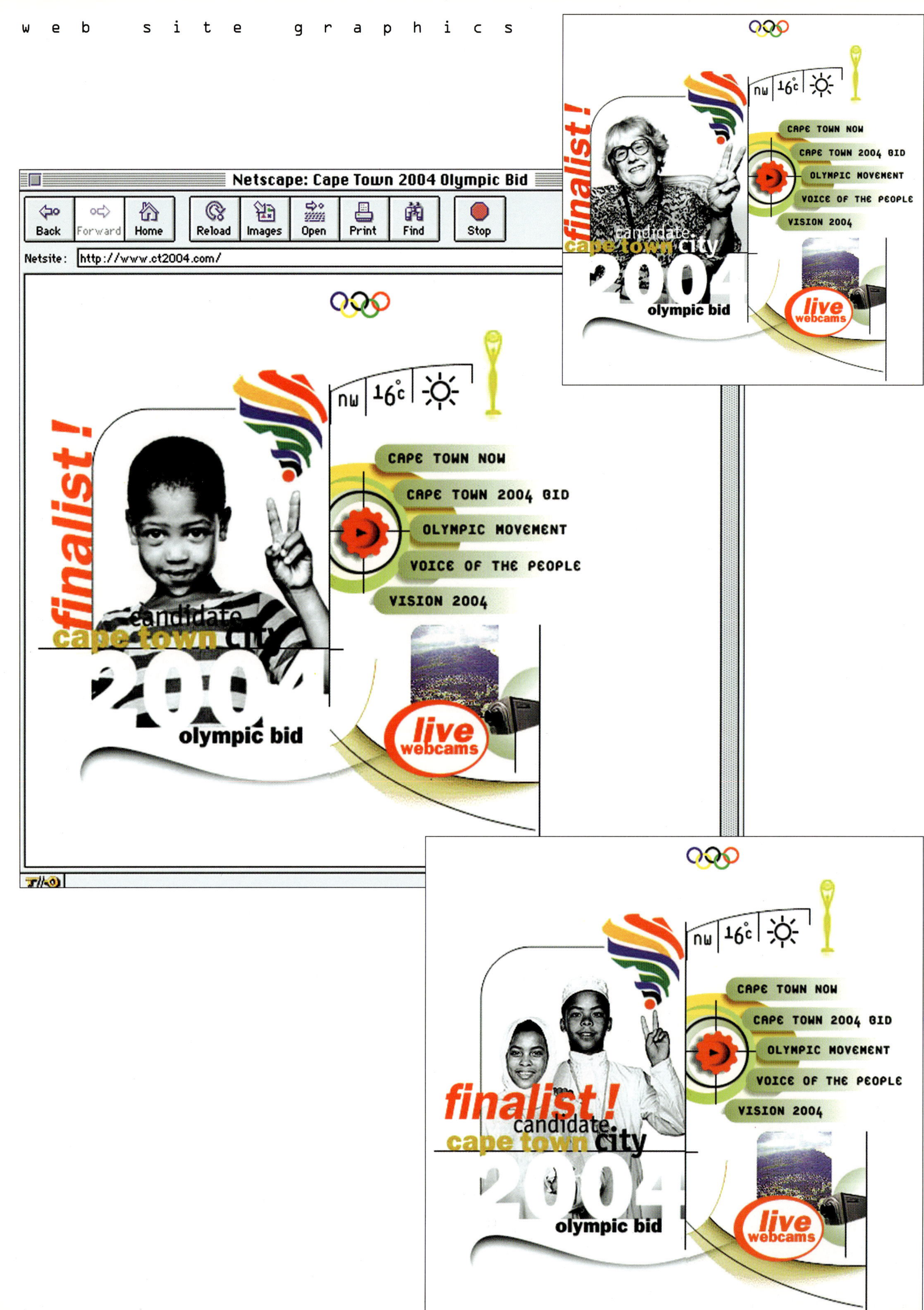
Netscape: Cape Town 2004 Olympic Bid
Back
Forward
Home
Reload
Images
Open
Print
Find
Stop
Netsite: http://www.ct2004.com/
finalist!
candidate
cape town city
2004
olympic bid
nw 16°c
CAPE TOWN NOW
CAPE TOWN 2004 BID
OLYMPIC MOVEMENT
VOICE OF THE PEOPLE
VISION 2004
live webcams

Title
cape town 2004
URL
http://www.ct2004.com/
design firm
electric ocean
designer/illustrator
nicholas wittenberg
programmer
stephen garratt

The typefaces used here are not unusual, but the designer's placement of the text is notable. If the copy were run into one column, readers may lose interest. However, breaking up the text in alternating blocks that straddle the vertical center of the page gives the text enough breathing room to be read leisurely.

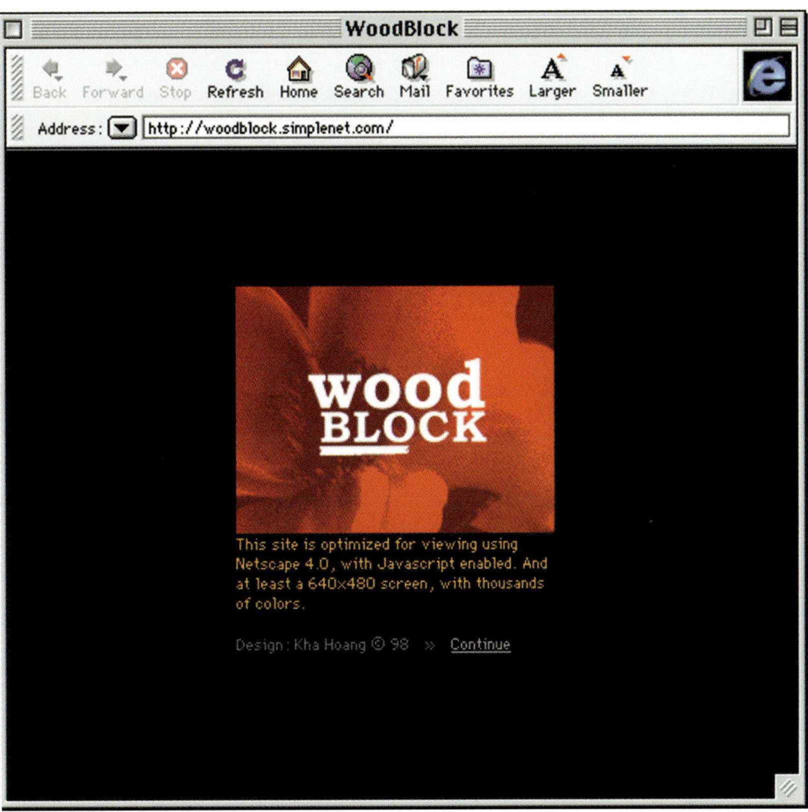

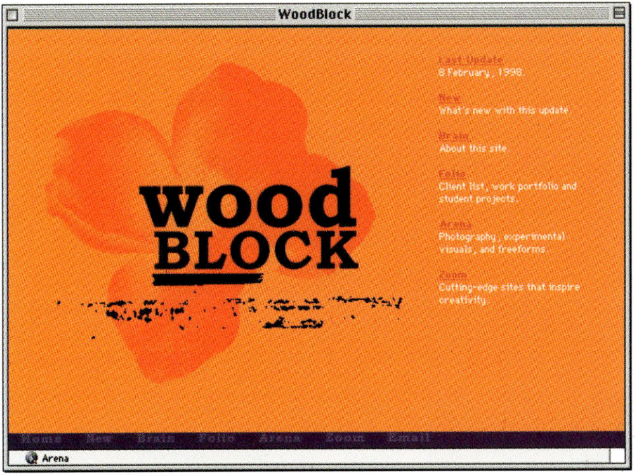

Title
woodblock
URL
http://woodblock.simplenet.com/
designer/illustrator/programmer
kha hoang
authoring platform
mac

Woodblock is a great example of minimalism in the use of type. Virtually all of the type on the site is the same size, using only boldface to differentiate headings. The zoom page makes great use of a custom shadow outline square coupled with the list format that uses a square as a bullet.

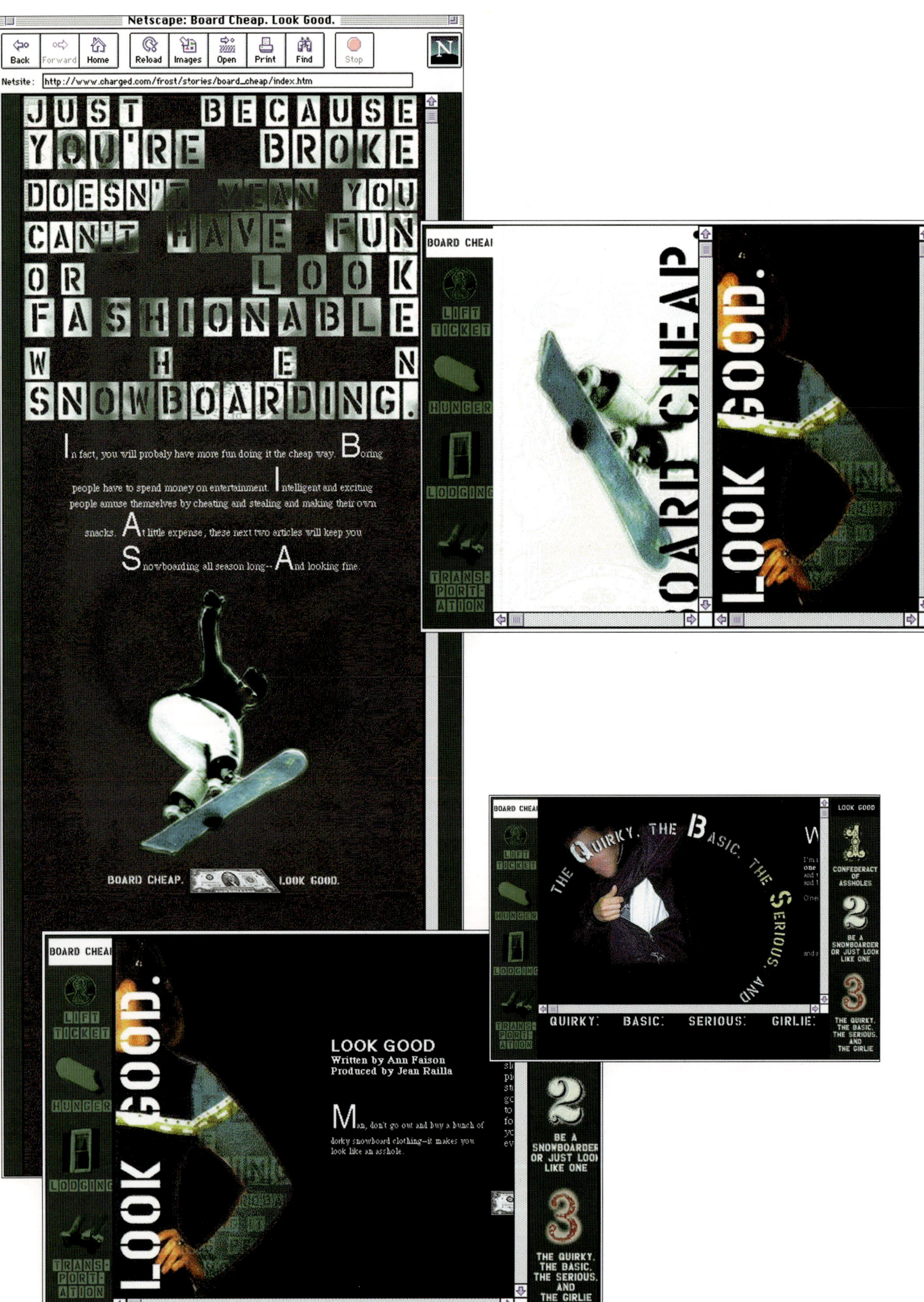

Netscape: Board Cheap. Look Good.
Back Forward Home Reload Images Open Print Find Stop
Netsite: http://www.charged.com/frost/stories/board_cheap/index.htm
JUST BECAUSE YOU'RE BROKE DOESN'T MEAN YOU CAN'T HAVE FUN OR LOOK FASHIONABLE WHEN SNOWBOARDING.
In fact, you will probaly have more fun doing it the cheap way. Boring people have to spend money on entertainment. Intelligent and exciting people amuse themselves by cheating and stealing and making their own snacks. At little expense, these next two articles will keep you Snowboarding all season long-- And looking fine.
BOARD CHEAP. LOOK GOOD.
BOARD CHEAP
LIFT TICKET
HUNGER
LODGING
TRANS-PORT-ATION
BOARD CHEAP.
LOOK GOOD.
LOOK GOOD
CONFEDERACY OF ASSHOLES
BE A SNOWBOARDER OR JUST LOOK LIKE ONE
THE QUIRKY, THE BASIC, THE SERIOUS, AND THE GIRLIE
LOOK GOOD
Written by Ann Faison
Produced by Jean Railla
Man, don't go out and buy a bunch of dorky snowboard clothing—it makes you look like an asshole.
THE QUIRKY. THE BASIC. THE SERIOUS. AND
QUIRKY. BASIC. SERIOUS. GIRLIE.
CONFEDERACY OF ASSHOLES
BE A SNOWBOARDER OR JUST LOOK LIKE ONE
THE QUIRKY, THE BASIC, THE SERIOUS, AND THE GIRLIE

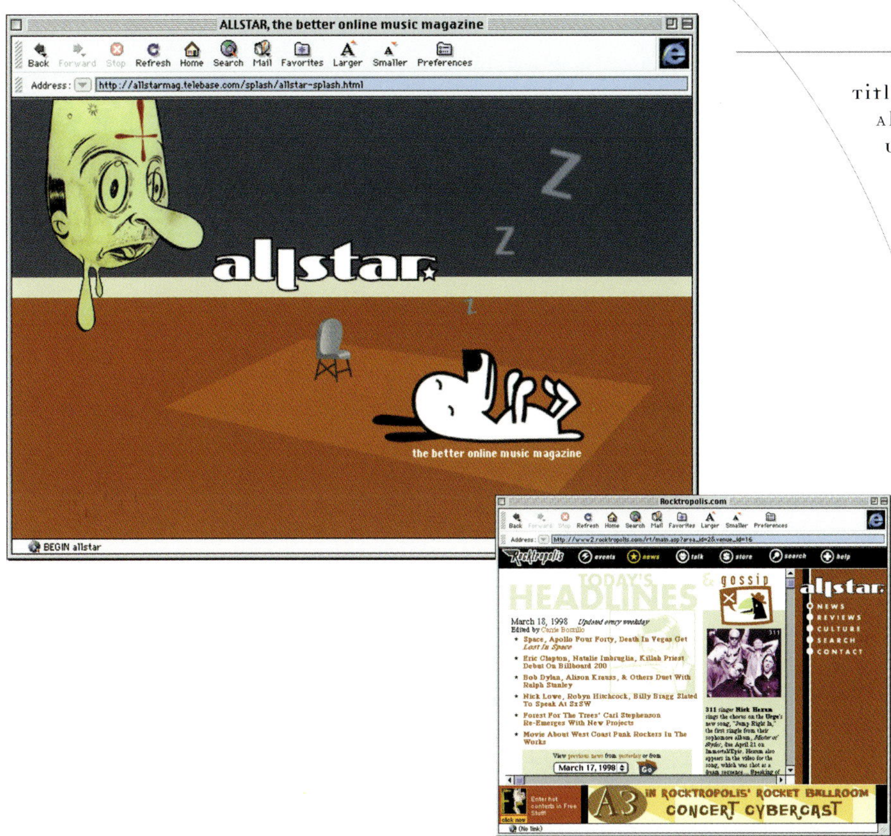

TITLE
  Allstar Magazine
URL
  http://www.allstarmag.com/
DESIGN FIRM
  N2K Entertainment
DESIGNERS
  Robert Lord, Trevor Gilchrist,
  Michelle Comas, Victor Bornia
ILLUSTRATORS
  Adriane Tomine, J. Otto Seybold
PROGRAMMERS
  Robert Lord, Victor Bornia
AUTHORING PLATFORM
  Mac, PC

The logo for the site picks up on the retro theme, giving the site a 1950s feel. The main navigation bar (for Rocktropolis, the site under which Allstar lives) uses a sans-serif italic face that has the same weight as the circles surrounding the icons for each area on the site.

TITLE
  Board Cheap/Look Good
URL
  http://www.charged.com/frost/stories/
  board_cheap/index.html
DESIGN FIRM
  Entropy8 Digital Arts
DESIGNER
  Auriea Harvey

The appeal of this page is clearly focused toward the snowboard enthusiast with little or no income, which makes the stencil-pattern typeface an attractive draw. Custom-coloring the letters takes an otherwise standard font variation (especially with its perfectly aligned baselines) and gives it a bit of rebel-in-the-snow character.

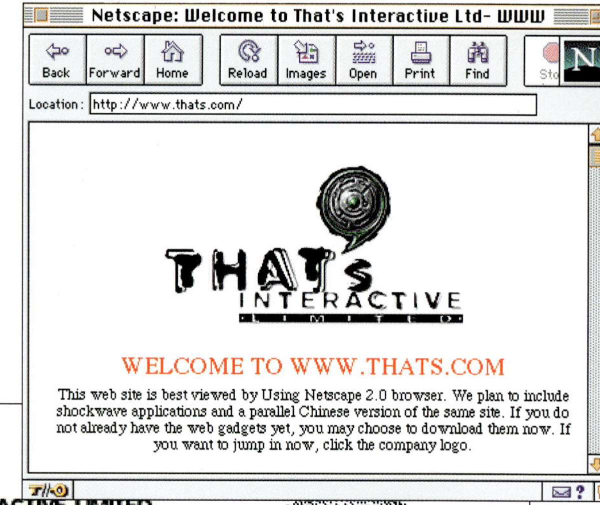

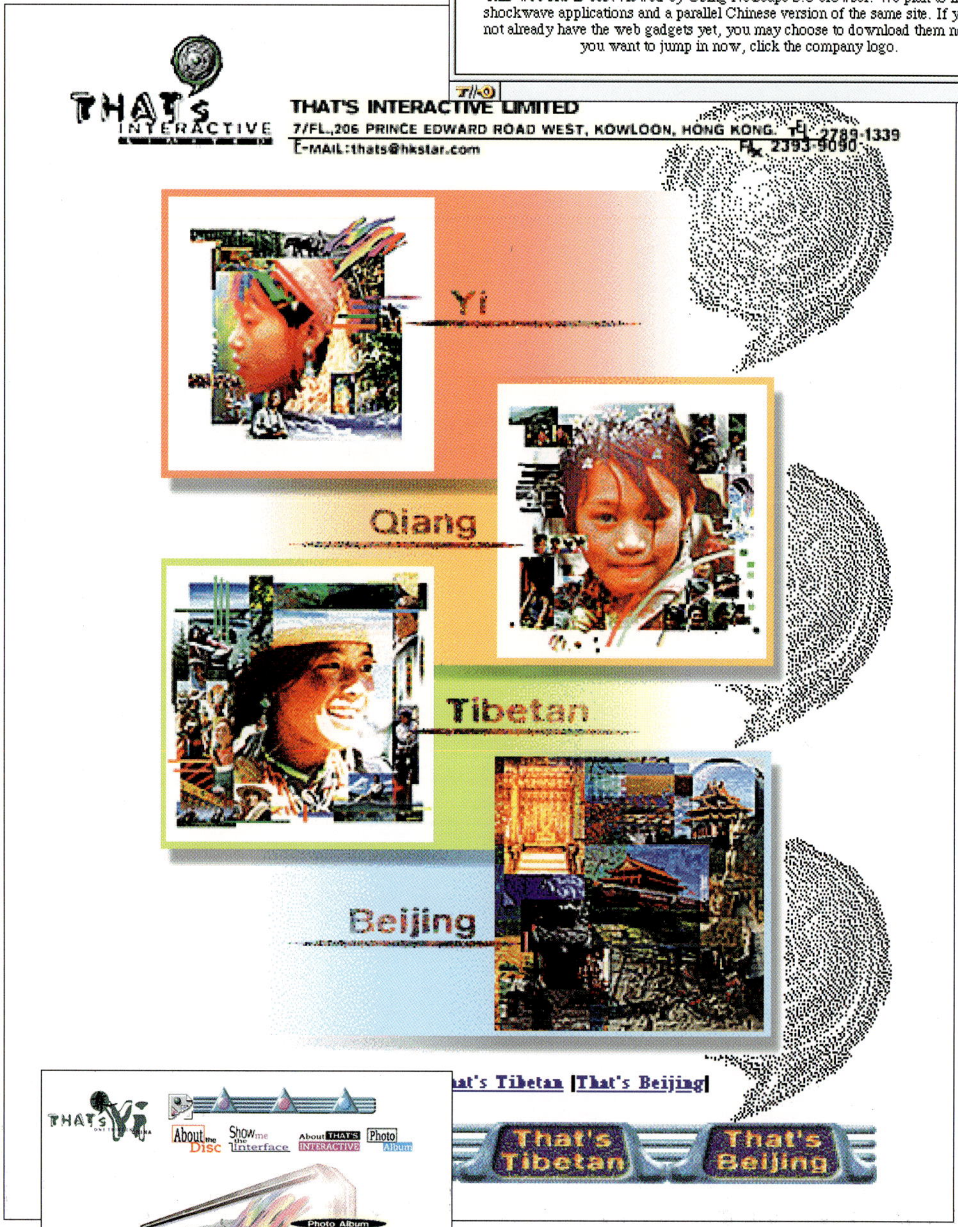

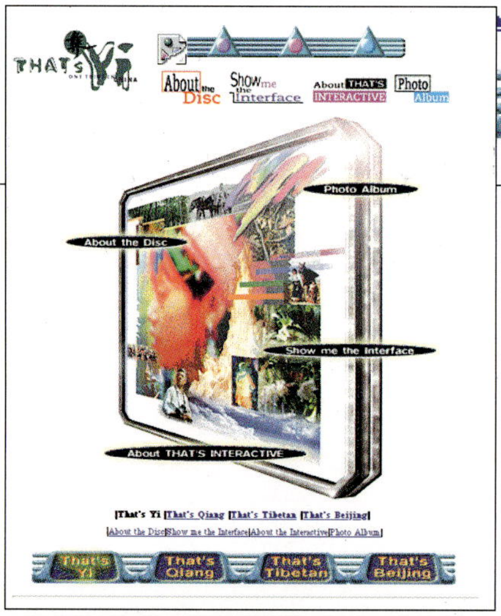

title
That's Interactive
URL
http://www.thats.com/
Design firm
That's Interactive Limited
Designers
Foley Kwok, Joey Pun
producer
Stephen Kam
programmer
Canty Lee
Authoring platform
HTML

Designers have been trying to get away from bitmapped typefaces since the early days of desktop publishing (even bitmapped "computer-looking" fonts are in smooth PostScript format now). Here, however, much of the text is not only bitmapped, but multicolored and highly dithered. The resulting grainy text accentuates the digital nature of the company's CD-ROM products.

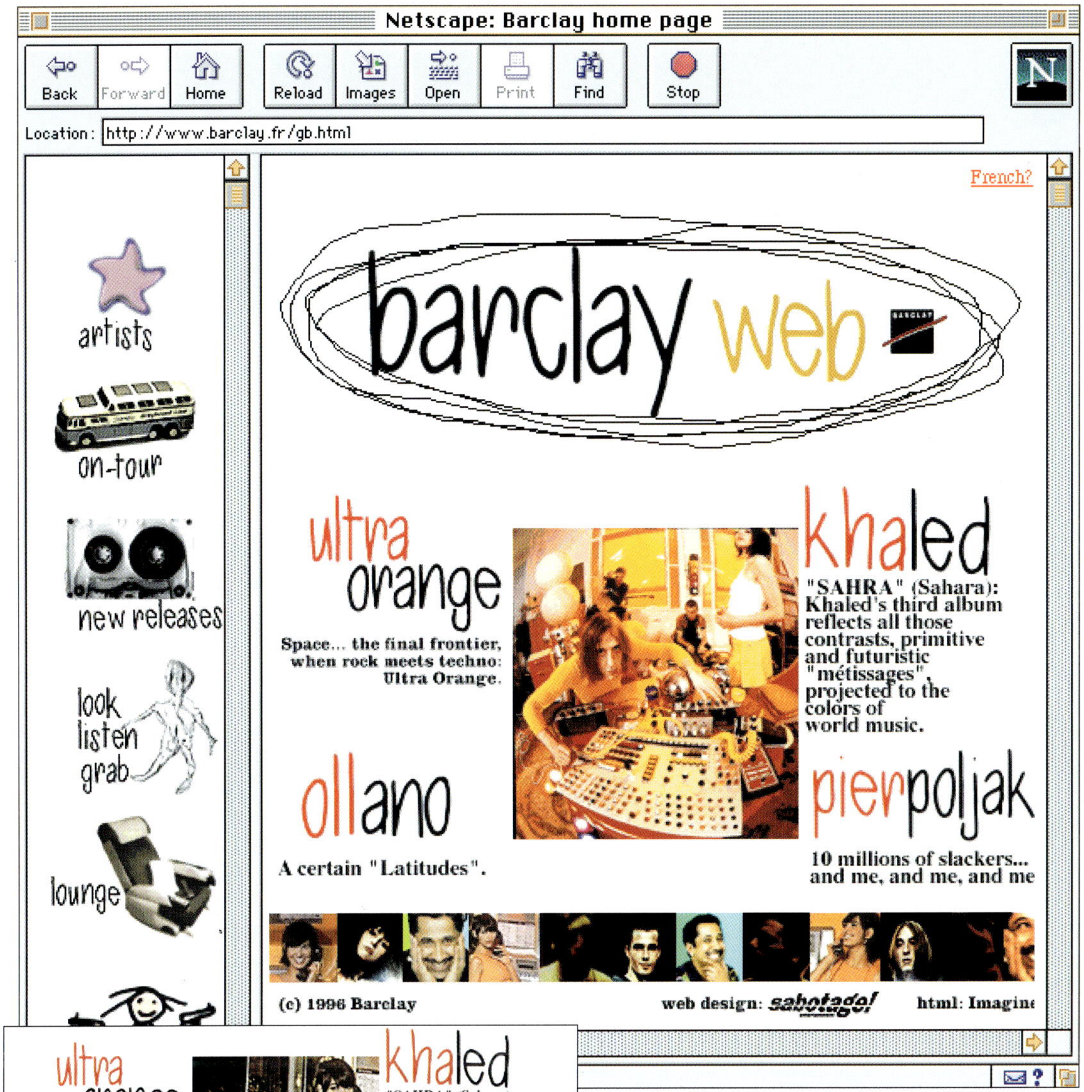

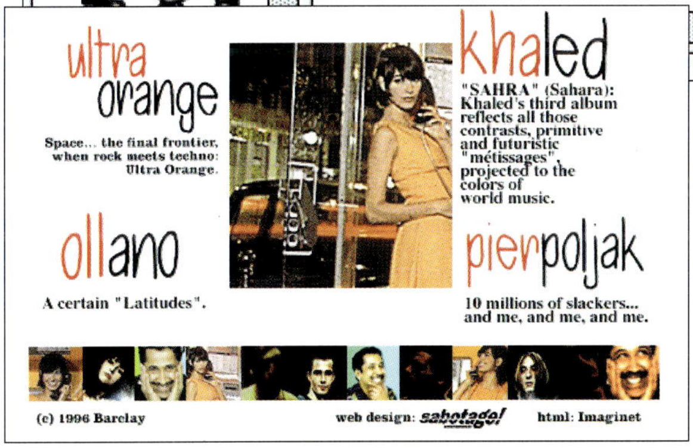

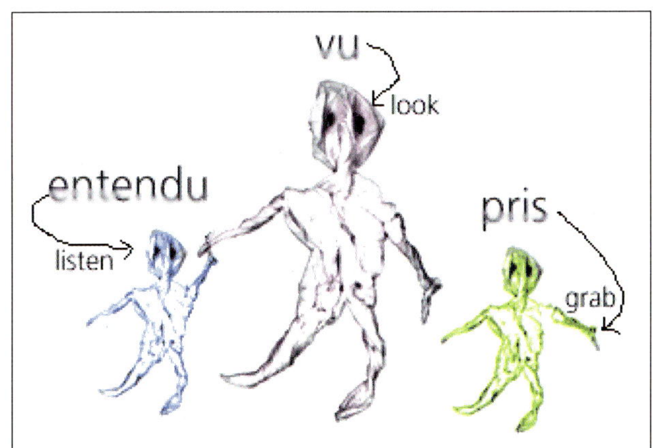

title
Barclay Web

URL
http://www.barclay.fr/gb.html

Design firm
sabotage! entertainment

Designers
Guillaume Wolf, Amaziane Hammouche

Many music publications strive for glossy, streamlined looks that reflect the cutting edge of the industry. Barclay Web takes a different approach, using a handwritten font and sketches to suggest that the editors are sharing their personal picks with the reader; it almost feels like swapping notes in the back of a high-school classroom.

typography

TITLE
DUNCAN HOPKINS WEB SITE
AND GALLERY
URL
http://www.syndeticdesign.
com/dhpkins/main.html
DESIGN FIRM
SYNDETIC DESIGN
DESIGNER
DUNCAN HOPKINS

It almost seems like cheating. The main page of this site uses a Helvetica-like font, but the designer has rotated the words to follow the finger lines created by the outstretched hand. The type on the accompanying gallery page exhibits more creativity, adding a faint blur around the letters to bring them off the screen.

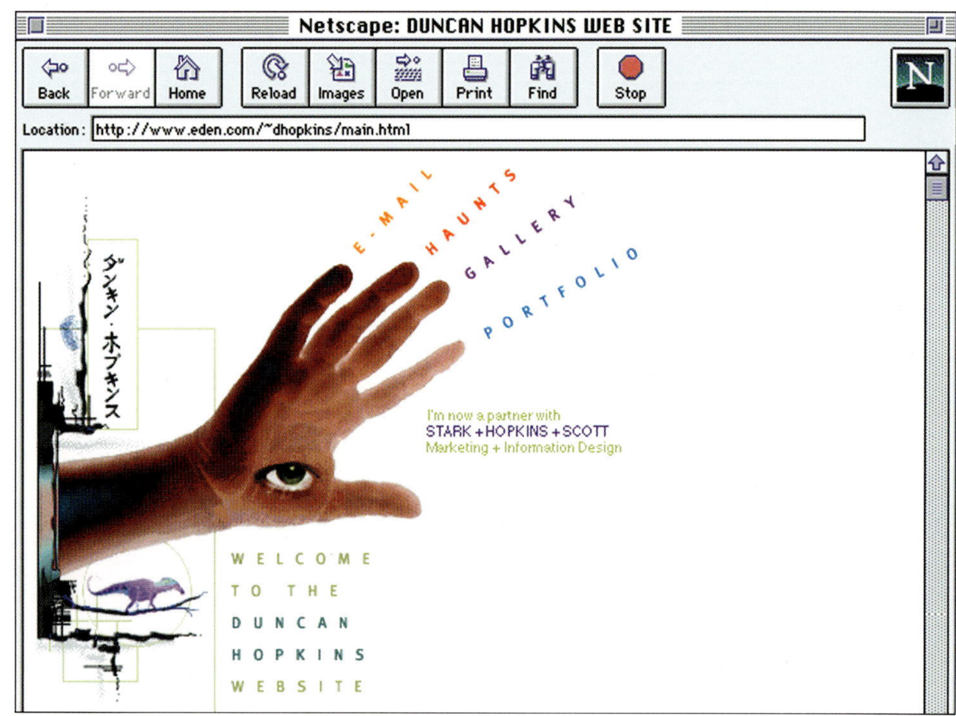

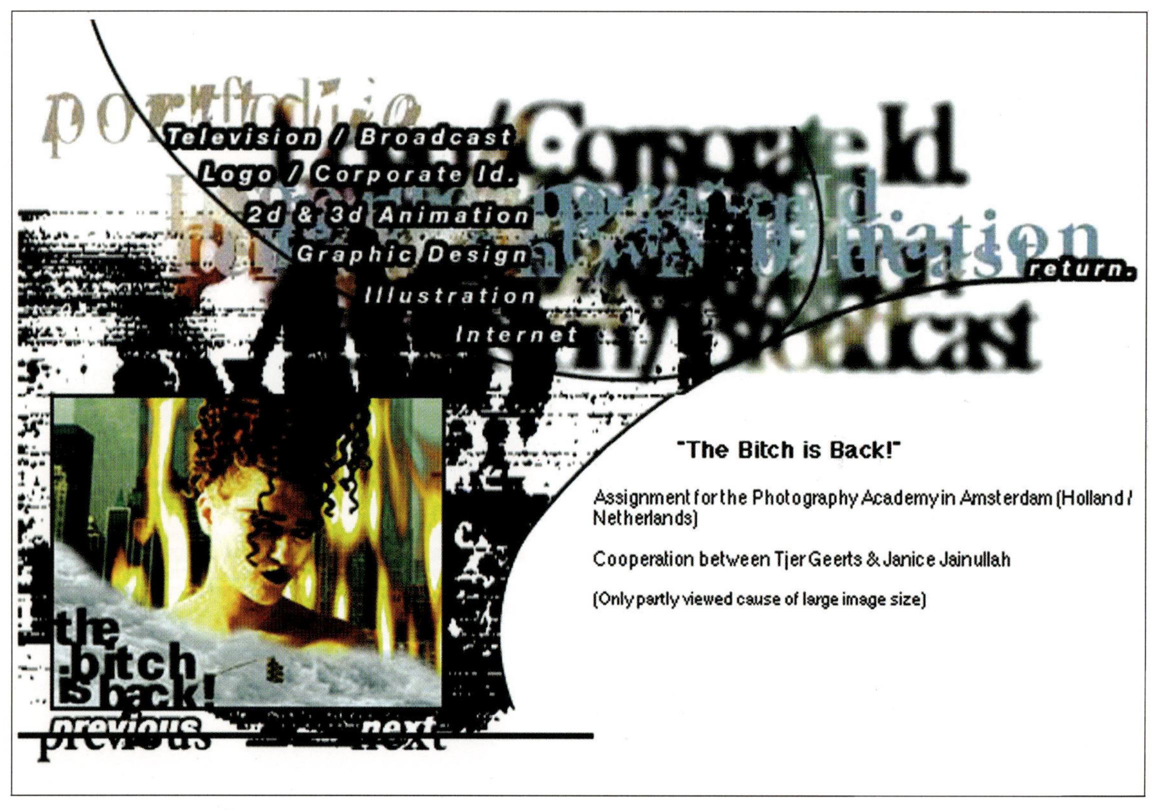

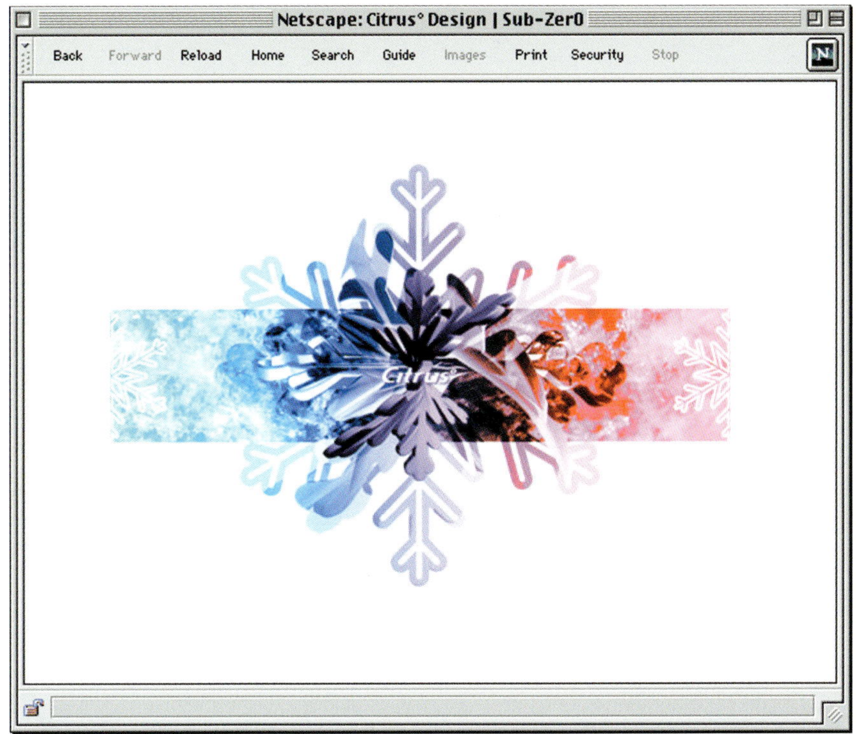

Possibly the most perfect site on the Internet, Citrus conforms to all the best principles of Web design—and all in just two pages of a placeholder site. The first page uses a simple, black background combined with elegant typography and elements that are used in a typographic fashion: the snowflake and small grids of pixels on either side of an animated GIF. The second page explodes the snowflake into the primary graphic element (now in color), while the company's name is neatly placed in the center.

Much has been said about grunge typography in the last few years—enough to warrant its own category. What's interesting about this site is that it's creating a grunge look, but with classic typefaces. By layering, slicing, rearranging, and reversing characters, the viewer is treated to controlled chaos rooted in traditional typography.

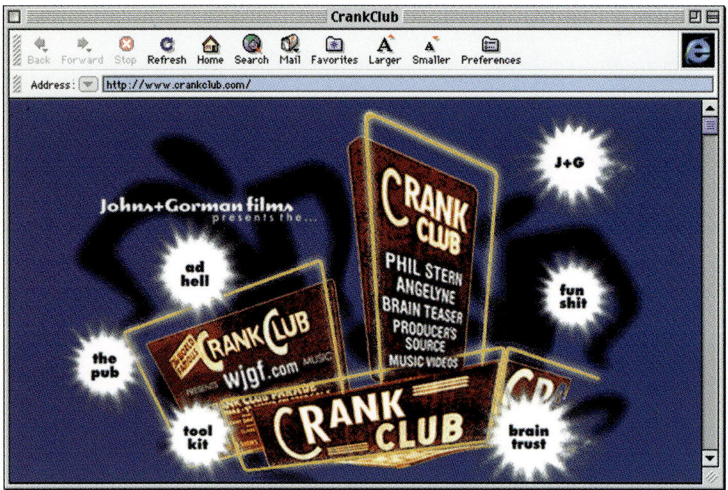

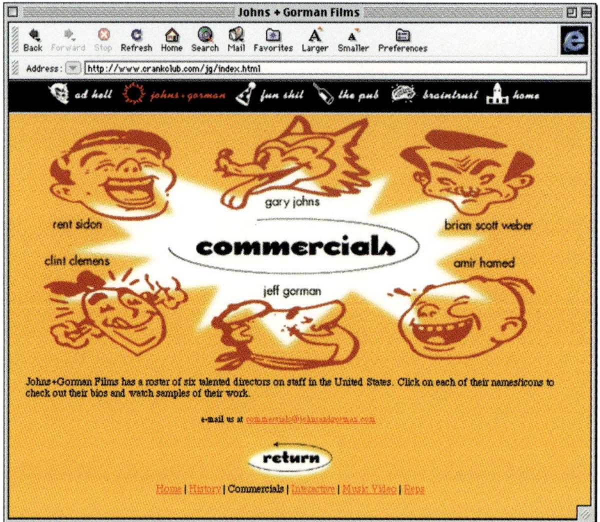

title
crankclub
URL
http://www.crankclub.com/
Design Firm
Johns+Gorman/Interactive
Designer/Illustrator
Rick Moris
Programmers
Glenn Morrissey, Ed Gildred
Creative Director
Gary Johns
Producer
Sylvia Kahn
Authoring Platform
Mac, PC

The typefaces chosen for this site are consciously ironic and backwards-hearkening. Although there's a lot of flash and color, only three display faces are used: a cursive in the top navigation bar, Futura (mostly in all caps) for navigation on a page, and a funky face with a lowercase *e* like a sickle moon that has a distinctly different uppercase and lowercase.

Title
iconoclast: where have all the designers gone?
URL
http://www.prophetcomm.com/iconoclast/
Design Firm
prophet communications
Designer
Josh Feldman

It's interesting that in creating a page that tries to differentiate digital design from print design, the designer of this page uses fonts that approximate the often variable quality of paper-and-ink publishing. The text appears layered and uneven, which accentuates the digitally-created background image in the upper-right corner.

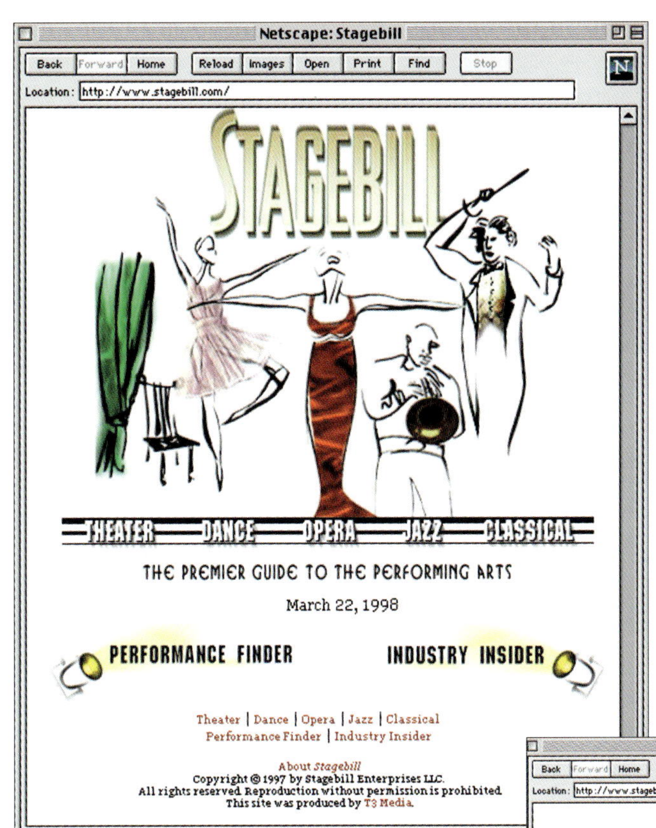

Pulled directly from the lettering that would adorn a performance hall's marquee, the typography of the blocked section titles could clue you to the site's content even if the words weren't related. With appropriate grandiose flourish, *Stagebill* leaps from the screen in graduated gold colors against a 1920s narrow typeface.

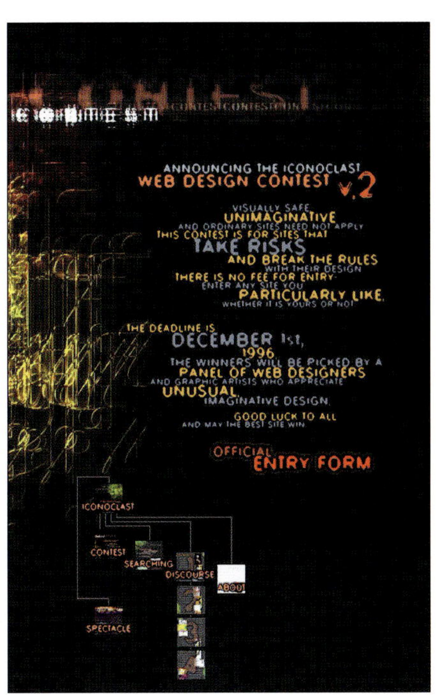

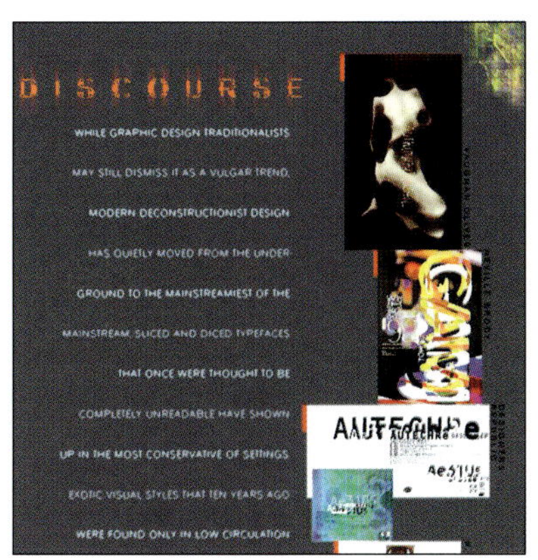
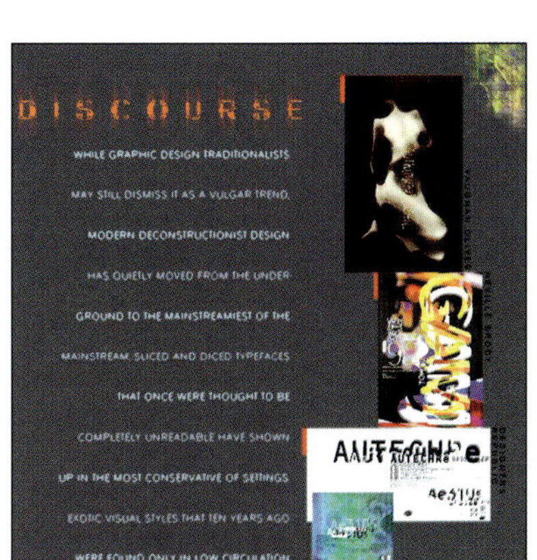

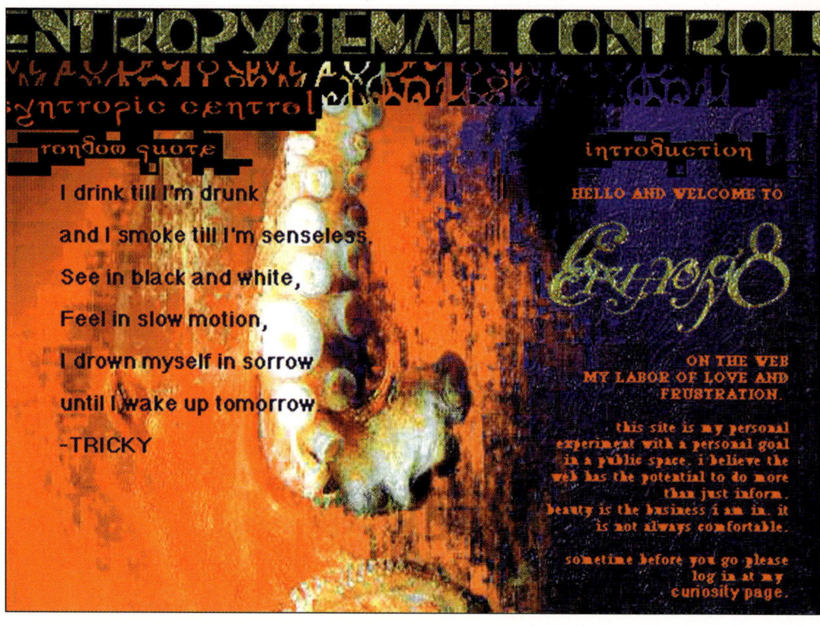

title
entropy8 email control
url
http://www.entropy8.com/
design firm
entropy8
designer
Auriea Harvey
programmers
Auriea Harvey, Marc Antony Vose

Many designers today are challenging the convention that type must be immediately readable in order to work. The Entropy8 site uses a few different typefaces to set its tone as much to inform the visitor. The repeated, overlapping *Entropy8* along the left side of the page ceases to have meaning as text, working instead as a varied texture.

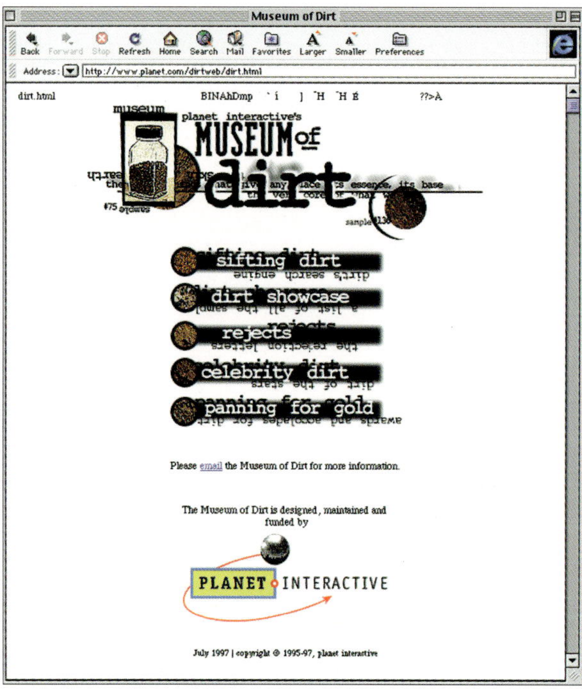

title
museum of dirt web site
url
http://www.planet.com/dirtweb/dirt.html
design firm
planet interactive, inc.
designer
Brian Cook
photographer
Chris Mascio
programmer
Rich Martin
art direction
Glenn Johanson
authoring platform
Mac

It is in fact a museum of dirt, and the designers have played on that theme in the Web site. The museum-label-like type is a big, closely spaced typewriter font. The explanation of each category on the home page is upside down and partially obscured, but still entirely legible.

The striking background color here surrounds the customized title lettering—clearly English, but styled and spaced to resemble futuristic Chinese characters. That combination, along with the bold sans-serif body text, imparts the sense of command and control required to boast of "revolutioniz[ing] design." It's also worth noting the activity generated by the wrapped text on the Faye Wong and This Mortal Coil pages.

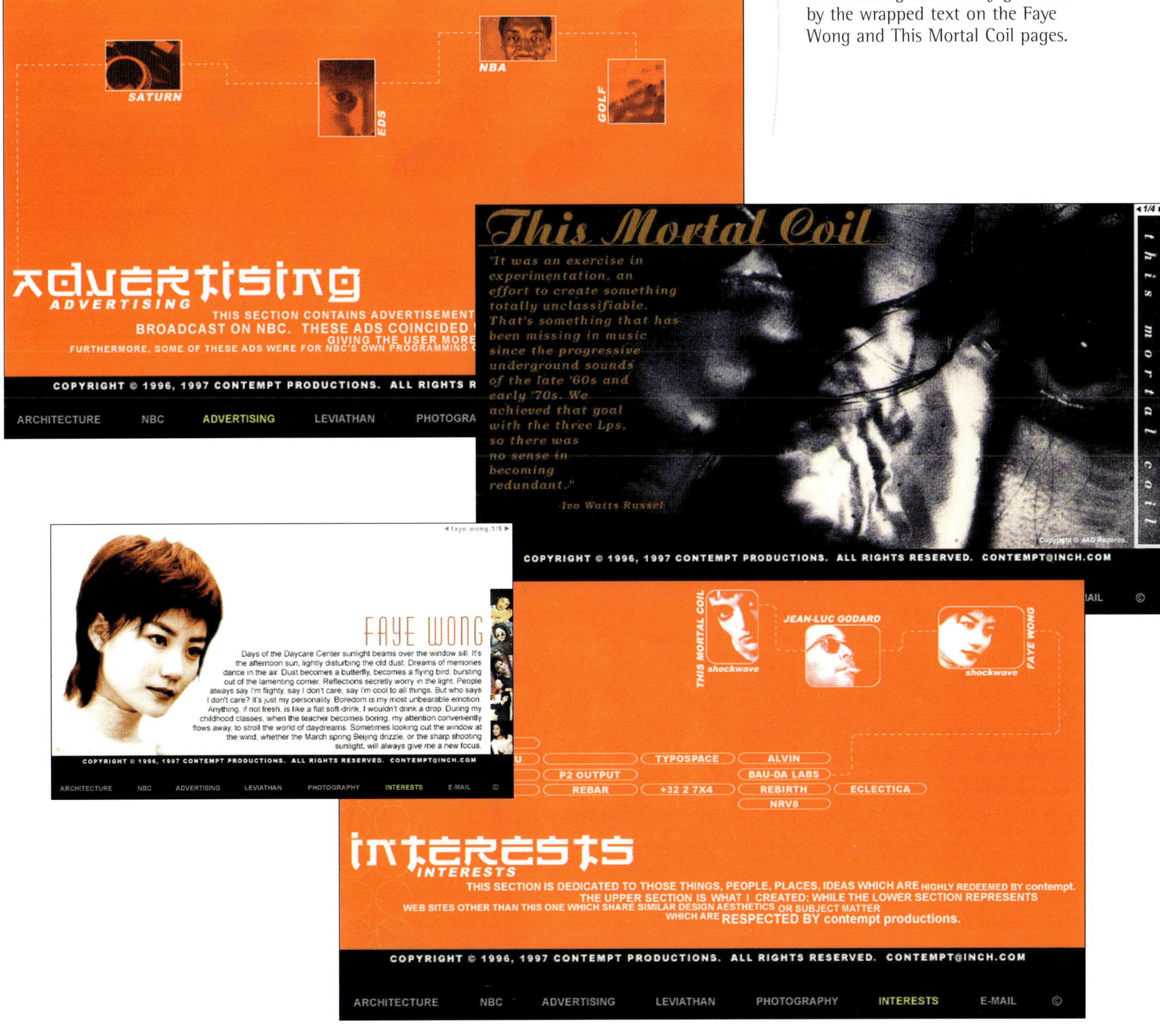

TITLE
Dreamless Studios
URL
http://www.dreamless.com/
DESIGN FIRM
Dreamless Studios
DESIGNER/PROGRAMMER
David Decheser
ILLUSTRATOR/PHOTOGRAPHER
Eric Dinyer

By itself, the term *dreamless* evokes empty darkness. Expressed in the morphing and often decaying typography of the Dreamless Studios site, however, the word becomes as fitful as any night consumed by mental images. The type here can be characterized as modern medieval, a mixture of traditional calligraphic letterforms and stylized scripts that blur, distort, burn, and glow.

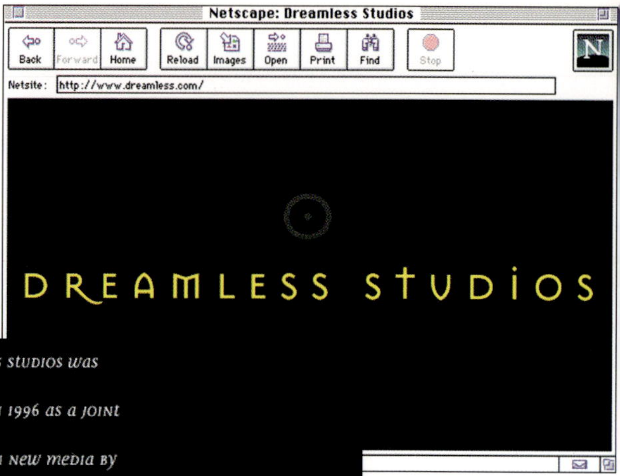

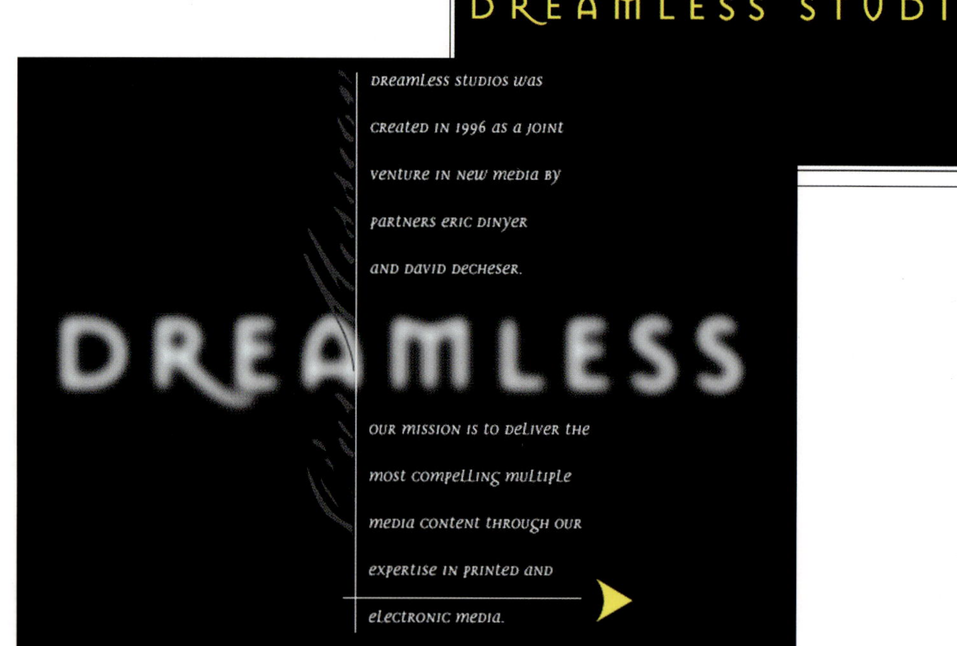

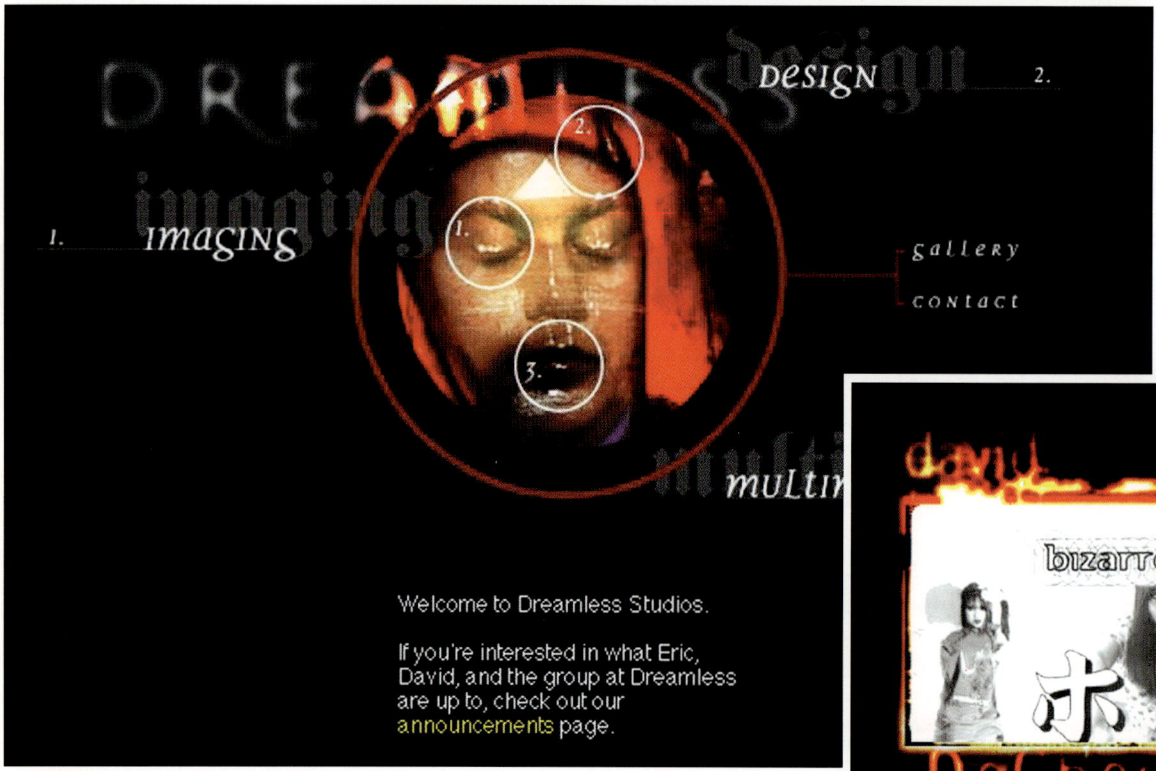

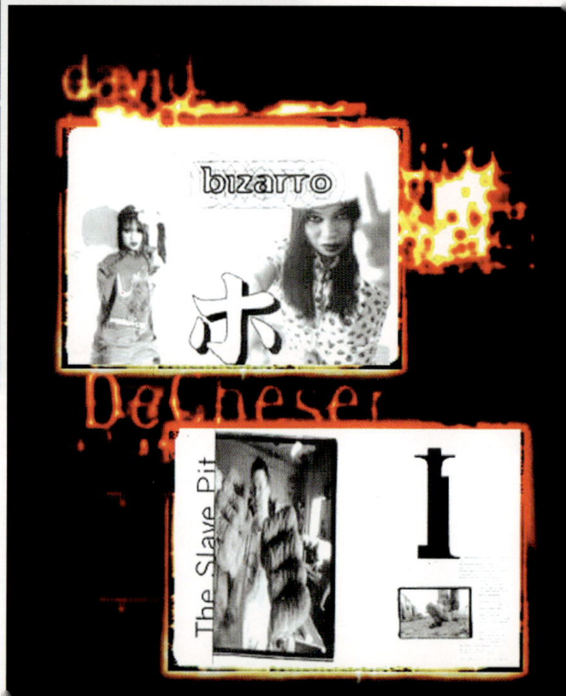

title
Dreamless Studios Multimedia
URL
http://www.dreamless.com/
multimed.htm
design firm
Dreamless Studios
designer/programmer
David Decheser
illustrator/photographer
Eric Dinyer

Without directly employing effects such as GIF89a animation or Shockwave files, the manipulation of the type puts the words and the pages in motion. Instead of looking like a page where each element has been measured and placed with precision, the word *media* appears as if it's been frozen mid-frame from a movie or animation.

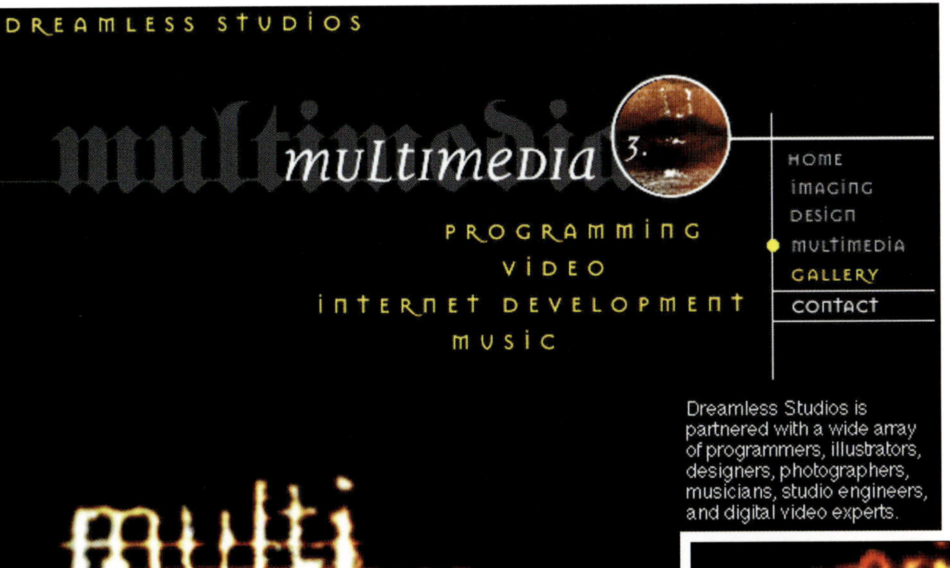

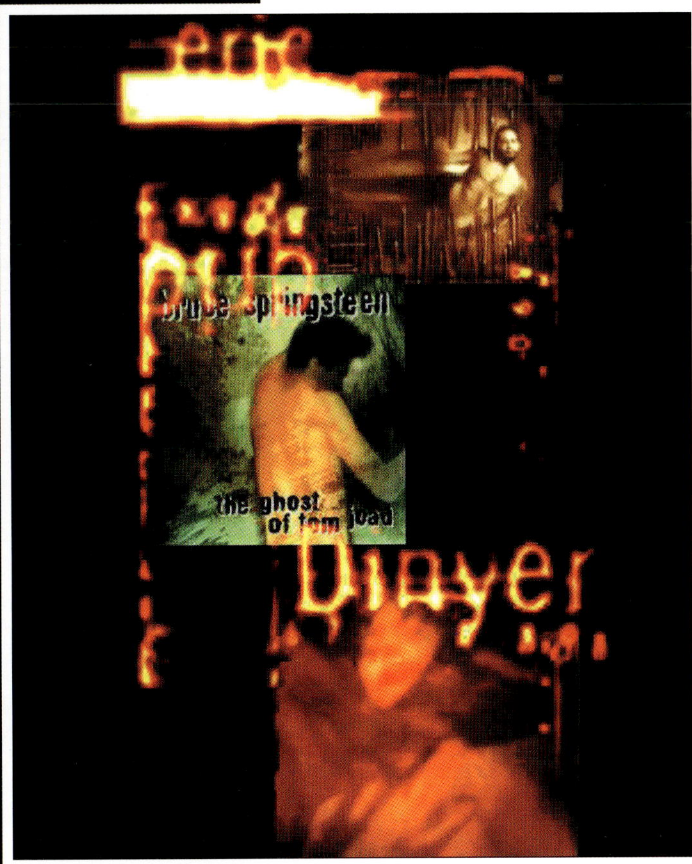

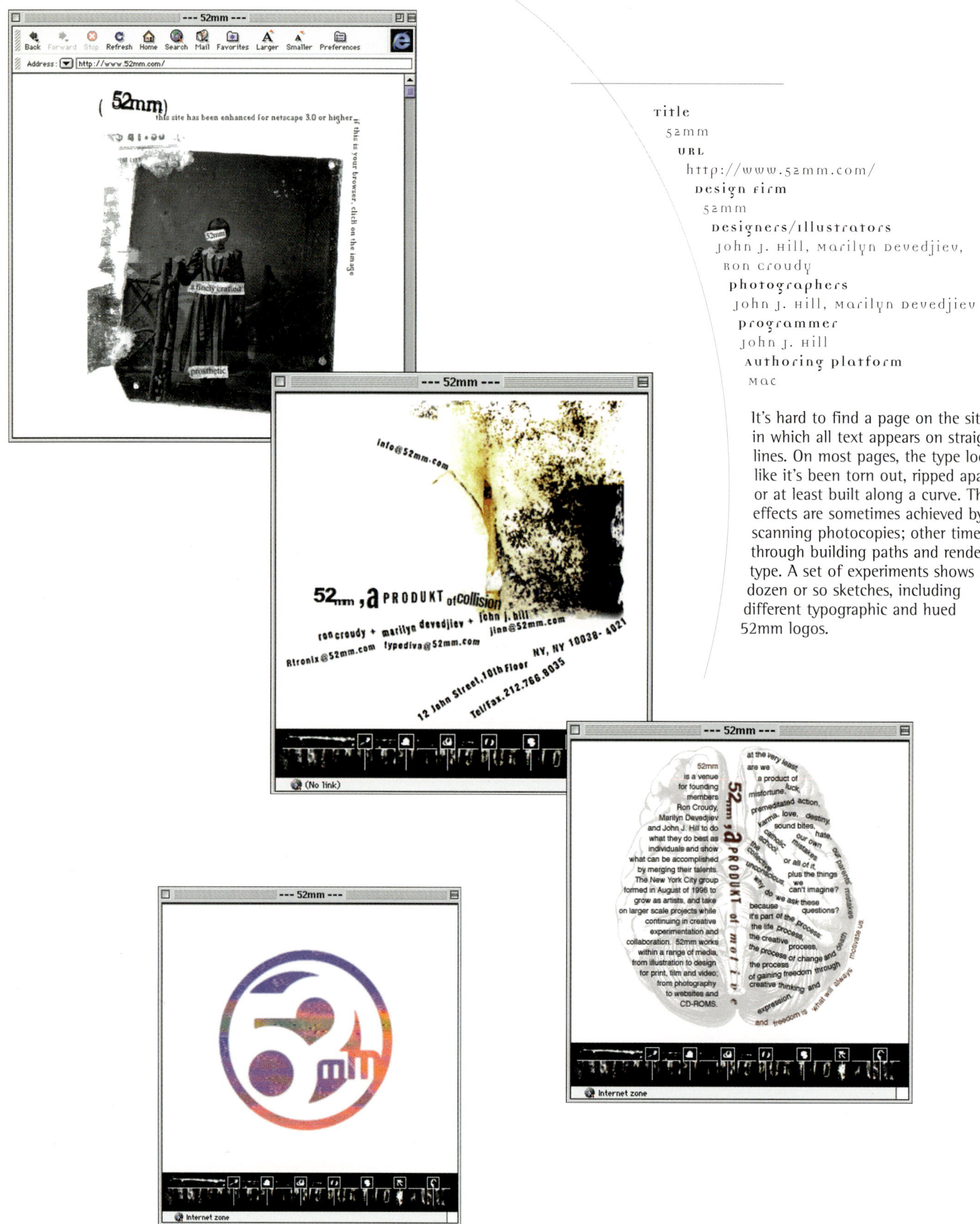

TITLE
52mm
URL
http://www.52mm.com/
DESIGN FIRM
52mm
DESIGNERS/ILLUSTRATORS
John J. Hill, Marilyn Devedjiev,
Ron Croudy
PHOTOGRAPHERS
John J. Hill, Marilyn Devedjiev
PROGRAMMER
John J. Hill
AUTHORING PLATFORM
Mac

It's hard to find a page on the site in which all text appears on straight lines. On most pages, the type looks like it's been torn out, ripped apart, or at least built along a curve. These effects are sometimes achieved by scanning photocopies; other times, through building paths and rendering type. A set of experiments shows a dozen or so sketches, including different typographic and hued 52mm logos.

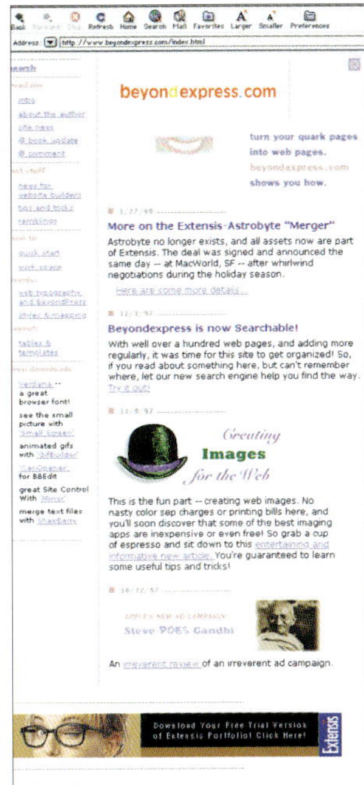

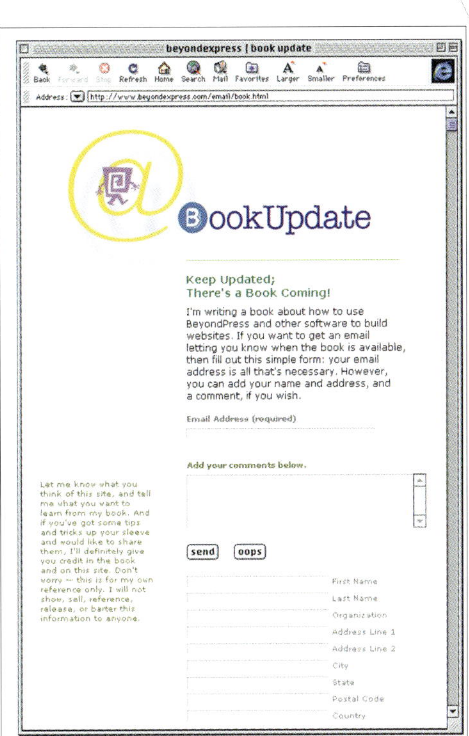

title
beyondexpress.com
URL
http://www.beyondexpress.com/index.html
design firm
pageworks
designer/illustrator/programmer
kip shaw
photographer
chris jones
authoring platform
mac

This site feels typographically rich without much rendered type. Headlines are made by using the <FONT> tag to increase the size of the type. Most paragraph or longer sections of type are bumped up above normal browser size through the same means. Type is also used effectively as ornament, as with the giant @ sign on the feedback page.

title
prophet communications
URL
http://www.prophetcomm.com/
design firm
prophet communications
designer
josh feldman
programmer
jason monburg

The designers clearly revel in the atmosphere that a dark background can lend. This site is warmed by the glowing, blurry text in many of the titles, which offsets the screens' darkness; the titles also draw one's view down the many blocks of text on each page.

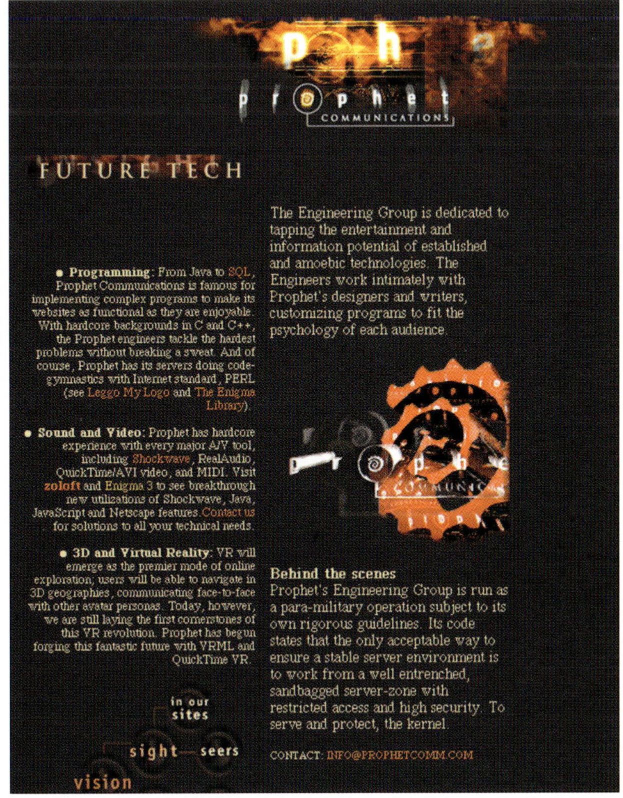

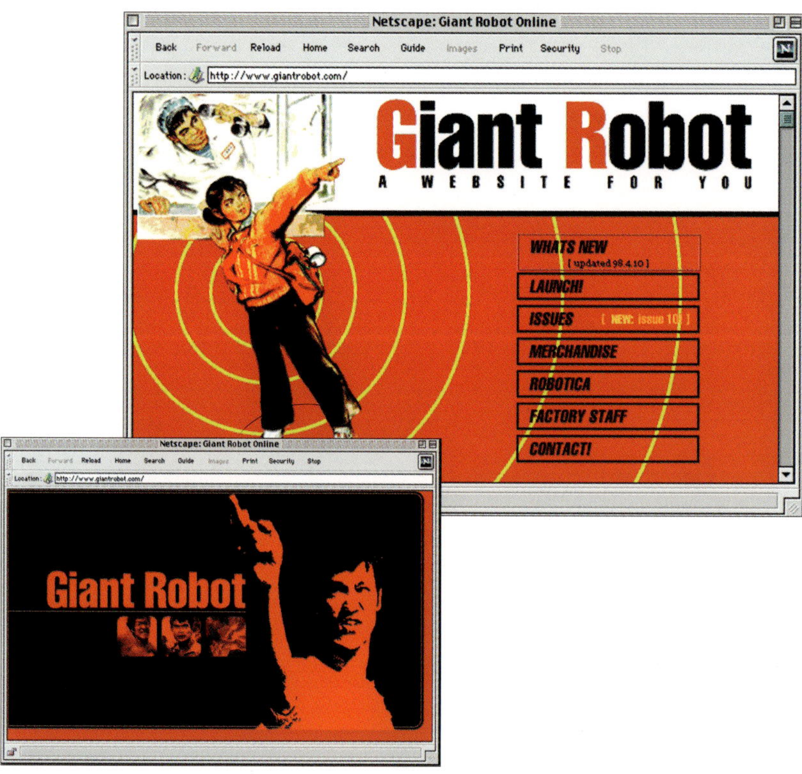

title
giant robot
URL
http://www.giantrobot.com/
designer/programmer
david yu
illustrator/photographer
staff of giant robot magazine
authoring platform
mac

It's hard to argue with a bold font. In order to quickly make an impact, the title here is big, bold, and painted an attention-grabbing red and black. Its heaviness allows the all-capped subtitle to be letterspaced cleanly, while italicized variations point you into the site.

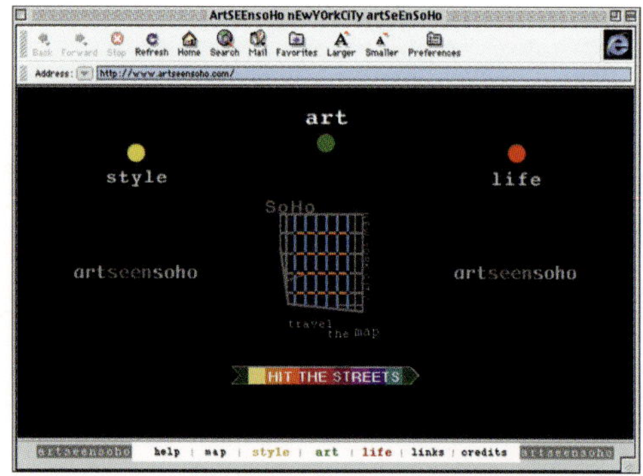

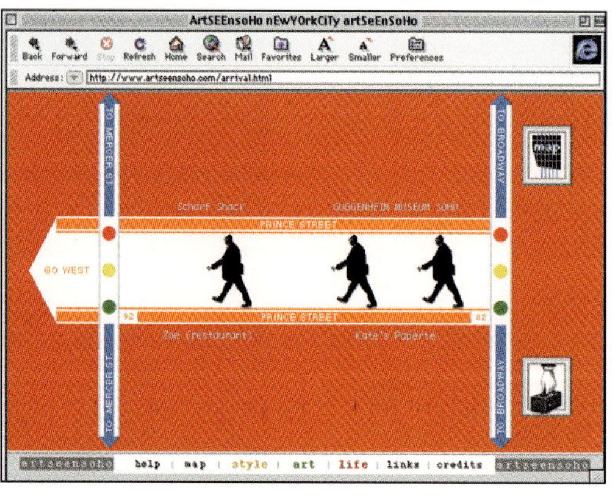

title
artseensoho
URL
http://www.artseensoho.com/
designer/illustrator
tim trompeter
photographers
peter cunningham, tim trompeter
authoring platform
mac

A typewriter face is used on the home page for the main areas of navigation, while the maps use all the same size of a sans-serif face. It's capitalized (and knocked out of color bars) to make the directional navigation stand out, but spacing is used to simply, geographically lay out where the shops are along the streets.

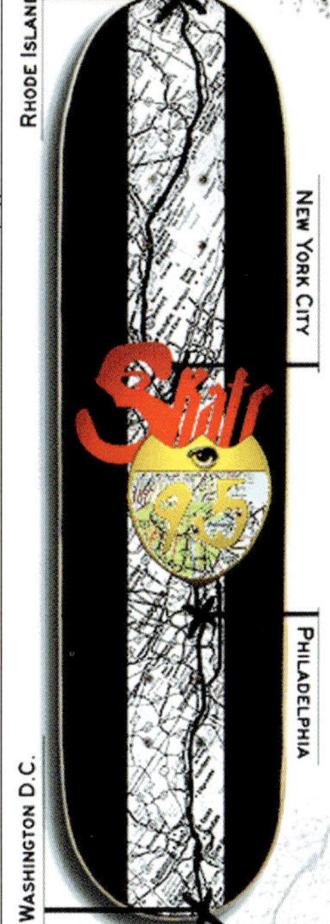

Now the east coast industry is a success.

and the primary reason is economic, explains Zimmer. The California market was saturated, with more than 20 companies in southern California alone shipping at least 70 percent of their product east to capitalize on its growing market. Kids here realized they could get in on the action and shake off California's monopoly. These skater-entrepreneurs didn't just start skateboard companies, they also set up manufacturing plants: Chapman Boards on Long Island and Dynamic in Wilmington, North Carolina, supply wood for decks, while Creative Urethanes in Virginia supplies wheels. Owning the means of production and the magazines lets East Coast skaters shape their own industry. And as Mike Agnew, the owner of a D.C.-area company, pointed out,

Having an industry based here on the east coast means that skateboarding can grow even larger.

More kids will be exposed to it, and skating will reach a bigger audience."

And East Coasters can't get enough of the local goods. Companies sell out their lines quickly. Kids here are hugely loyal to East Coast product, and it's doing well overseas. In England, skaters will only skate East Coast style, and now the West Coast wants in on the act. A recent advertisement for LA-based World Industries (which also owns Big Brother magazine) featured Maurice Key, a black skater who hails from Rhode Island, as "made in Brooklyn," with a photo-montage of Key skating over a Brooklyn subway map, and this copy:

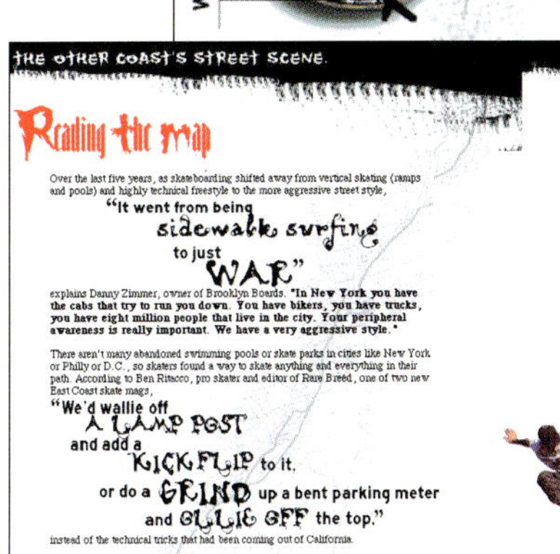

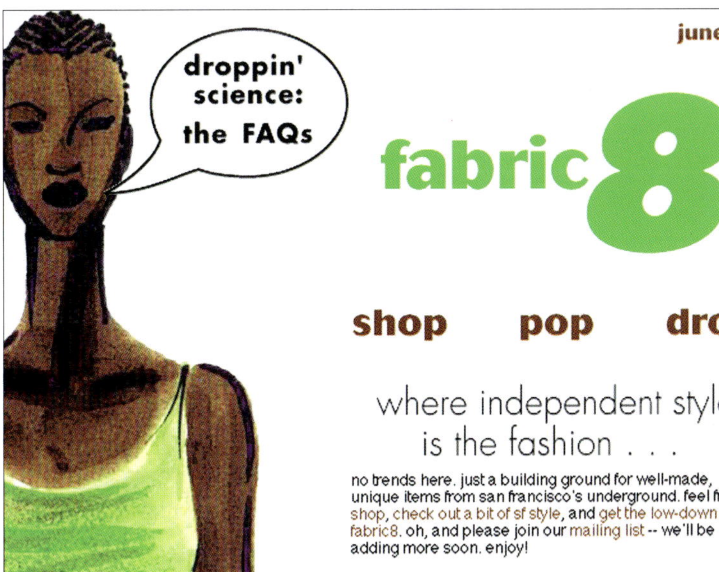

---

title
skate I-95
URL
http://www.charged.com/tar/stories/i95/
Design Firm
Entropy8 Digital Arts
Designer
Auriea Harvey

Yes, you can mix typefaces and not get your creative license revoked. The combination of stylized sans-serif and grunge-written title faces presents the attitude expected to draw in this site's skateboarding audience.

title
fabric8 online Boutique
URL
http://www.fabric8.com/
Design Firm
fabric8 productions
Designers
Olivia Ongpin, Antony Quintal
Photographers
Drea Donio, Keith Ross, Jackie Way
Programmers
Antony Quintal, Olivia Ongpin, Joe Emenaker

The variety of vendors and designers sharing space at Fabric8 leads to a mix of typographic styles, customized to fit the mood of the intended customers.

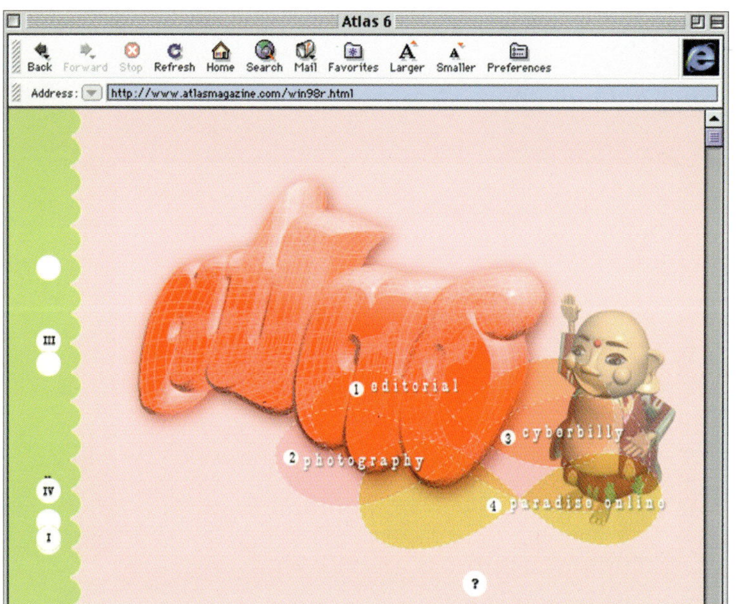

title
Atlas Magazine
url
http://www.atlasmagazine.com/win98r.html
design firm
Atlas
designer/illustrator
Amy Franceschini
photographers
Olivier Laude, Catherine Karnow,
Bob Sacha, Adam Kufeld, et al.
programmer
Michael Macrone
authoring platform
Mac, PC

Marcel Duchamp pioneered the use of repeated arbitrary forms called *the three standard measures*, which were curved lines instead of straight edges. Atlas magazine approaches the same kind of aesthetic by repeating odd forms, such as the scalloped edge and the figure-eights behind navigation links. Type and shape conform to this internal consistency.

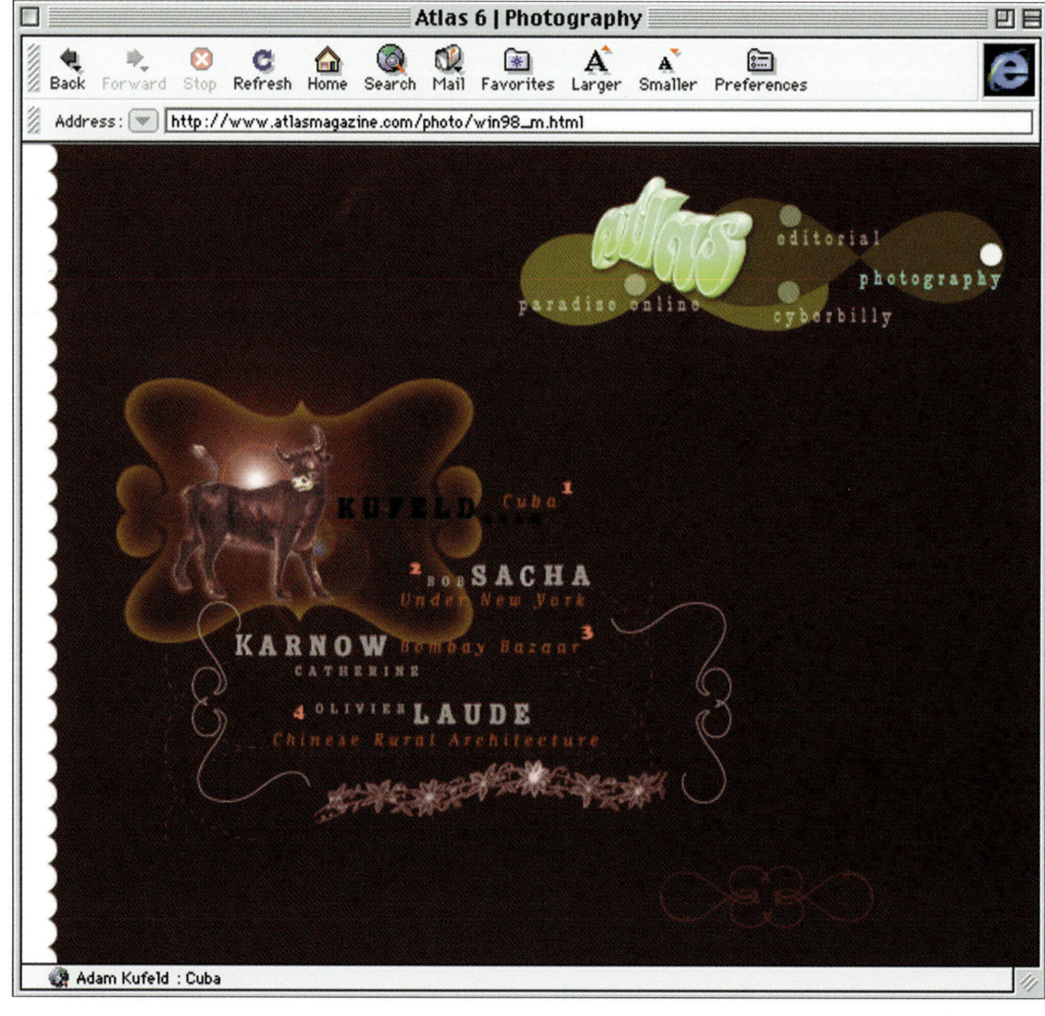

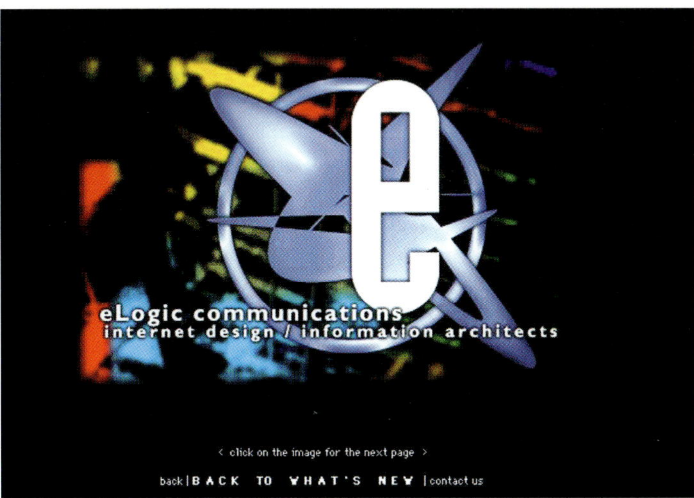

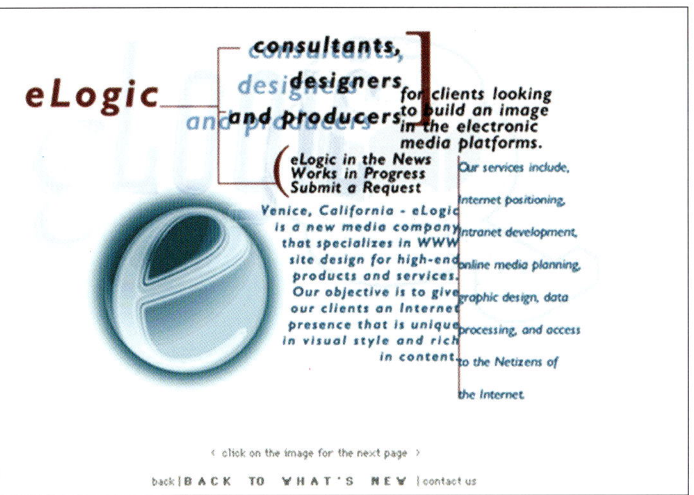

title
eLogic communications Typographics
URL
http://www.elogic.com/
Design Firm
eLogic communications
Designer
Jimmy Chen
Programmers
Jimmy Chen, Bill Nash

With the curves and lines inherent in typography, it's a wonder that relatively few designers use text solely as a design element. The What's New page contains a minimum amount of color variation and no illustrations, yet the layered and stretched type becomes the page's illustration.

title
Blue Marlin
URL
http://www.bluemarlincorp.com/home.html
Design Firm
Atlas Web Design
Designer
Olivier Laude, Atlas
Photographer
Joe Budd
Programmer
Michael Macrone, Atlas
Art Director
Francoise Sejourne, Blue Marlin
Authoring platform
Mac

Many designers strive for a vintage look, usually going over the top with their implementations. Here, a vintage feel is achieved with the help of a typeface that differs only slightly from a standard serif body font. Slightly condensed with squarish serifs, it resembles the standard lettering used on baseball fields of an earlier era.

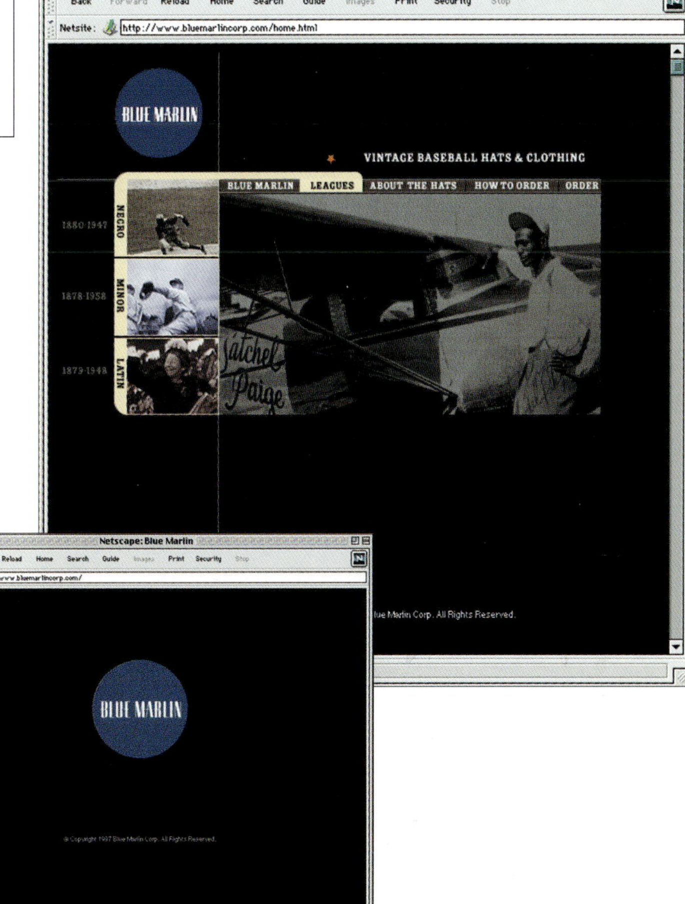

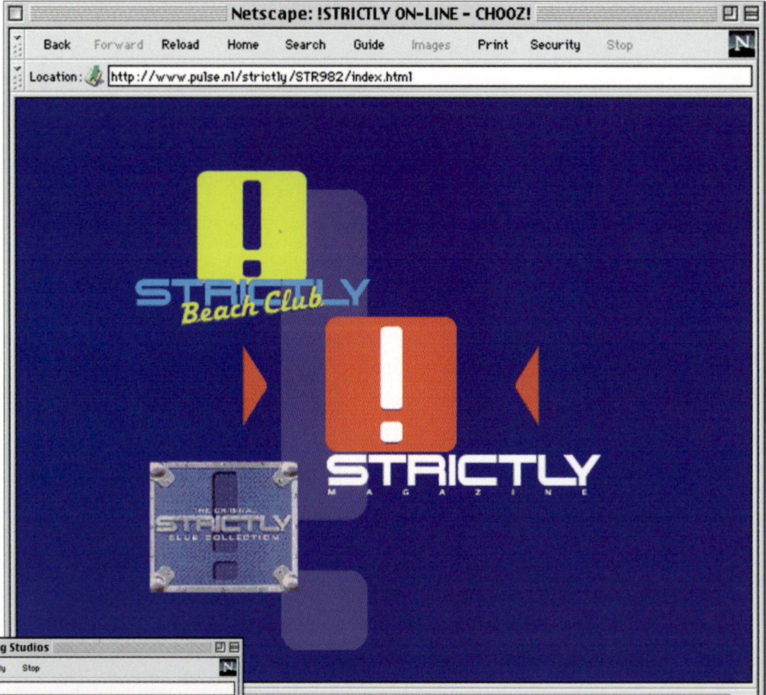

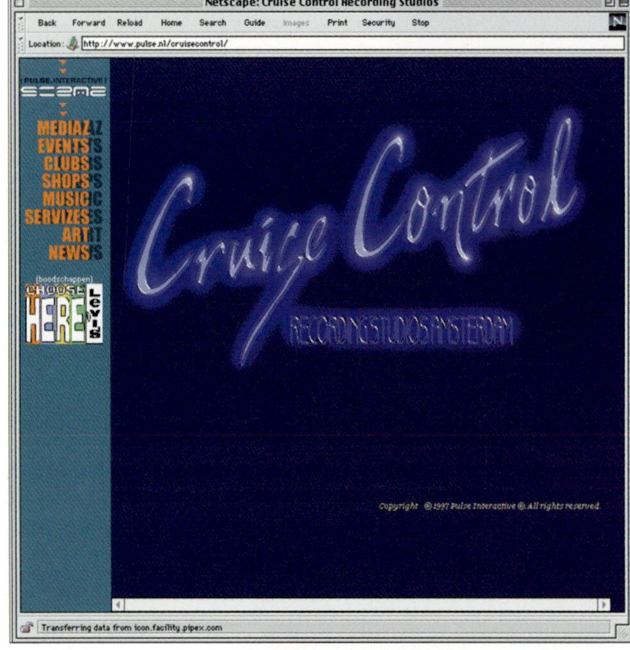

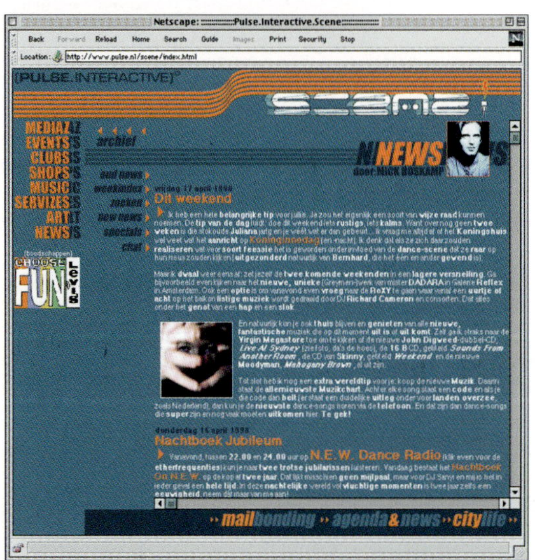

title
pulse.interactive scene magazine
URL
http://www.pulse.nl/scene/index.html
design firm
pulse.interactive
designer
Tino Nooten
editors
Mick Boskamp, Marthijn Klopper
authoring platform
Mac

Bold, rounded, and oblique, much of the typography on this site reflects its hyper-hip content. This is not a destination for brooding commentary, but for reports on the best of new music, art, and events. The fonts here help propel the reader into this mindset.

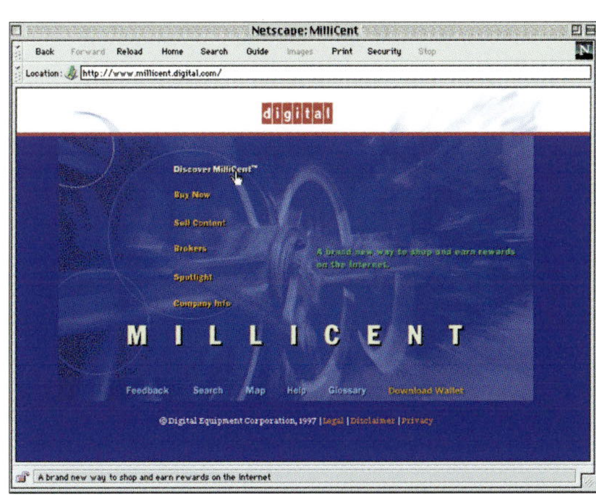

title
millicent

URL
http://www.millicent.digital.com/

design firm
organic online inc.

designer
Jennifer Martinez

information architect
Bjorn Heinrichs

account manager
Meghan O'Leary

producer
John Bagby

associate producer
Greg Black

engineer
Orion Letizi

content engineer
Rocky Mullin

strategic planner
Polly Arenberg

The typeface Helvetica, and sans-serif fonts akin to it, are often derided because of their outright simplicity. (As one of the Macintosh's default fonts, Helvetica has found its way onto more materials than one would like to count.) Here, however, the power of its clarity works to full effect: The type is professional, easy to read, and able to hold unusual colors (sea-green and pale orange) against a dark blue background.

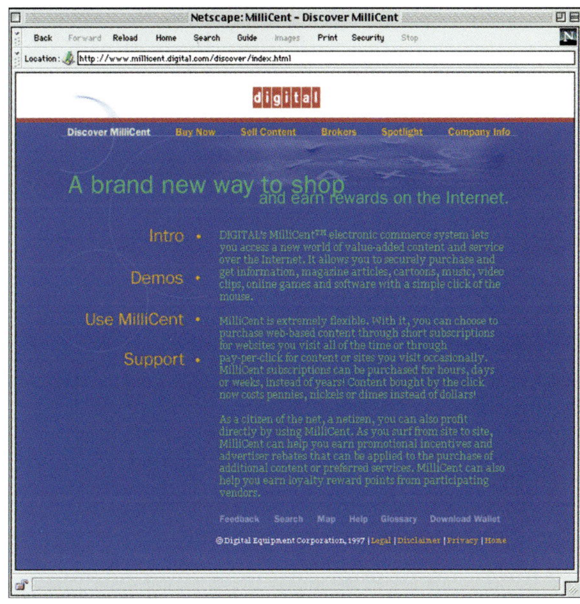

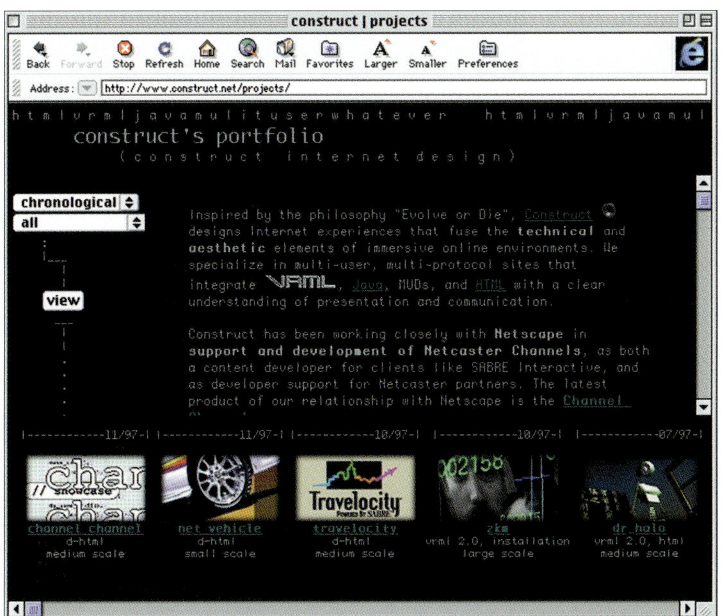

title
construct internet design

URL
http://www.construct.net/projects/

design firm
construct internet design

designer/illustrator
Annette Loudon

programmer
Cynsa Bonorris

authoring platform
Mac, SGI

Construct makes cutting-edge sites, and uses a reverse logic in its site design; by emphasizing functional type and using ASCII-art-like effects, they create a tour de force: the seemingly simple things they do are quite difficult to create. A clever and straightforward example is the use of the vertical bar (|) and hyphen in monospaced Courier (or the equivalent) to act as titles for their portfolio entries.

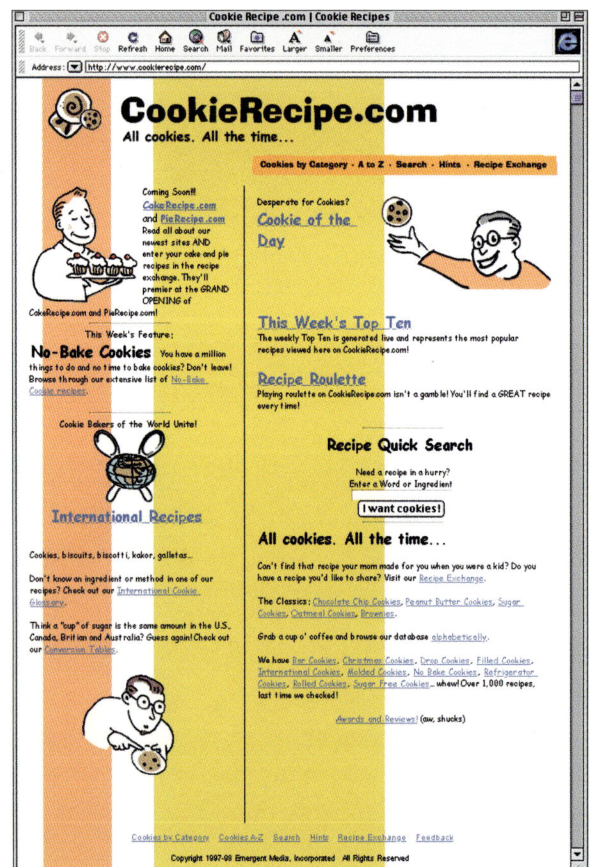

title
cookierecipe.com
url
http://www.cookierecipe.com/
design firm
emergent media, inc.
designer/illustrator
yann oehl
programmers
tim hunt, kala anderson, dan shepherd
authoring platform
pc

A site about cookies should feel childlike but not childish (to paraphrase *The Fantastiks*). Cookierecipe.com requires that the Microsoft-supplied (and free) Comic Sans face be installed to fully benefit from the whimsy, but the lighthearted and practical site doesn't need anything more to emphasize its nature.

title
mike motz: promotional portfolio
url
http://www.cal.shaw.wave.ca/~mmotz/
design firm
anythyme web design
designer/illustrator/programmer
mike motz

Mike Motz uses his site to promote his work, which includes excellent cartooning, so he has chosen four styles of writing (typefaces and handwriting) for navigation and headlines that have a cartoony feel. He doesn't overuse any of them, limiting use to specific areas and using regular type for longer passages. His signature in his own handwriting is prominent on each page.

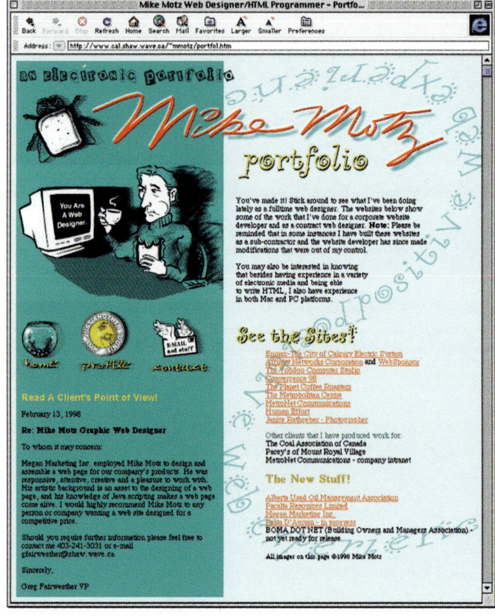

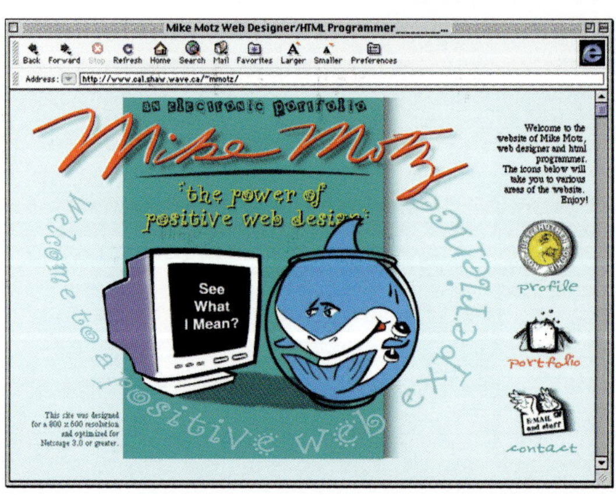

Designers often aim for clarity, but at the Blind site, clarity is intentionally elusive. Mocking the familiar look of a doctor's eye-exam chart, the opening page features a Shockwave-based sliding focus bar that sharpens a swath of text while blurring the rest of the title.

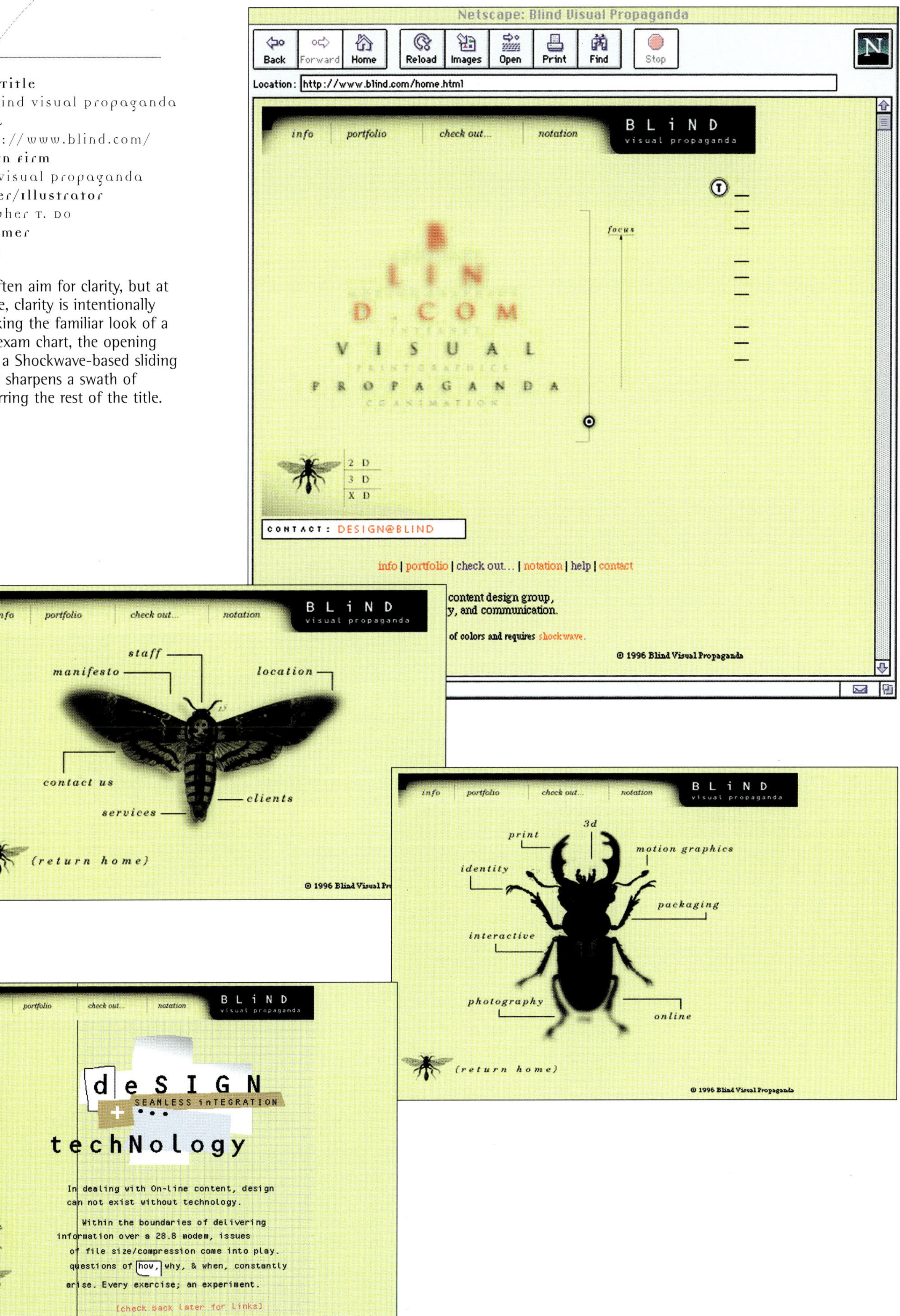

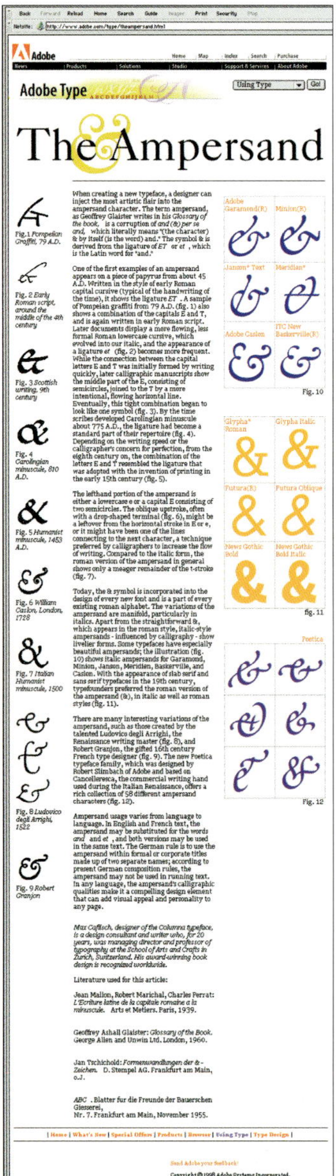

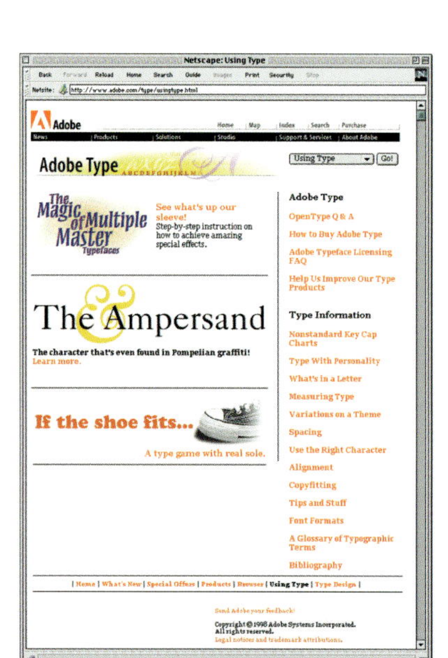

Title
adobe systems

URL
http://www.adobe.com/type/main.shtml

Design firm
adobe systems web department

Authoring platform
mac, pc, sun sparc

Adobe has been at the forefront of digital type for years, and their pages devoted to typography reflect this. The title image on the opening page manages to demonstrate the breadth of the company's offerings without falling into the trap of cramming multiple faces on one page. Credit the generous amount of white space throughout the site for providing balance and allowing the typefaces to draw attention to themselves.

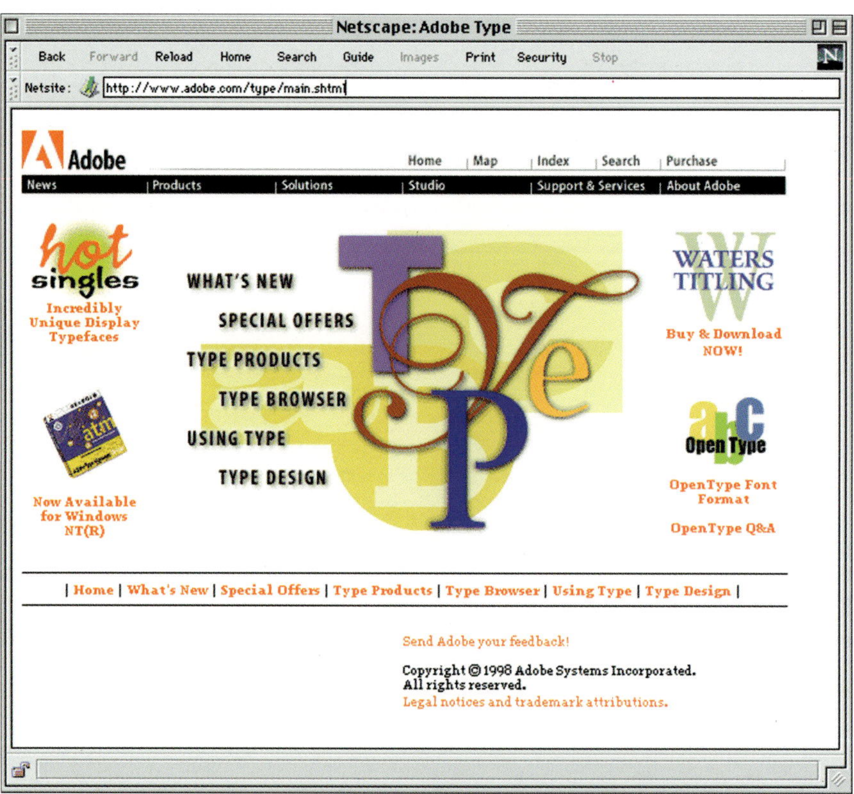

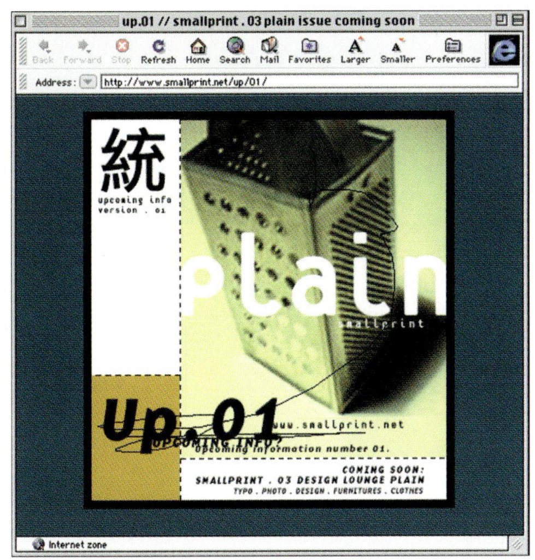

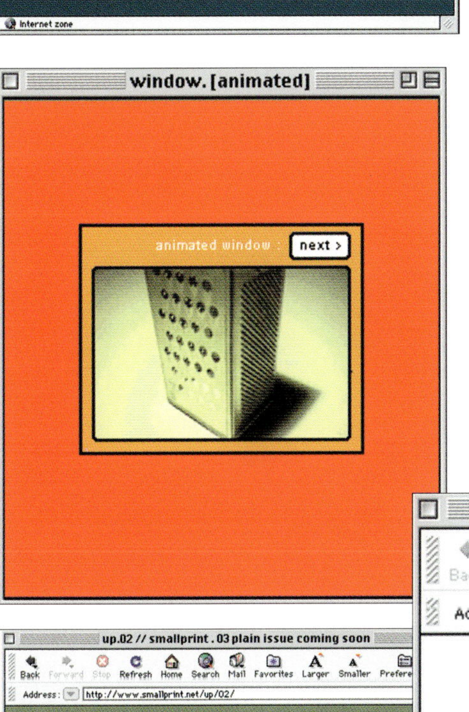

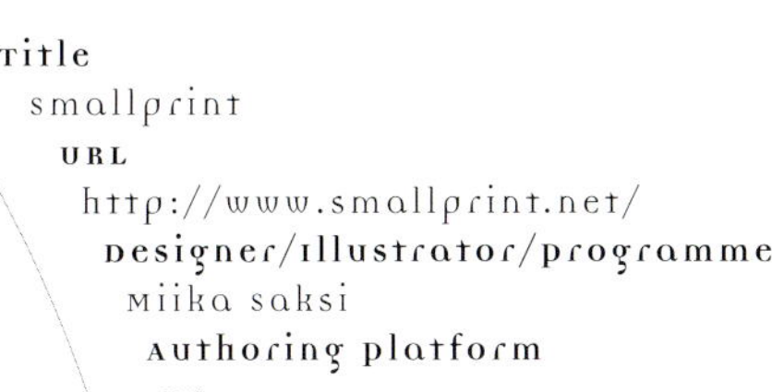

Smallprint: the site that dares to scribble on itself. Using mostly rendered, very legible type—a face in which a lowercase *l* has that extra flip to help differentiate itself at low resolution—only a few bits of repeated text serve as navigation. Greater-than (>) signs are used instead of arrows as emphasis that an item should be clicked on to get to another page.

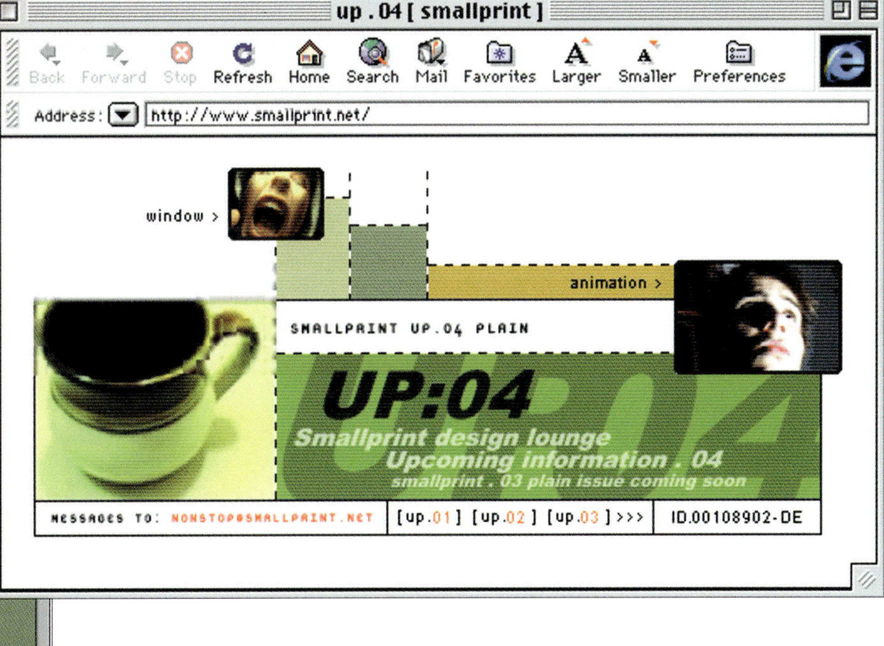

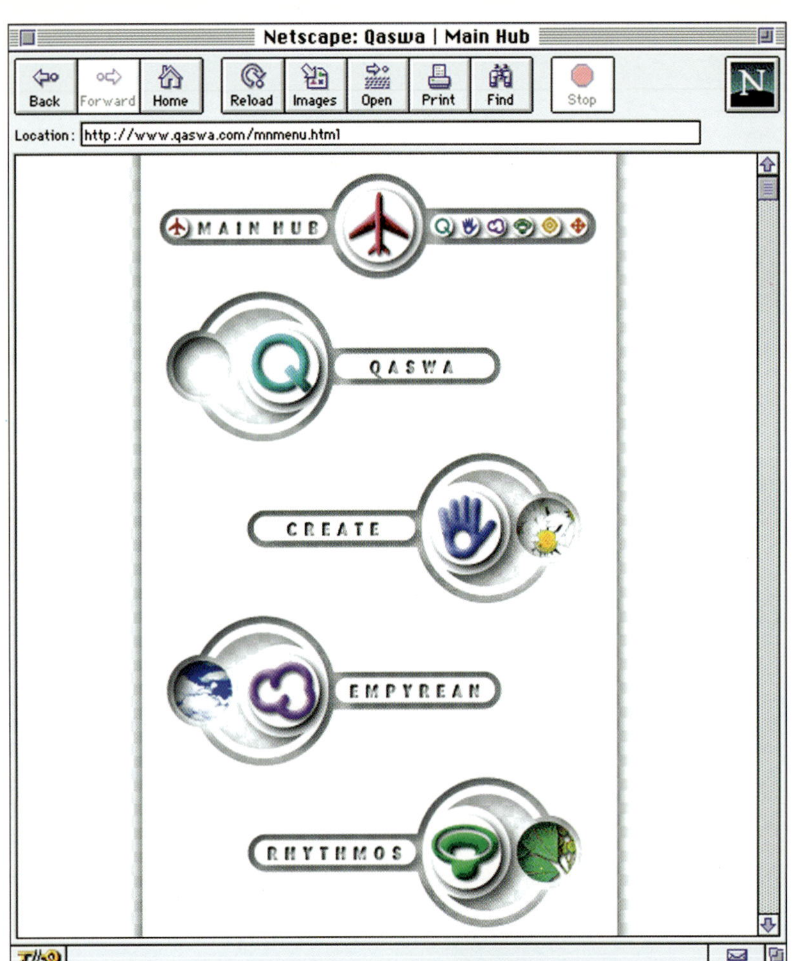

Title
qaswa shockwave hub
URL
http://www.qaswa.com/shock.html
Design firm
qaswa communications
Designer
ammon haggerty

One shortcoming of much Web typography is a limitation shared by its print cousin: letters are, in most cases, flat characters on a flat surface. It's refreshing when designers add the perception of depth, as in the Qaswa Shockwave Hub. Well-placed drop shadows, reinforced by the navigation cut into the screen, turning a bold sans-serif font into something more eye-catching.

Title
popi music magazine
URL
http://www.popi.com/
Design firm
hyperhead new media
Designer/programmer
ross teasley
Authoring platform
mac, pc

Can too much typographical variety sabotage good design? Definitely. However, thanks to the subject matter of this site (a music magazine), combining exaggerated typefaces enhances the pages' character. Uneven, layered, illuminated—these are musical concepts rendered in letter form.

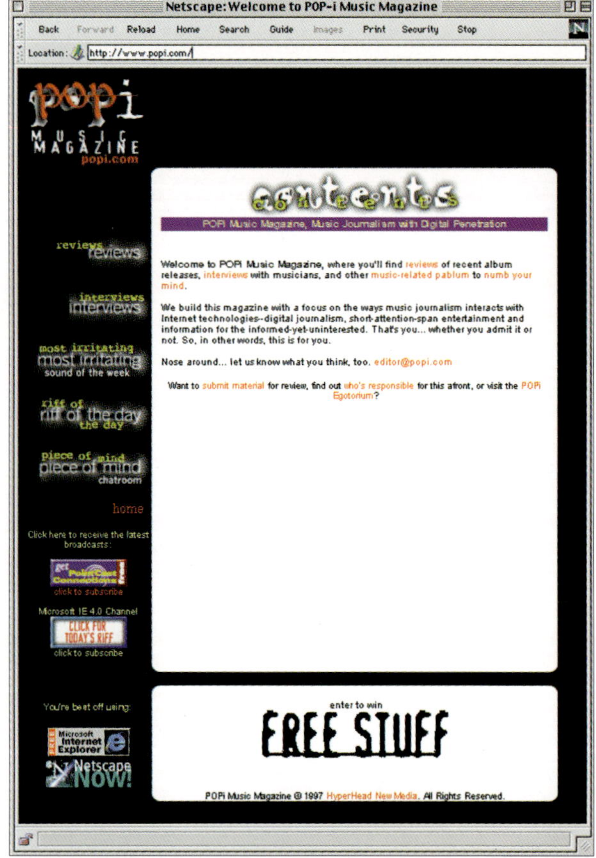

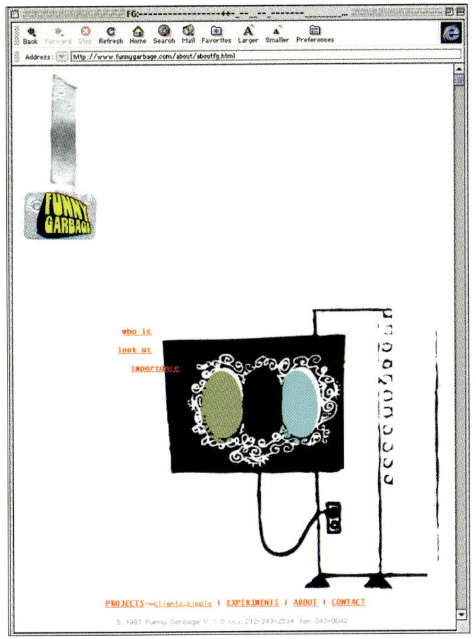

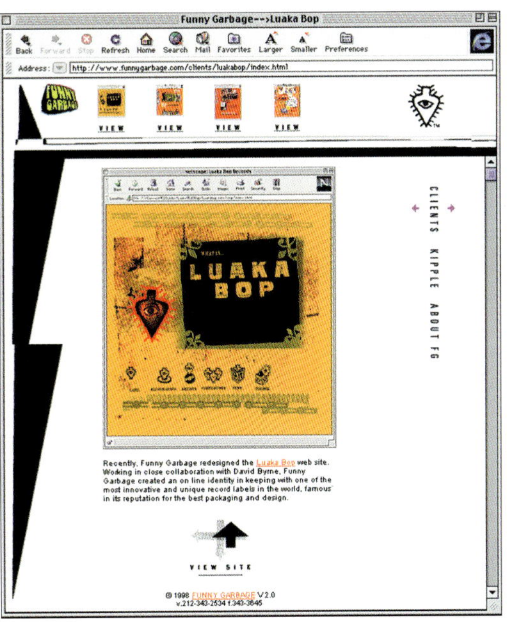

Title
funny garbage
URL
http://www.funnygarbage.com/about/aboutfg.html
Design Firm
funny garbage
Designers
peter girardi, chris capuozzo
Illustrators
todd james, devin flynn
Programmers
fred kahl, dan wyszynski, nina ong
Producers
fred kahl, kristin ellington, esther robinson
Authoring Platform
mac, pc

The 1970s (or maybe late 1960s) cannot be evoked better than through the balloon-like letterforms of the Funny Garbage logo. That logo is combined with the modern equivalent of photocopier art, including type that's actually struck-through—an amazing development. Every page features careful placement of type, but the type is artistically messed up: sometimes all caps, sometimes lowercase, sometimes intercapped, often slightly different sizes in the same word.

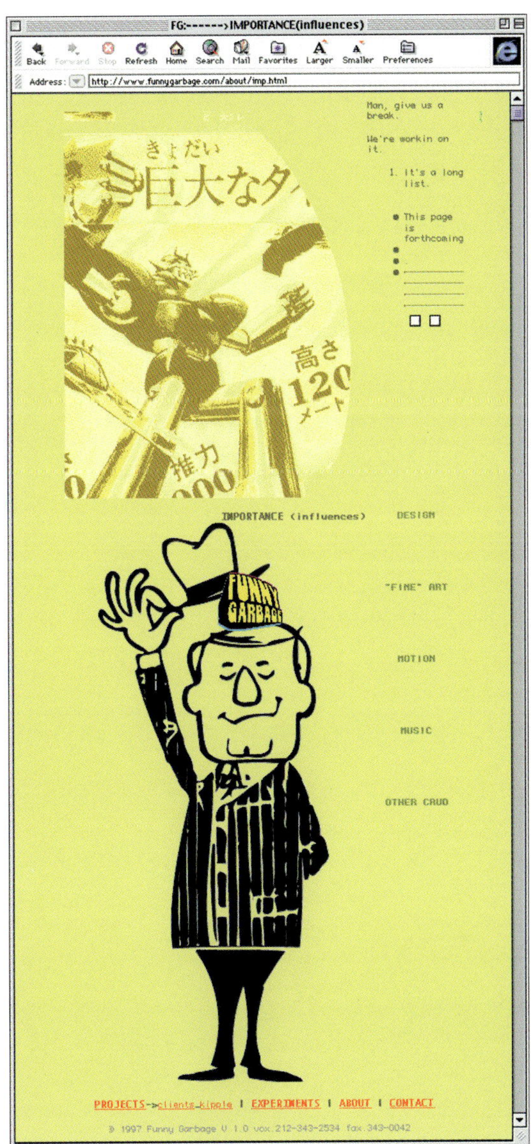

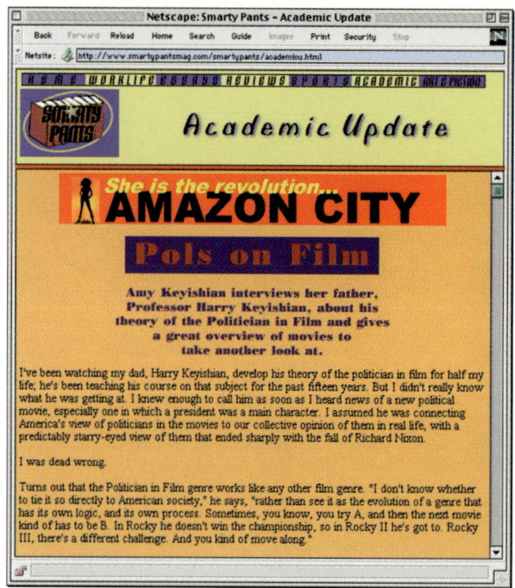

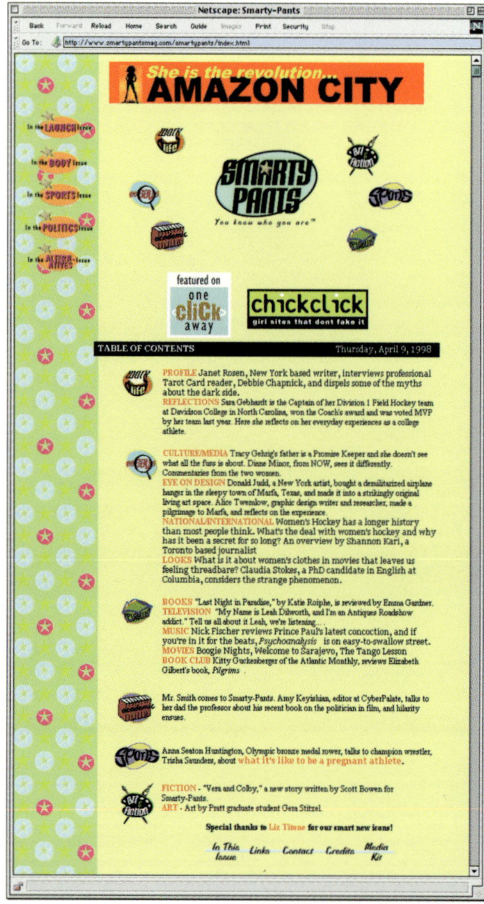

A 1970s aesthetic has snuck back into design, as evidenced by the angular, stylized font used in the title and the top navigation on inside pages. Coupled with an italicized faux-handwritten typeface for titles, the message here is that modern design does not have to use modern typography.

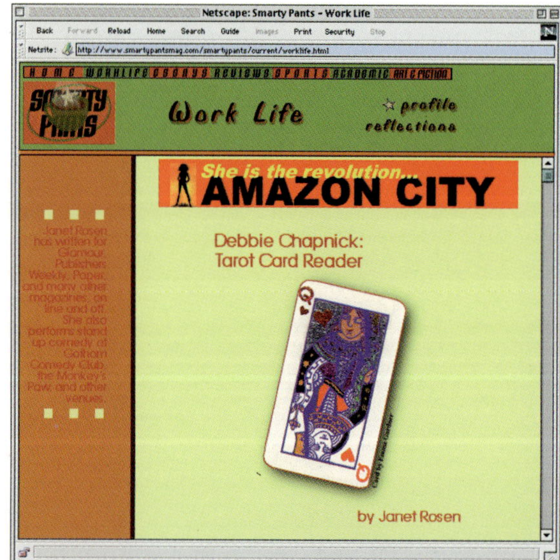

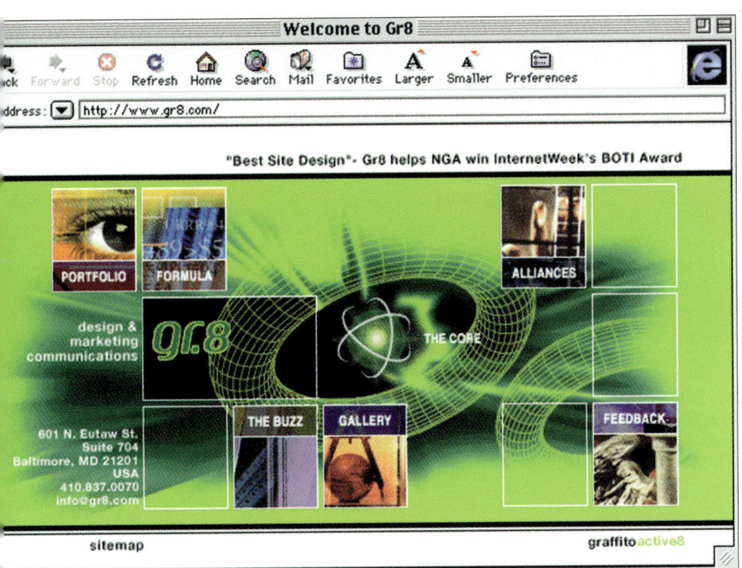

The site map exactly matches the home page substituting large numbers for the illustrations. The numbers correspond typographically (and navigationally) to the subdivisions of the site. The numbers, wherever they appear, are always the largest element, whether in the graphic site map, the more text-oriented one, or in the section headings.

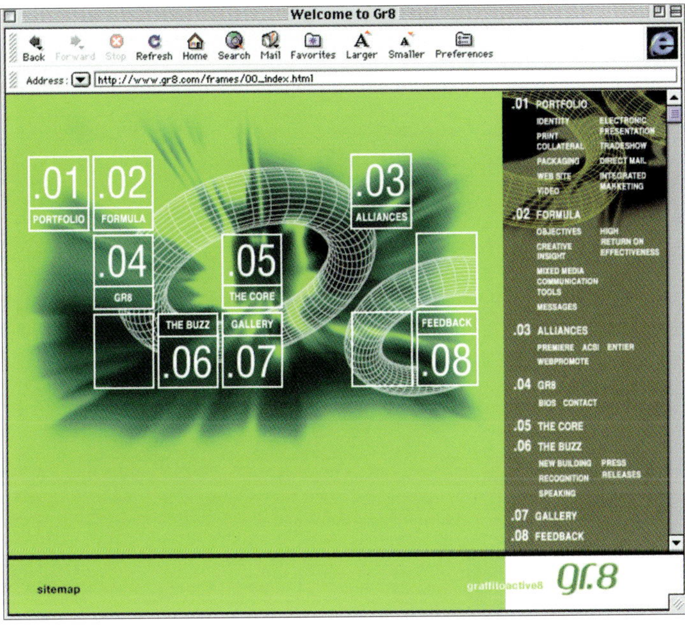

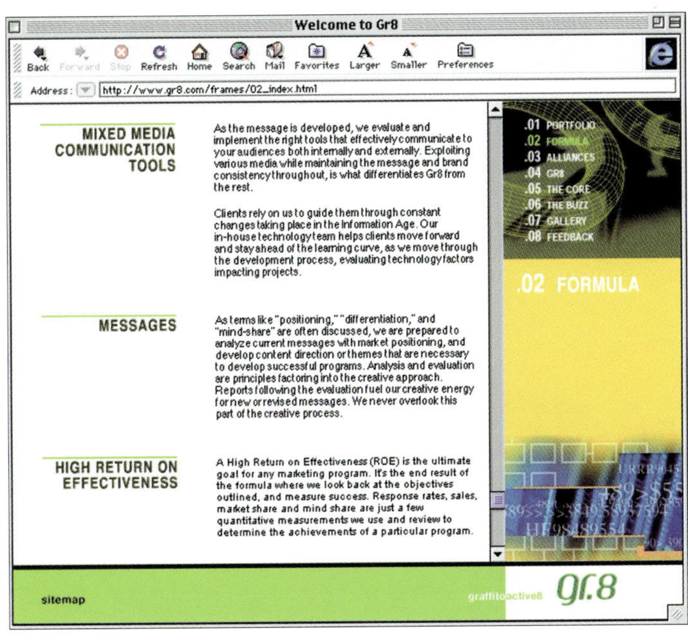

Title
Haynes and Boone website
URL
http://www.hayboo.com/
Design Firm
Phinney/Bischoff Design House, Inc.
Designer
Neil Robertson, Dean Hart
Illustrator
Dean Hart
Programmers
Glenn Fleishman, Neil Robertson
Creative Directors
Karl Bischoff, Leslie Phinney
Responsible Attorney
Rona Mears
Authoring platform
Mac

Elegant rendered type on the home page gives way to simpler (and easily legible) type on subsequent pages. The embossed type on the home page aren't links: they're concepts underlying the law firm's approach. Type in black, with lines running to pieces of illustration that repeat on each section's page, attach to concrete parts of the site, like briefings or recruiting.

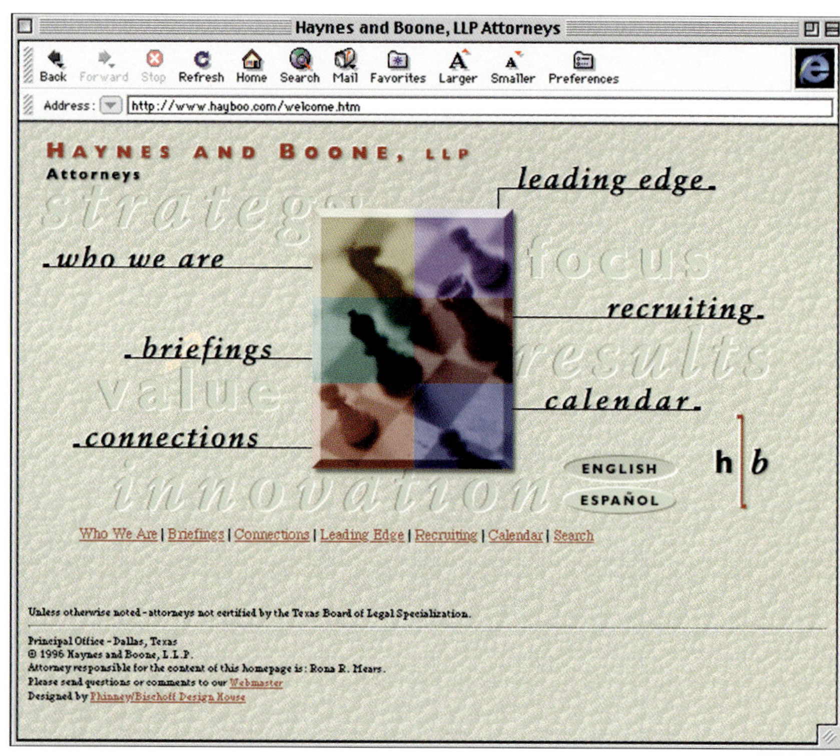

Title
Circumstance Design
URL
http://www.circumstance.com/
Design Firm
Circumstance Design
Designers/Illustrators
Tim Barber, David Bliss
Programmer
David Bliss

Despite the multimedia capabilities afforded by the Internet, the Web is still largely flat. Although you can make text move with JavaScript and other technologies, not every browser will display them. The solution is to create motion in motionless imagery, like the layered titles here, where the relevant title comes to the front on its page.

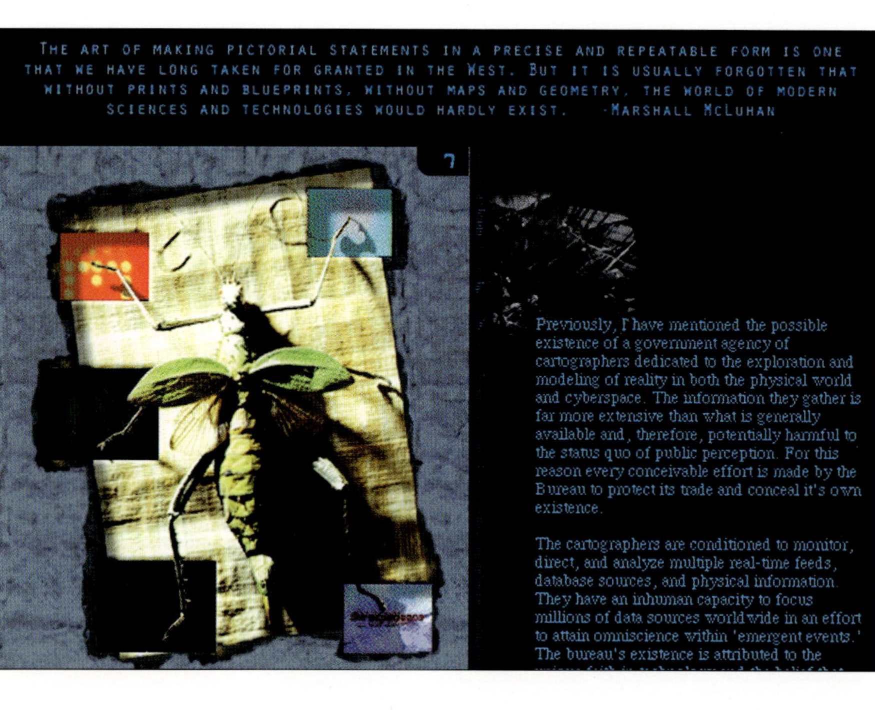

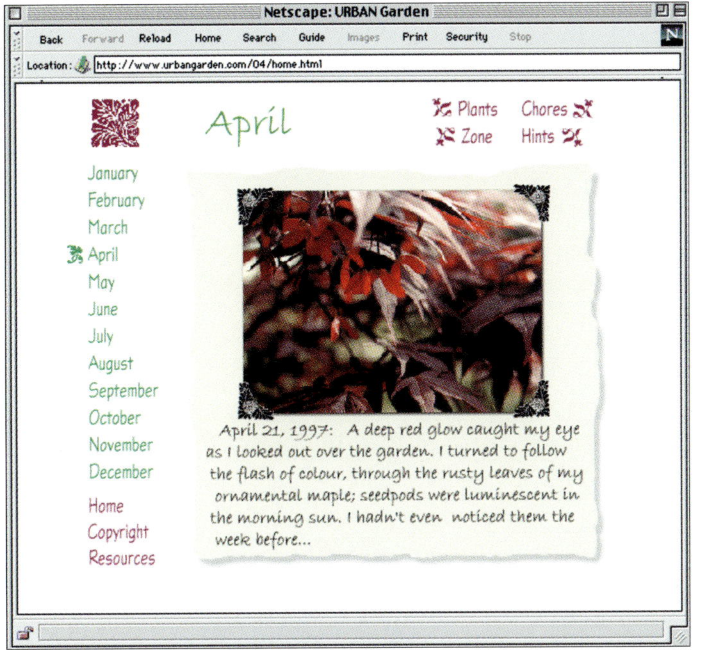

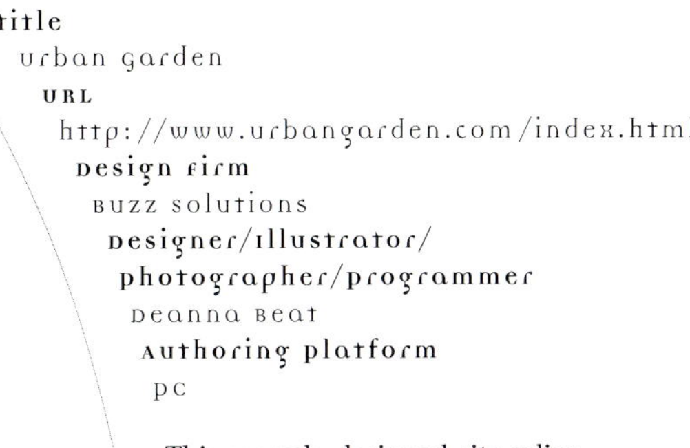

This sparsely designed site relies almost entirely on its typography. Built using images instead of actual text, the body typeface here suggests carefully handwritten journal entries; the relatively tall X-height makes the words particularly readable. Flowery dingbat characters, used as navigation aids, do not detract from the botanical content of the site.

title
The Iconfactory
URL
http://www.iconfactory.com/
design firm
The Iconfactory
designers/illustrators
Corey Marion, Talos Tsui, Gedeon Maheux
programmer
Craig Hockenberry
authoring platform
mac

For a site that has as its sole mission the dissemination of custom icons, it's appropriate that the typefaces found in the rendered type have a blocky but high-quality feel to them. The site's name is extra-chunky, but they've even taken the subtle step of using the same font in the visitor counter at the bottom of the page.

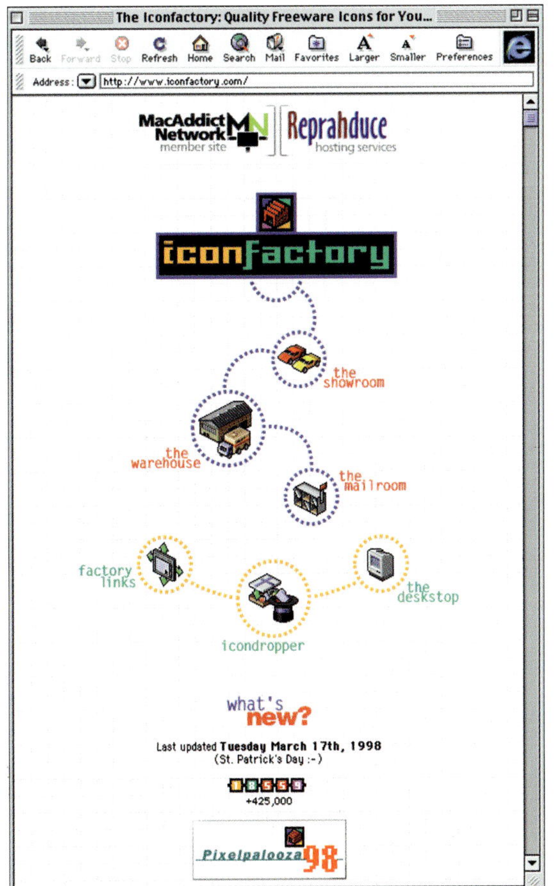

typography

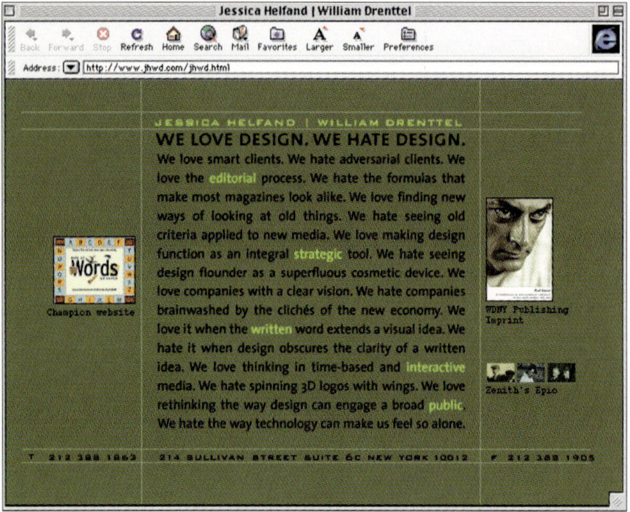

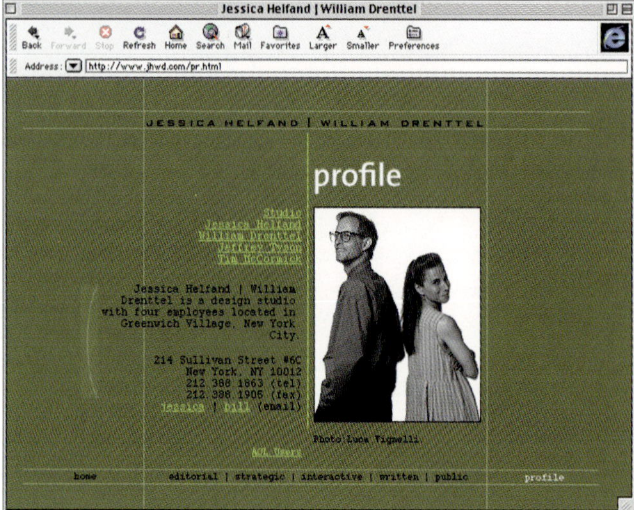

title
jessica helfand | william
drenttel
URL
http://www.jhwd.com/jhwd.html
design firm
jessica helfand | william drenttel
designers
jessica helfand, william drenttel,
jeffrey tyson
programmers
jeffrey tyson, steve bull (java)
editor
timothy mccormick
authoring platform
mac

Without using much but Courier, the site manages to look elegant. The type is carefully placed and sized, yet remains somewhat unpredictable. Courier is used in a few sizes: one for text, another for navigation links, and a third for captions (where italic is thrown in). Section headings and the firm name are the only rendered type on lower-level pages; the home page is a carefully set block of text.

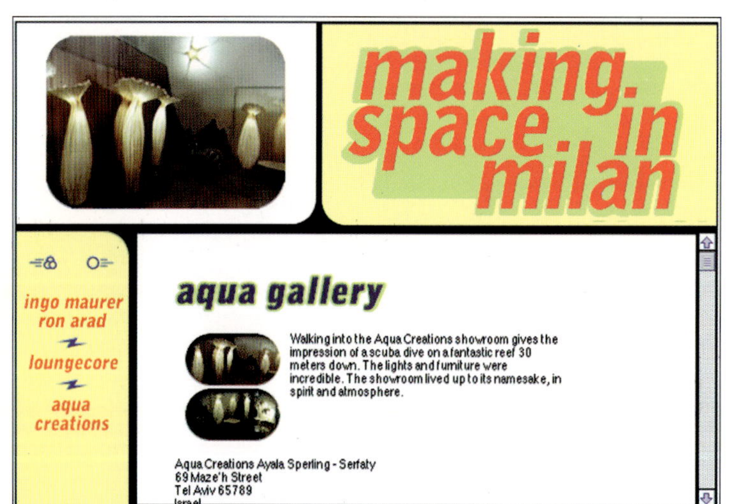

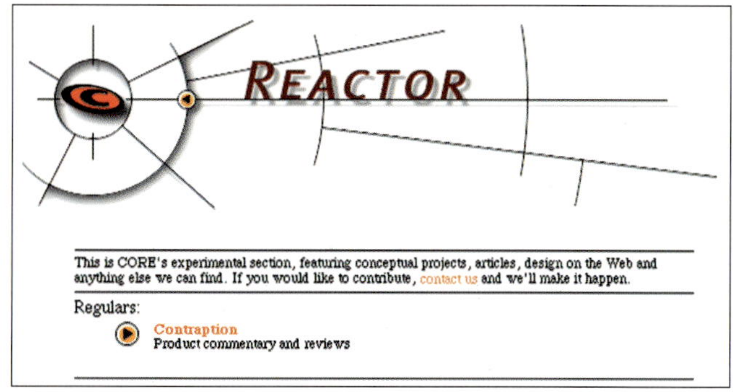

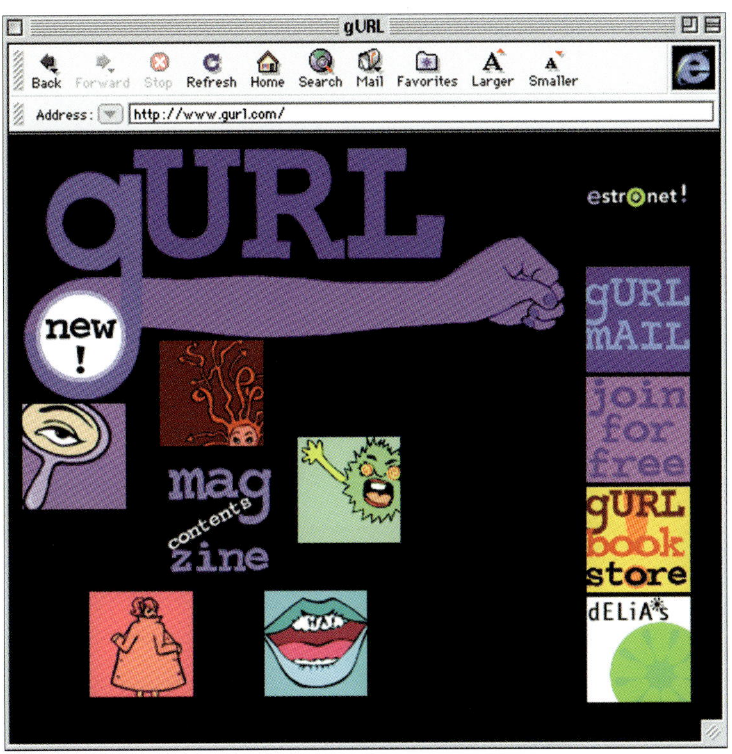

title
gURL

URL
http://www.gurl.com/

Design Firm
gURL

Designer/Illustrator
Rebecca Odes

Programmers
Sonya Allin, Esther Drill

Authoring Platform
Mac

With its many hand-drawn illustrations and spot colors, this site pushes a fun, down-to-earth atmosphere that invites exploration. The blocky typeface almost looks as if it's been cut from construction paper, making it ideal for placement anywhere in the layout and flexible when applying different colors.

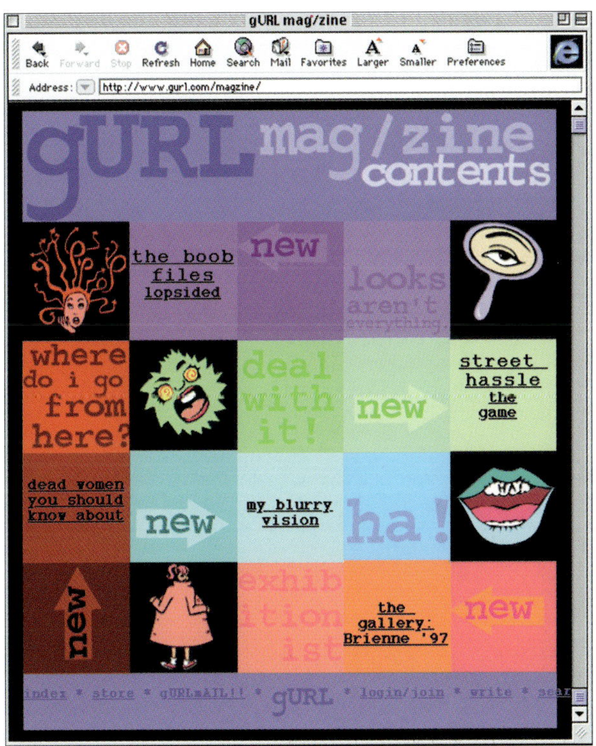

title
Core77

URL
http://www.core77.com/

Designers
Eric Ludlum, Stuart Constantine

Industrial design is often sleek, progressive, smooth, and new. So it comes as no surprise to find italicized sans-serif fonts at Core77. The all-caps titles seem to push the viewer's eye to the right, into the center of the circular navigation framework.

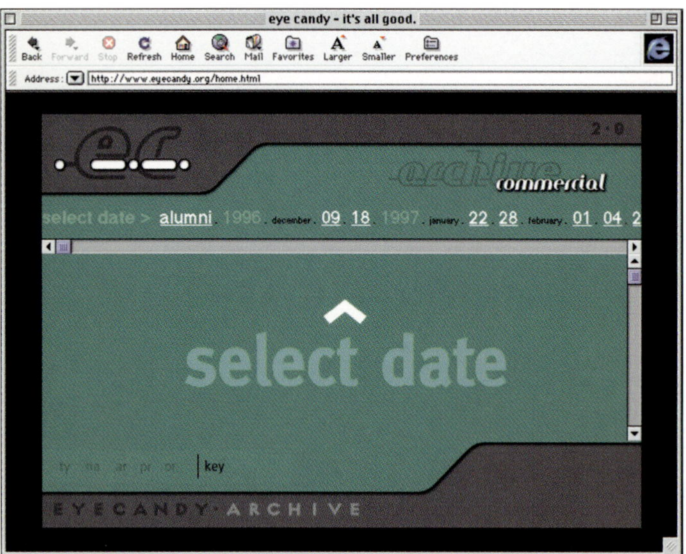

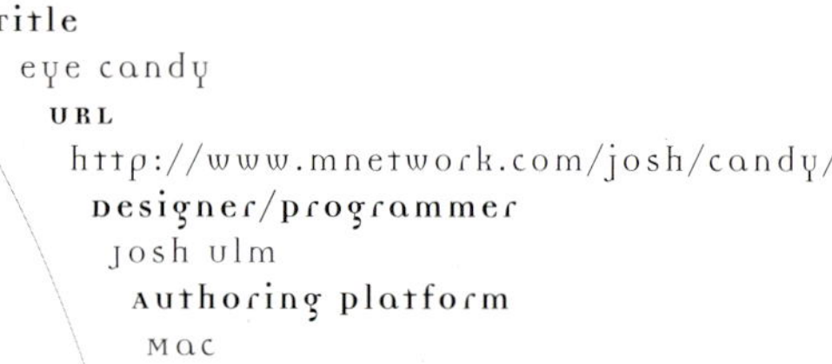

Eye Candy makes great use of one really interesting typeface, using it in multiple colors, with stroked outlines, and reversed-out of background colors, for both logotypes (like the site's name and section names) and for headlines. The typographic treatment throughout relies on rendered type to provide the visual interest, while plainer text conveys the longer messages.

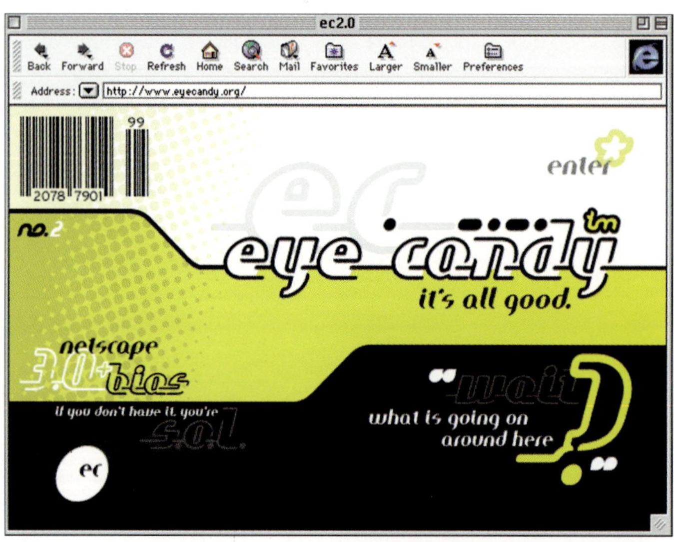

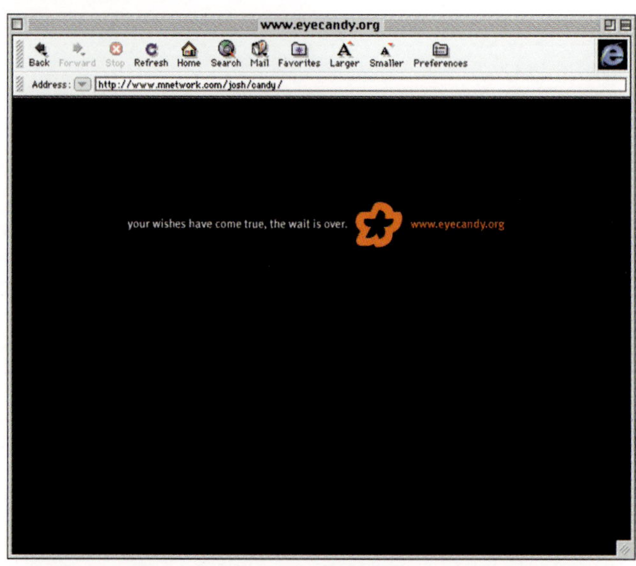

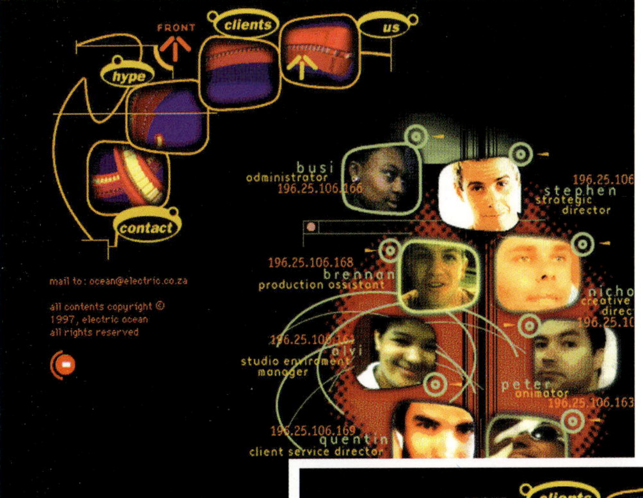

Title
Electric ocean

URL
http://www.electricocean.co.za/

Design firm
Electric ocean

Designer
Nicholas wittenberg

Programmer
Stephen Garratt

With so much going on
visually within these pages,
it's helpful that the typography
uses letterforms that are clear
and easy to read. The main
navigation uses sans-serif
italics, which pop out from
the surrounding images
without overpowering them.

Title
Emergent media, inc.

URL
http://www.emergentmedia.com/

Design firm
Emergent media, inc.

Designer
Yann oehl

Programmers
Tim hunt, Kala anderson, Dan
shepherd

Authoring platform
pc

All graphical elements, besides the color
field, are pieces of type or the logo. A little
animation rotates the elements of the logo,
making it look a bit like a set of abstracted
gears. The name of the company slides neatly
into place in crisp, simple type.

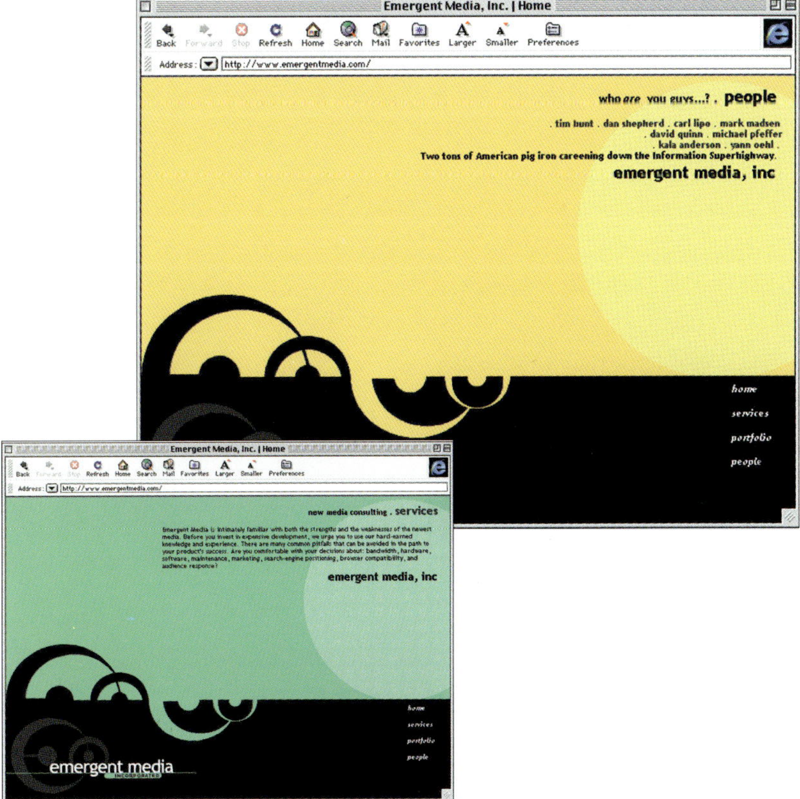

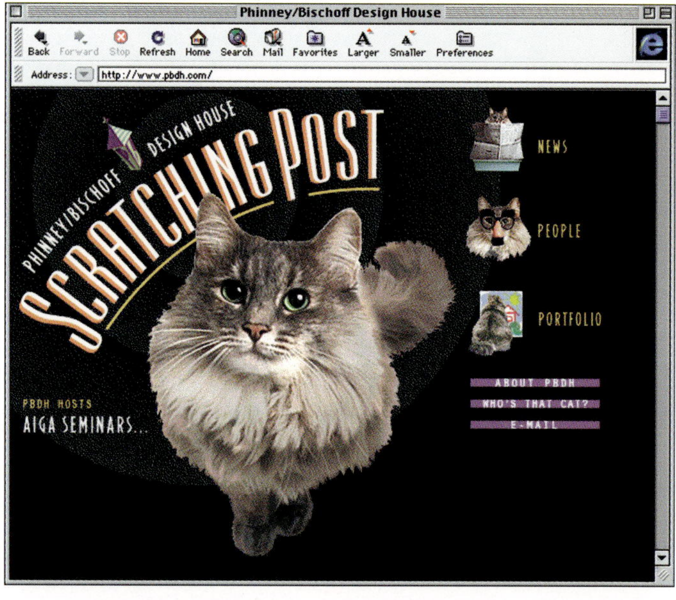

title
phinney/bischoff design
house, inc.
url
http://www.pbdh.com/
design firm
phinney/bischoff design house, inc.
designer/illustrator
Neil Robertson
photographer
Karl Bischoff
programmers
Neil Robertson, Scotty Carreiro
creative directors
Leslie phinney, Karl Bischoff
authoring platform
Mac

The narrow stylized sans-serif font found throughout this site does more than just stand out from the Web browser's default text font. Reminiscent of 1930s cinema and theater lettering, the typeface (especially curved and layered on the main screen) suggests that clients will receive work worthy of performance, not just standard viewing fare.

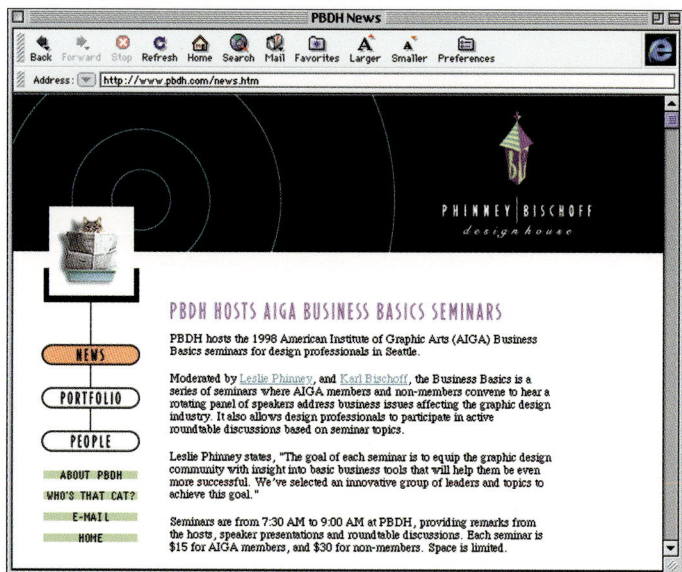

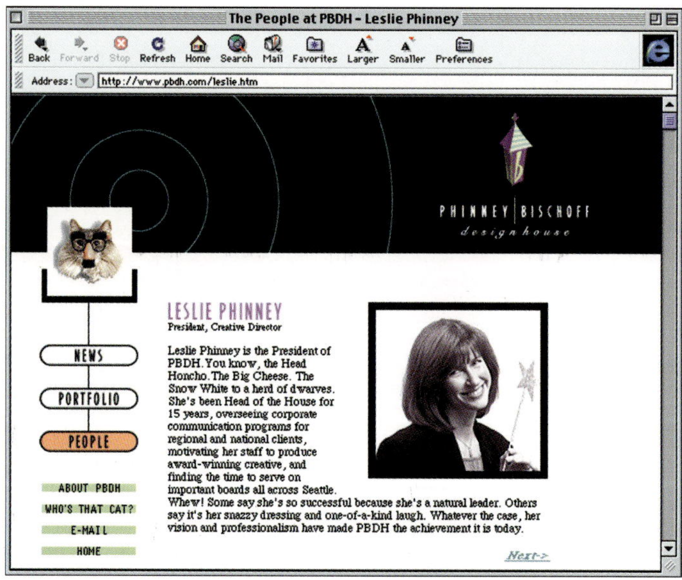

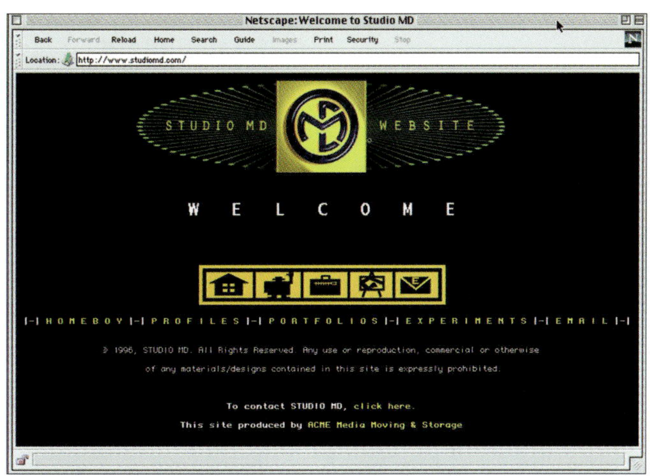

Title
studio M D

URL
http://www.studiomd.com/

Design firm
studio M D

Designers
Glenn Mitsui, Randy Lim,
Jesse Doquilo

Illustrators
Glenn Mitsui, Jesse Doquilo

Programmer
Tim Celeski

Authoring platform
Mac

In HTML, the <CODE> and <TT> tags are usually reserved for displaying programming examples or similar information using a fixed-width font such as Courier or Monaco. Here, the designers have chosen to run with this style for all body copy, which makes it very readable and a subtle change from most other sites.

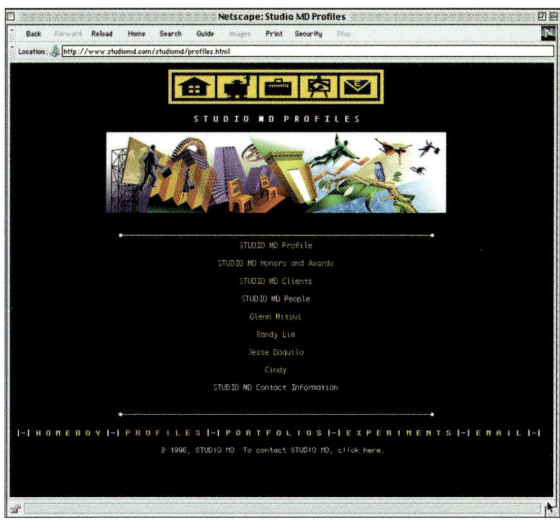

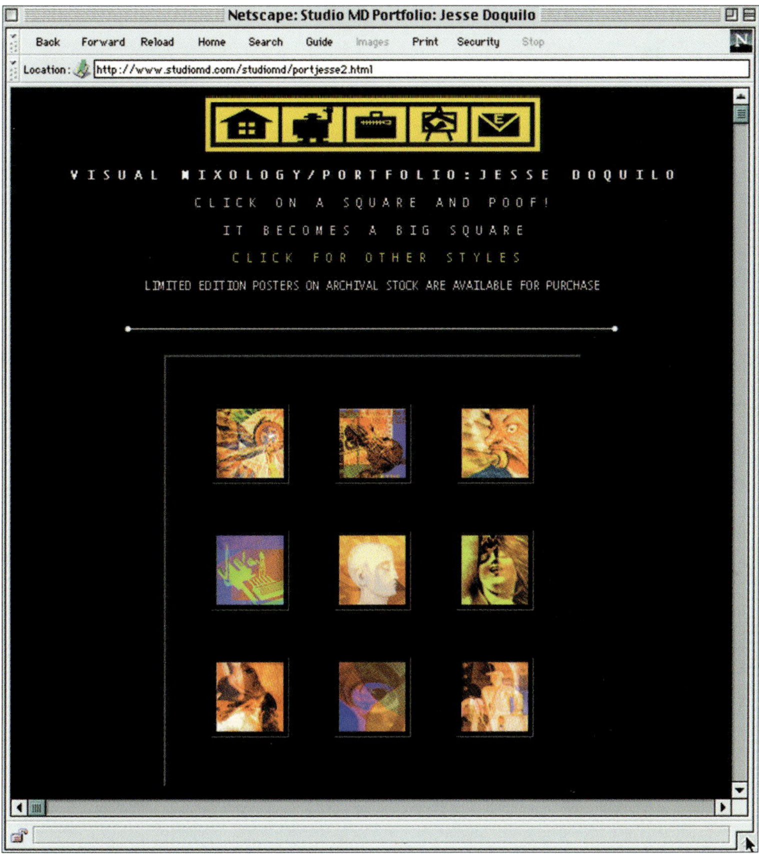

typography

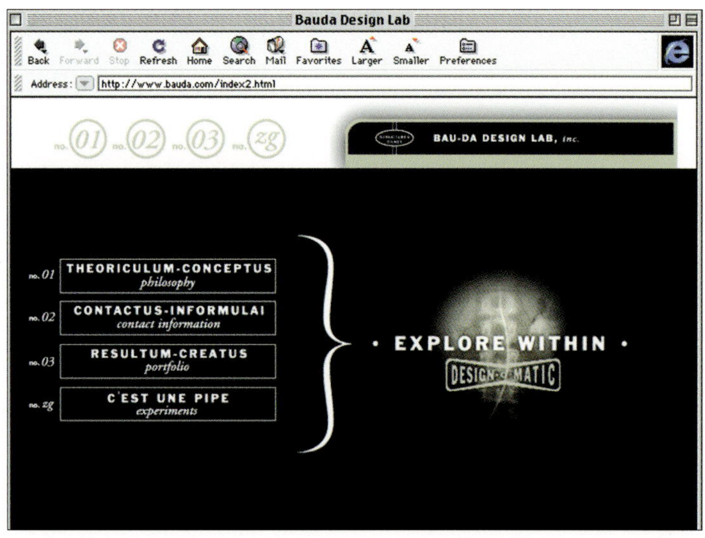

TITLE
Bau-Da Design Lab, Inc.
URL
http://www.bauda.com/
DESIGN FIRM
Bau-Da Design Lab, Inc.
DESIGNER/ILLUSTRATOR
P.R. Brown
PROGRAMMER
Eric Brown
AUTHORING PLATFORM
Mac

Bau-Da takes a fairly traditional approach combined with a pseudo-scientific whimsy. They use a heavy san-serif type in all caps coupled with lowercase, italic serif. This gives the site a certain solidity that doesn't take itself too seriously. Bau-Da favors rendering type to ensure exact placement, such as the list of album cover portfolio pieces, where each name is a separate graphic to allow navigation even without images loading.

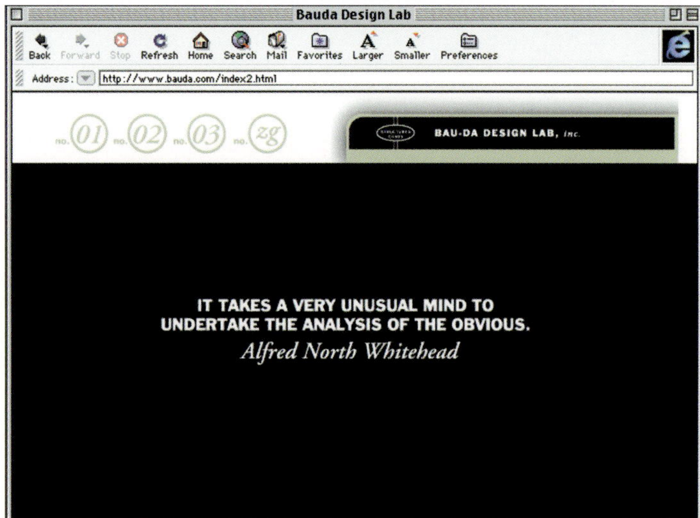

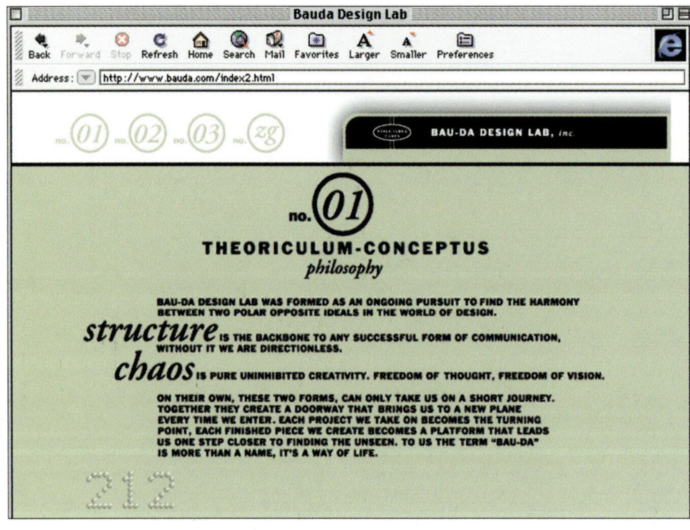

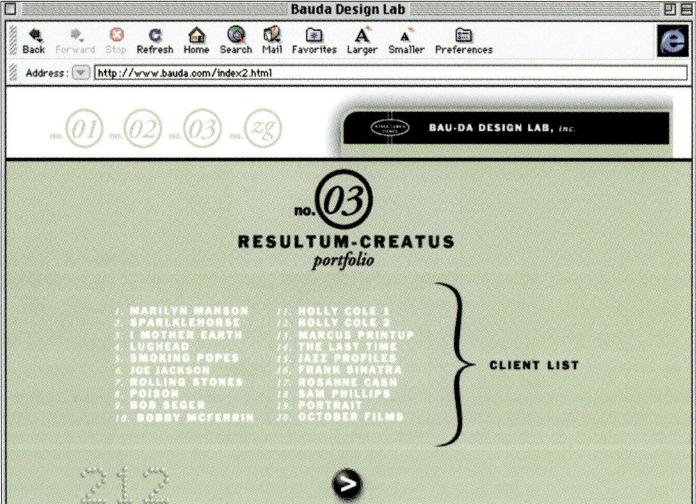

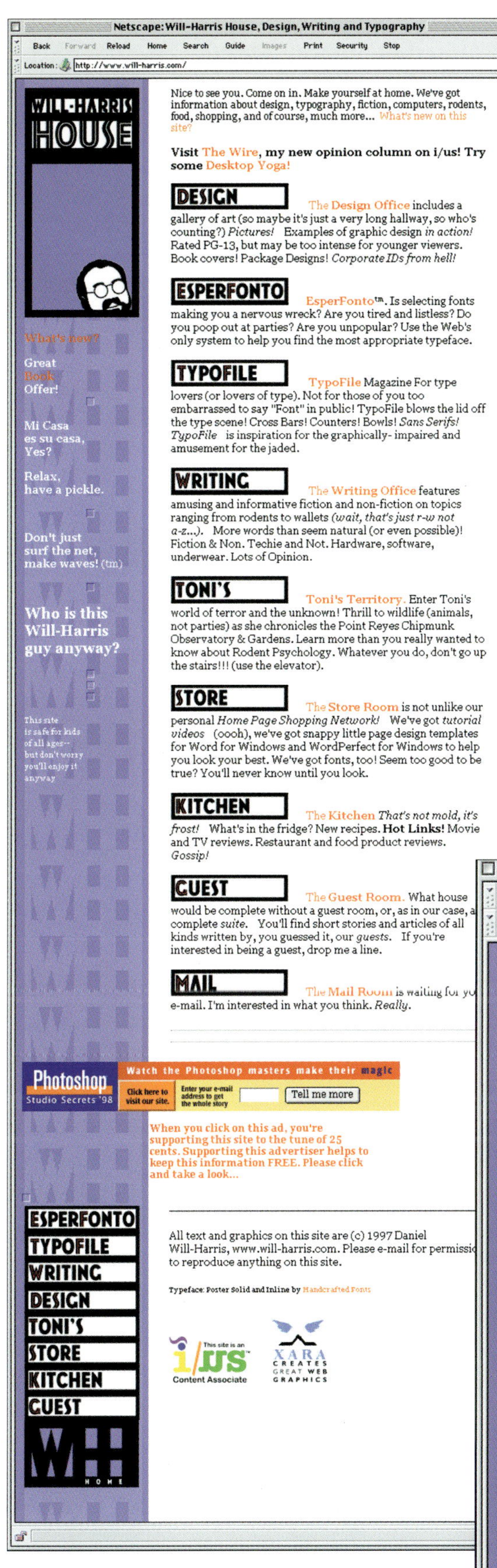

title
will-harris house
url
http://www.will-harris.com/
design firm
will-harris house
designer/illustrator/programmer
daniel will-harris
authoring platform
pc

One of the interesting aspects of this site's typography is not the unique fonts that are used, but their technical setup: for increased flexibility, each letter is rendered as its own file—words are constructed by placing the letter images side-by-side. This way, if the words or the fonts change, only the HTML has to be modified, instead of recreating new graphics from scratch.

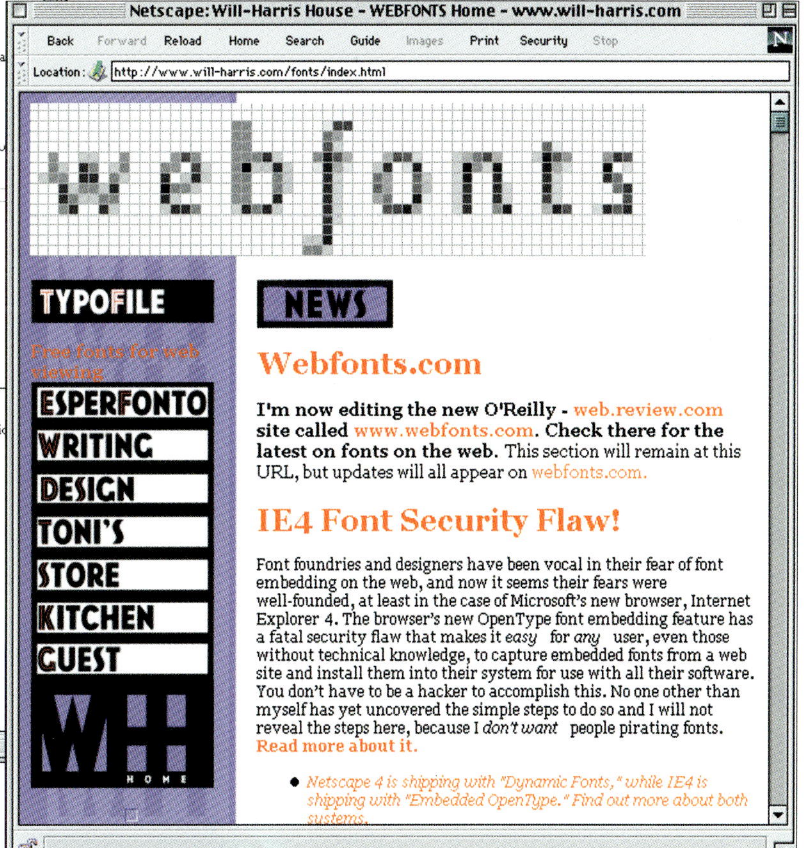

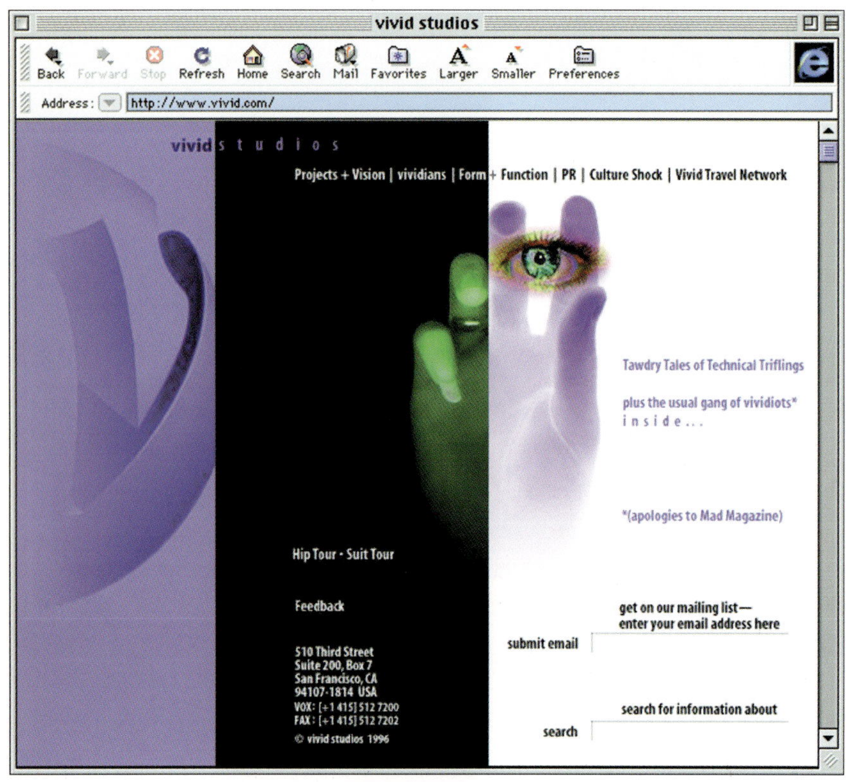

title
vivid studios
URL
http://www.vivid.com/
design firm
vivid studios
photographers
Brian Bell, Chuck Gathard,
Marsha Plat
programmers
Paul Guth, Nat Johnson
creative director
Nathan Shedroff
information designer
Drue Miller
visual designers
Jeff Davis, Nathan Shedroff,
Maurice Tani
writer
Drue Miller
authoring platform
Mac, UNIX

One of the two graphic elements on this site's home page is a V cut out of a sphere; it nicely shows both their typographic sensibility and their "cutting-edge" mentality. All of the type used for navigation is rendered, and outside of the name of the firm, is in the same size and weight. The type gets set in different colors, lit up, or knocked out to distinguish functions and location.

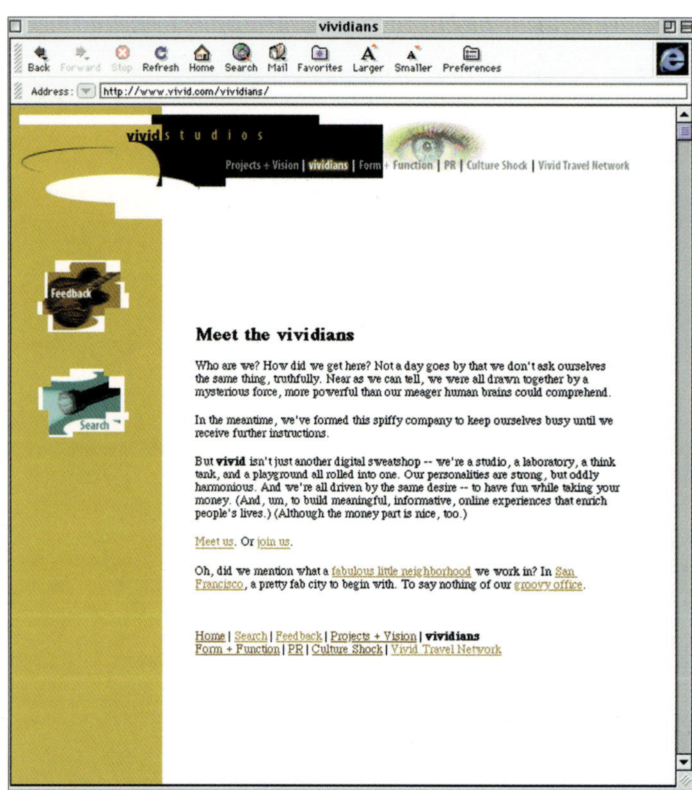

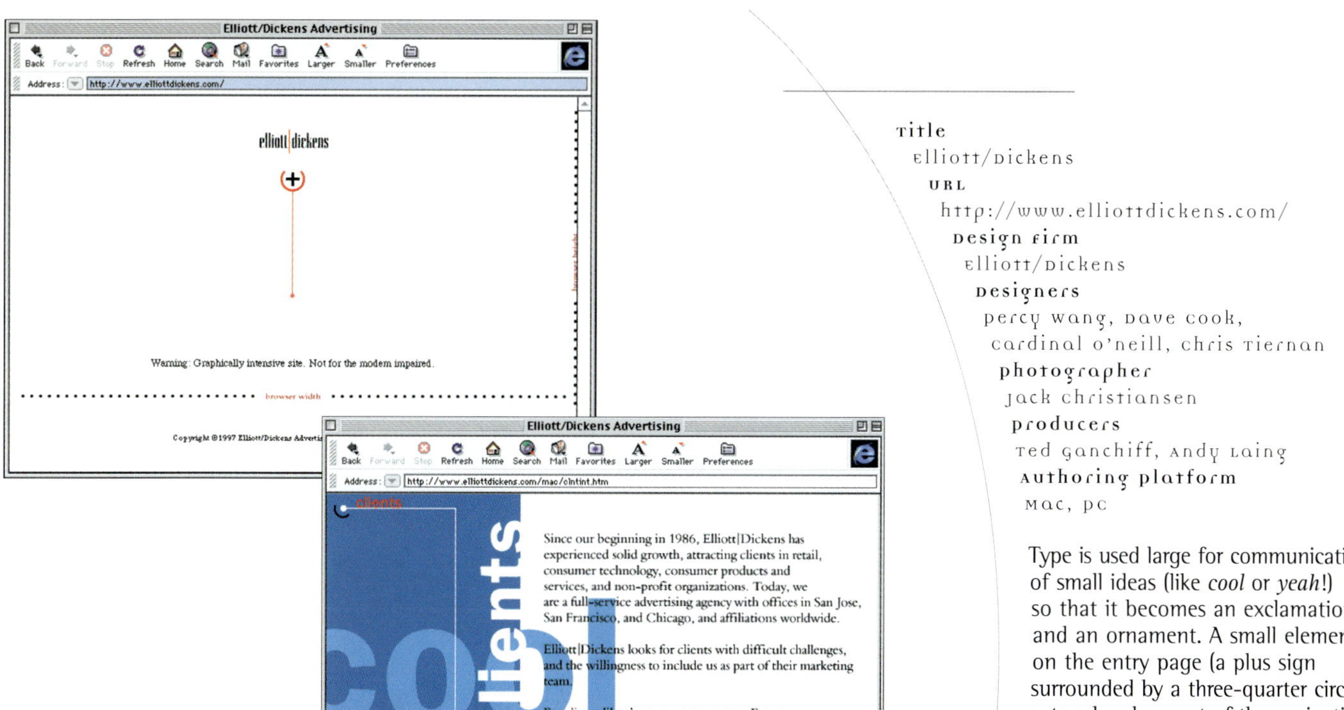

Type is used large for communication of small ideas (like *cool* or *yeah!*) so that it becomes an exclamation and an ornament. A small element on the entry page (a plus sign surrounded by a three-quarter circle) gets echoed as part of the navigation scheme on subsequent pages: the circle gets cut to one-half, but echoes the homepage element.

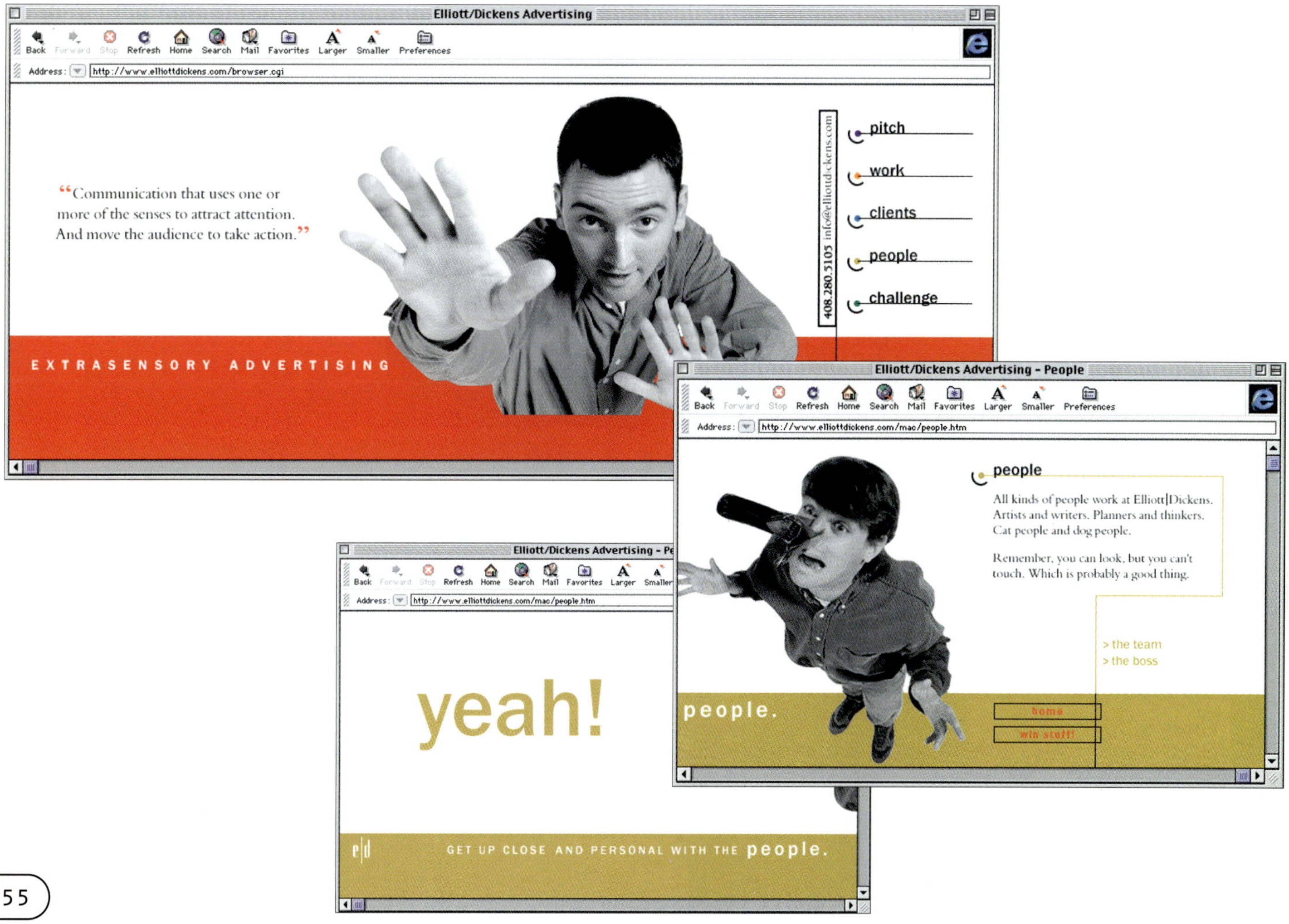

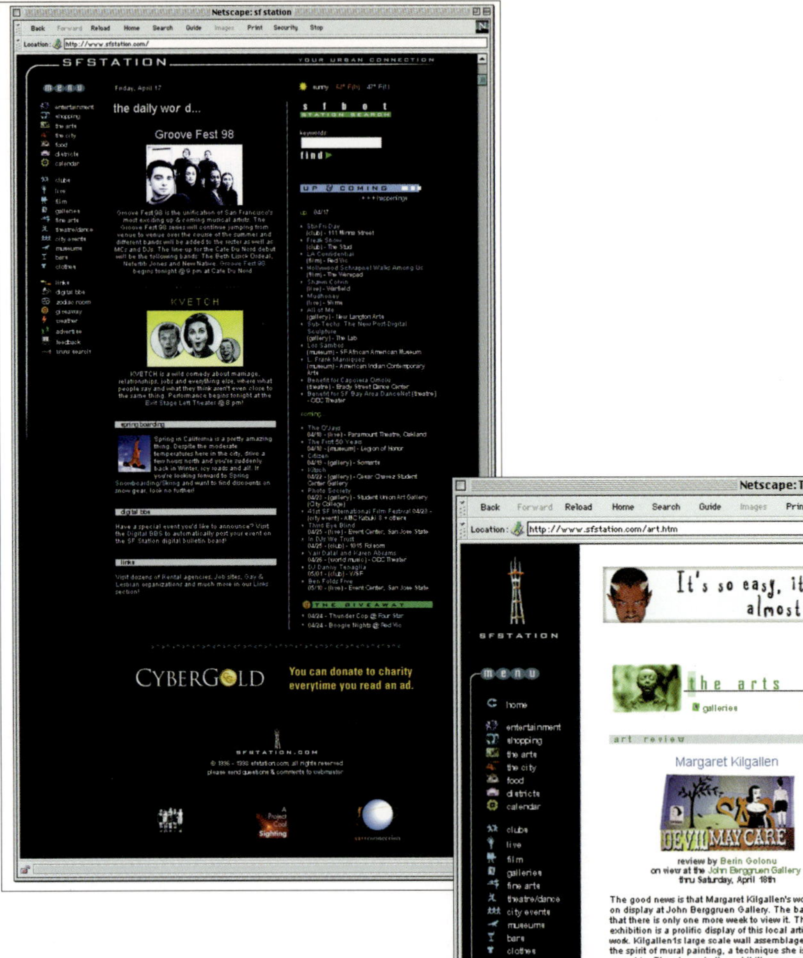

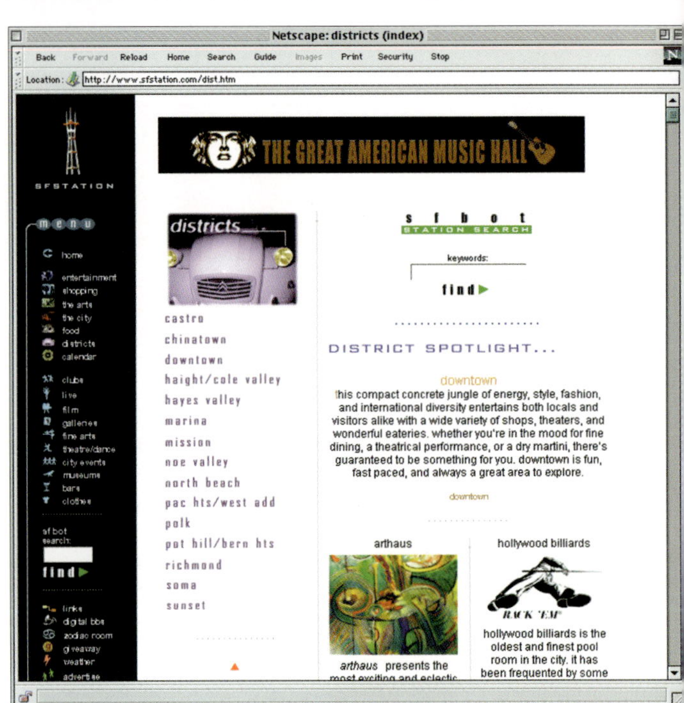

title
sfstation

url
http://www.sfstation.com/

design firm
sfstation

designers
mike richards, kyu kyung

illustrator
kyu kyung

photographer
curtis christophersen

programmers
vincent archuleta, kyu kyung, mike richards

authoring platform
mac, pc

The visual importance in this text-heavy site is weighted toward making a great deal of information as readable as possible. The designers have chosen to force the body text to display in a sans-serif font: The text is streamlined and meant to be skimmed by the reader, who is likely looking for a few nuggets of information, not the page as a whole. The sans-serif typography, even in title graphics, also adds to the site's modern feel.

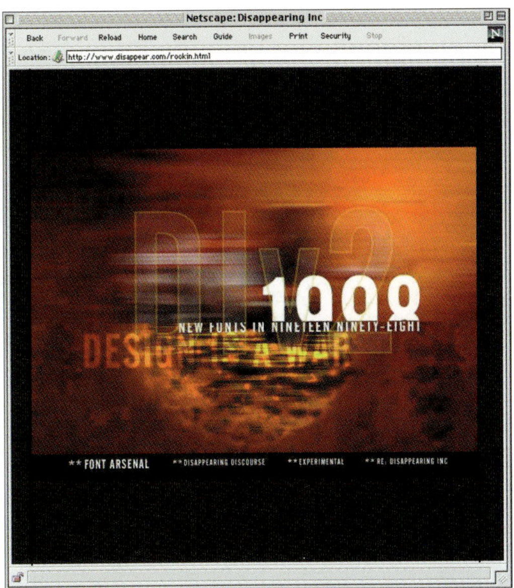

title
The Disappearing Inc Font Arsenal

URL
http://www.disappear.com/rockin.html

design firm
Disappearing Inc

designers/illustrators/photographers
Jason Lucas, Jeff Prybolsky

programmer
Al McElrath

authoring platform
Mac

Many inexperienced designers tend to look past plain fonts such as the condensed sans-serifs used here. Typefaces with solid fills are great for slicing, fading, blurring, outlining, layering, and applying other effects that do not obscure the words themselves but add to the design.

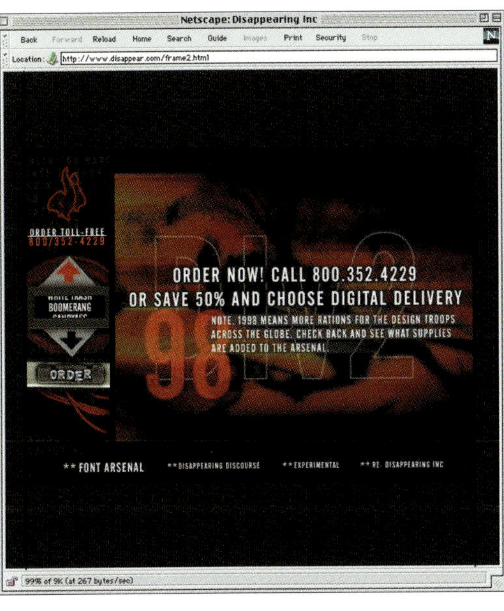

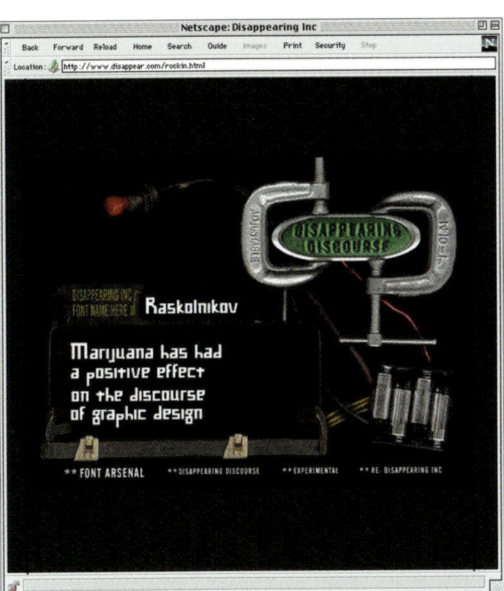

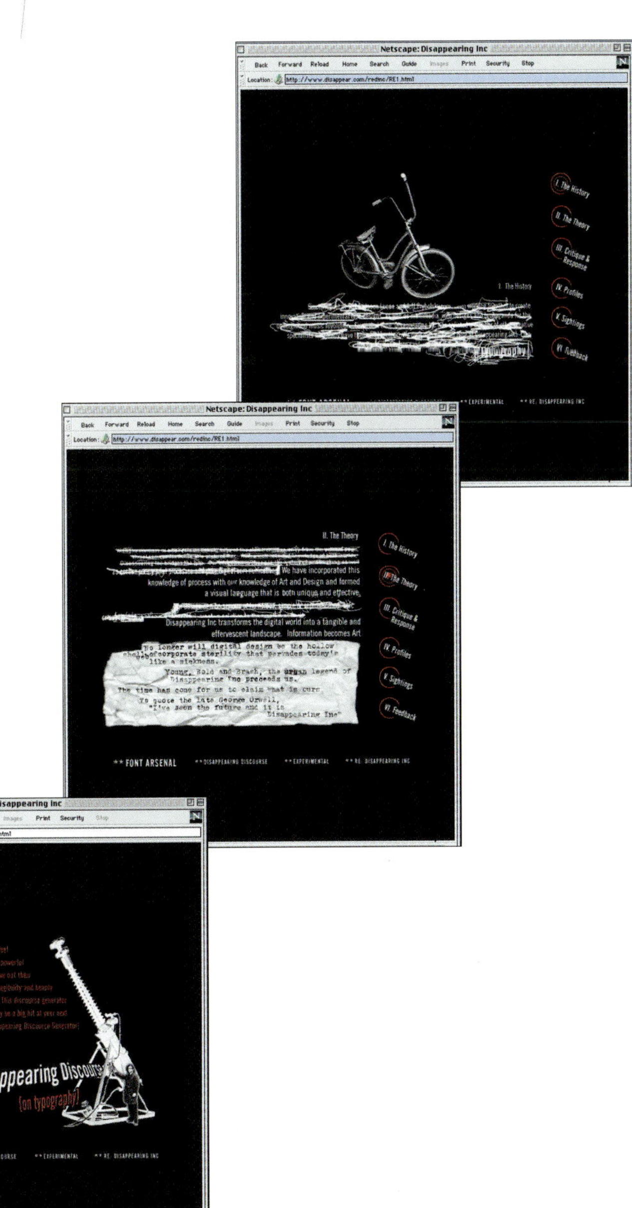

title
sub pop records
url
http://www.subpop.com/
designer
joe walker
programmers
ian dickson, ed slocomb,
joe walker

Although striving for a 1950s nuclear-family look, the fonts found here are appropriate for any time period. Certainly, the scripted Sub Pop on the main page echoes the chromed titling of big-finned automobiles; but "TRAFFiC REPORt" suggests a modern take on a retro font.

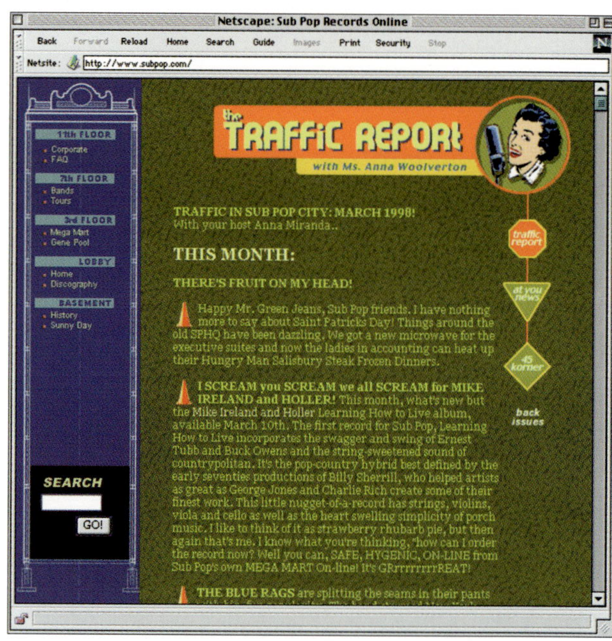

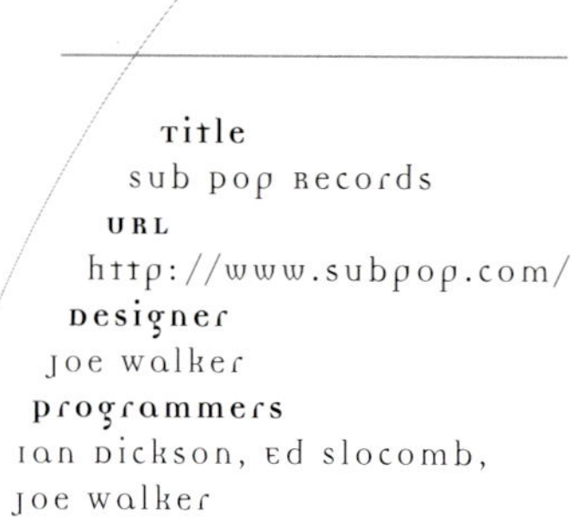

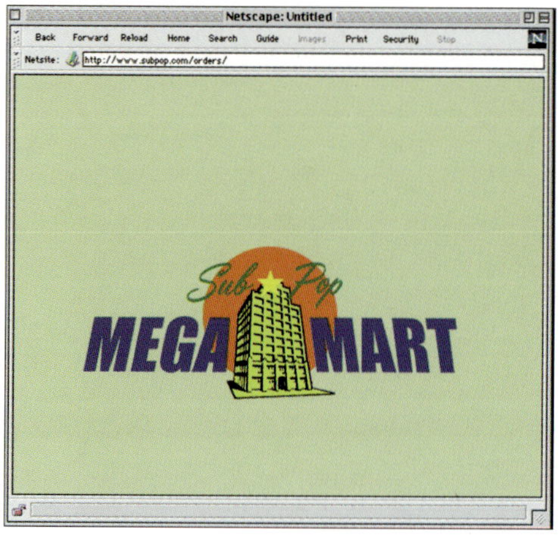

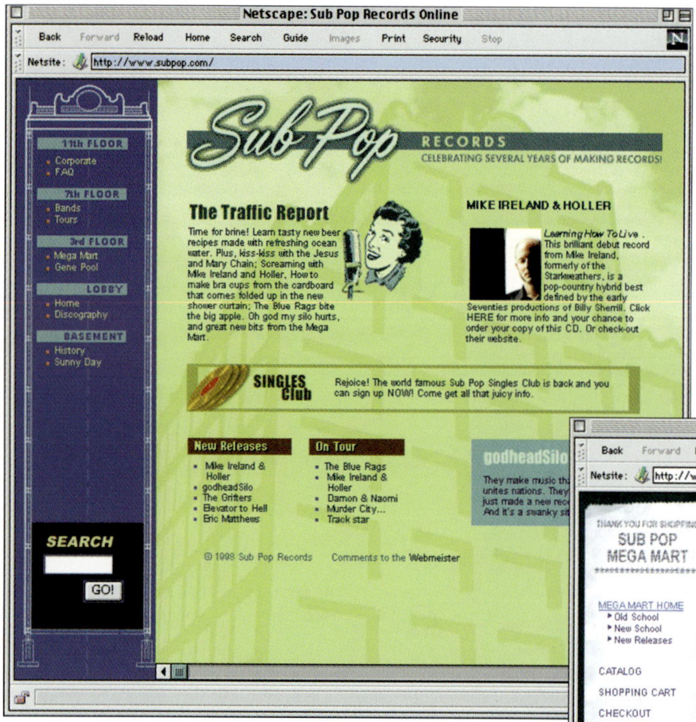

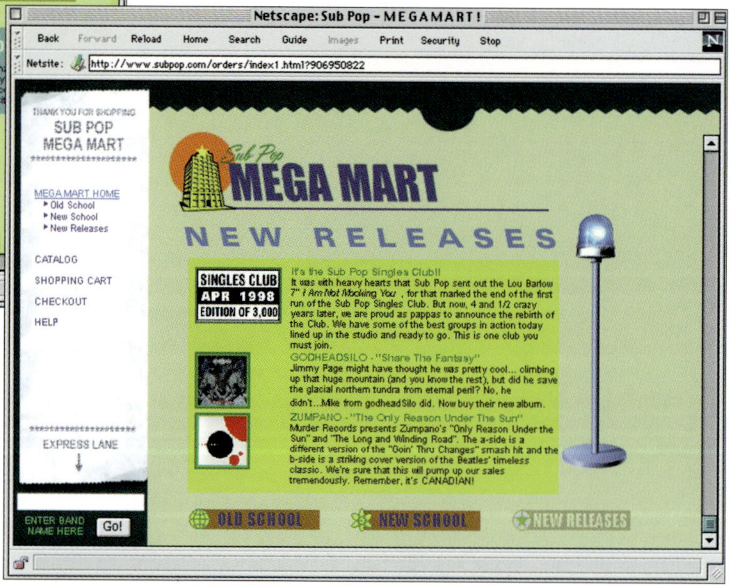

More than anything else, the typography of this site establishes its character. The simple lettering on the map suggests a note slipped surreptitiously by a friend. The hand-lettered typeface used in the navigation includes enough variation (especially with the flexible baselines) to signify membership in an informal club, while also containing the determined legibility of an astute letterer.

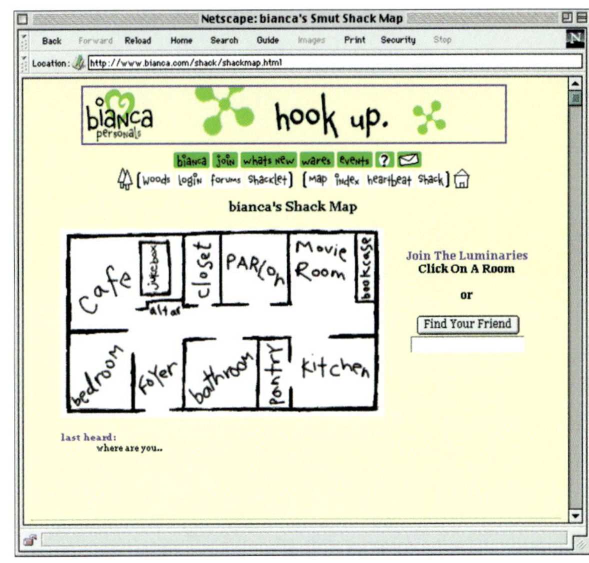

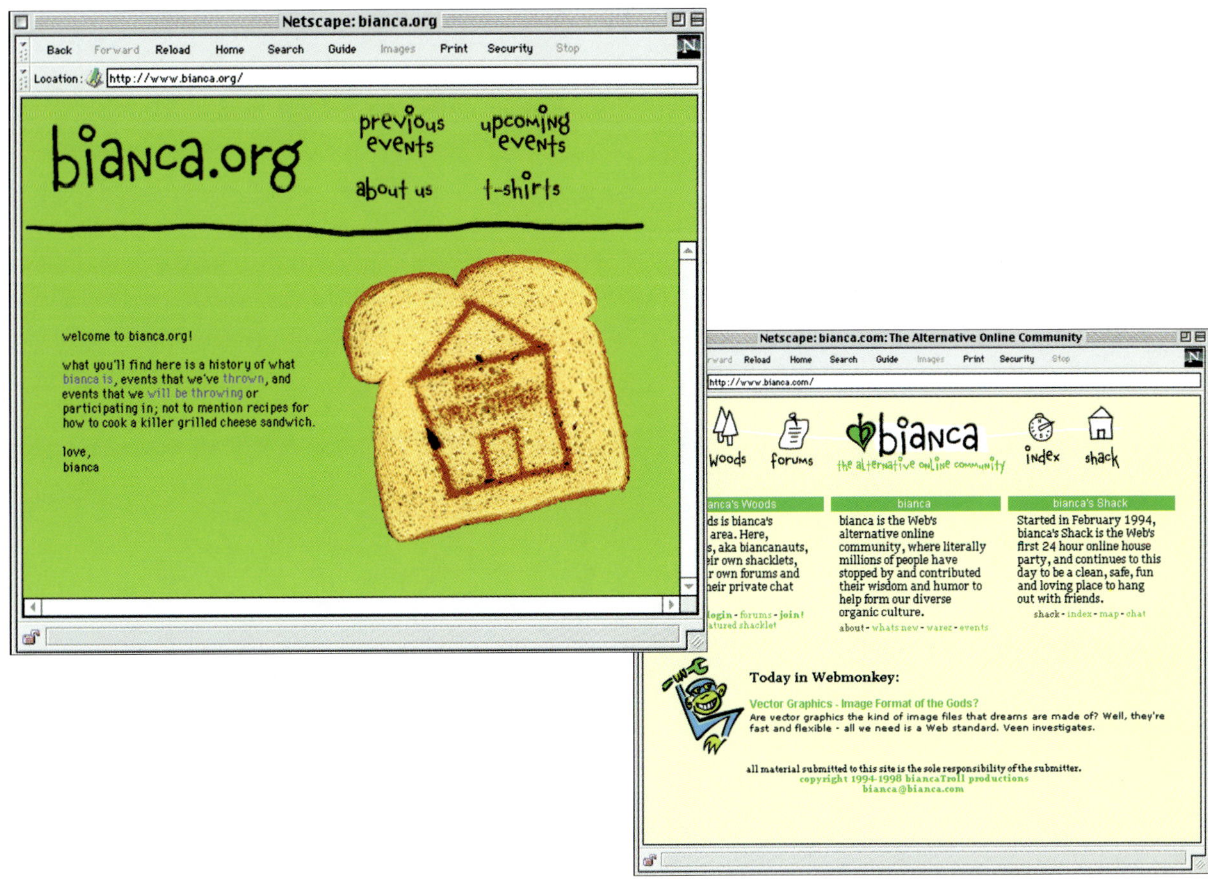

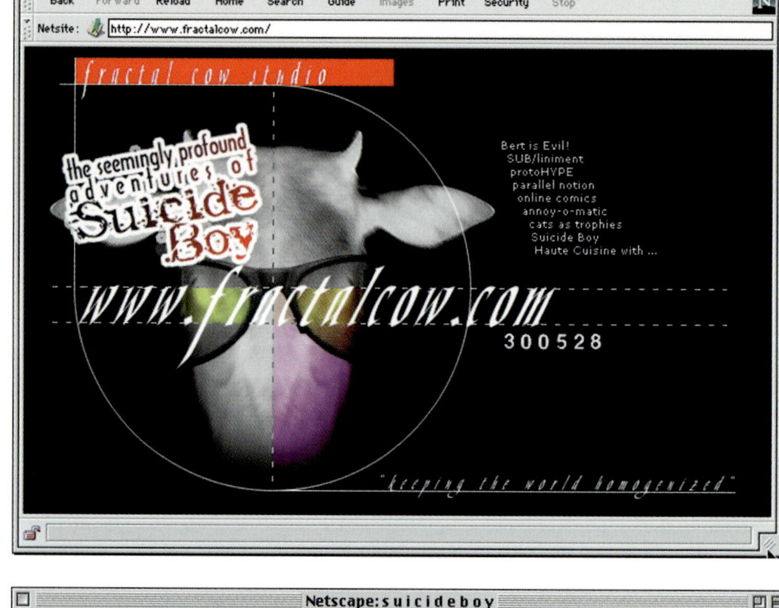

Title

fractal cow studio

URL

http://www.fractalcow.com/

Design Firm

http://www.binary-soup.com and fractal cow studio

Designer/Illustrator/ photographer/programmer

Dino Ignacio

Authoring Platform

pc

There are a number of typographic elements at work at this site. The teaser for Suicide Boy is striking partly because of its splattered serif font, and partly due to the red-to-black blended fill. The titles are variations of the same font, a stylized script that appears in two angles of italicization to denote a sense of cutting-edge, forward momentum.

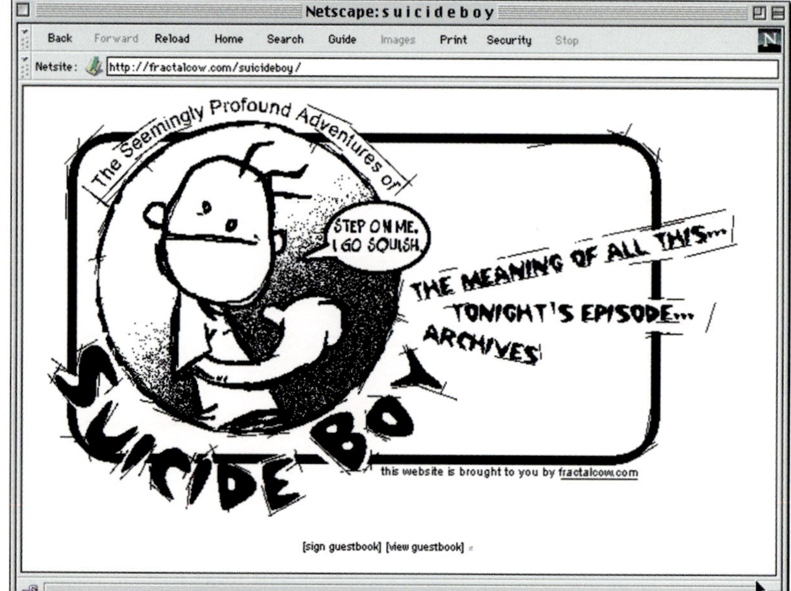

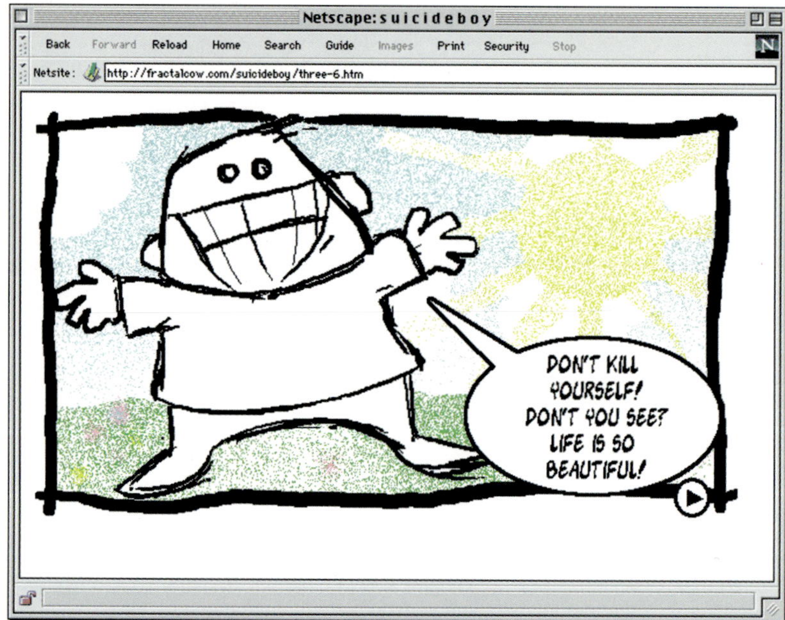

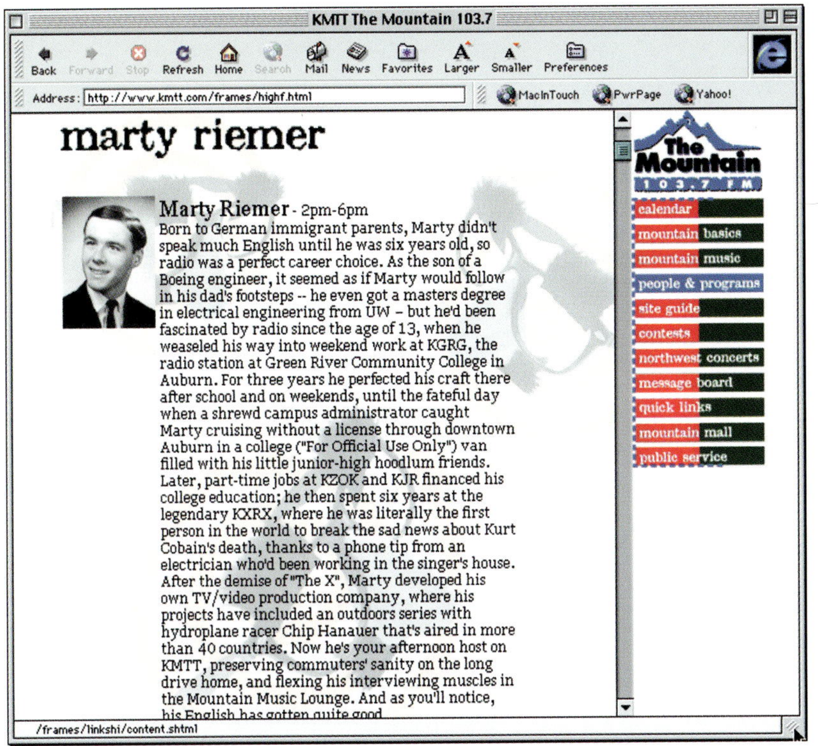

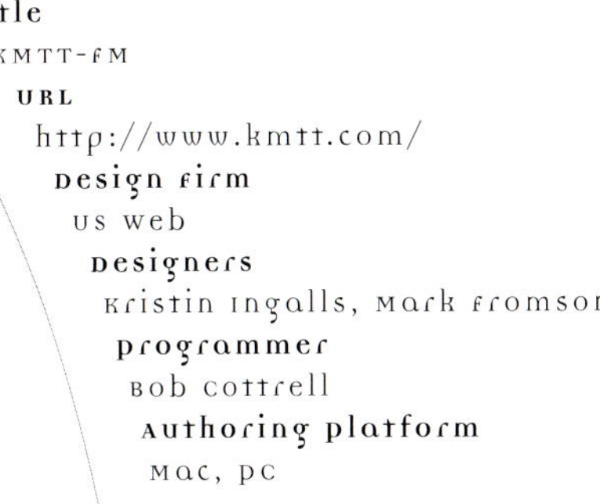

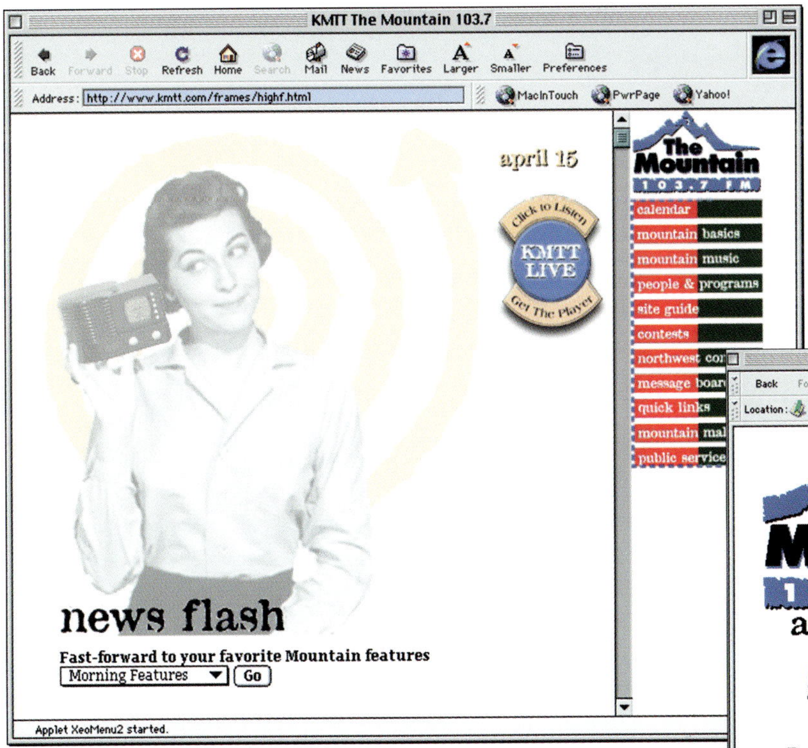

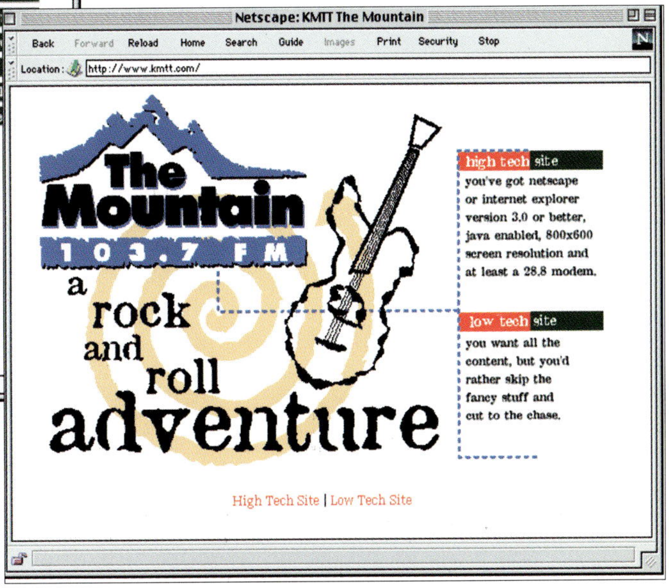

The radio station featured in this Web site caters to a broad middle spectrum of listeners between the ages of 20 to 70+. As a result, it's no surprise to see that the feel generated by the typefaces used here straddles the line between old-fashioned (manual typewriters with slightly uneven hammers) and progressive.

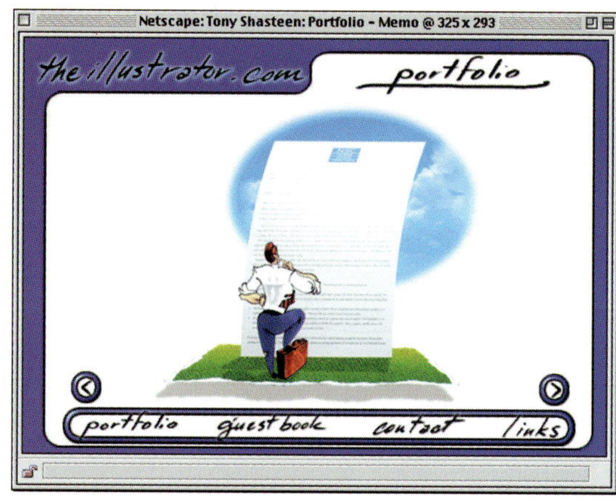

Title
The Illustrator

URL
http://www.theillustrator.com/

Design Firm
Tony Shasteen Illustration & Design

Designer/Illustrator
Tony Shasteen

Programmers
Digital Positions
David Taylor-Klaus, Beth Cooper

Authoring Platform
Mac

There are many typefaces out there that are based on personal handwriting, but sometimes it's better just to go with someone's original scrawls than try to force a font to achieve the same effect. These pages echo the designer's profession of illustrator, giving viewers a peek into a virtual sketch pad.

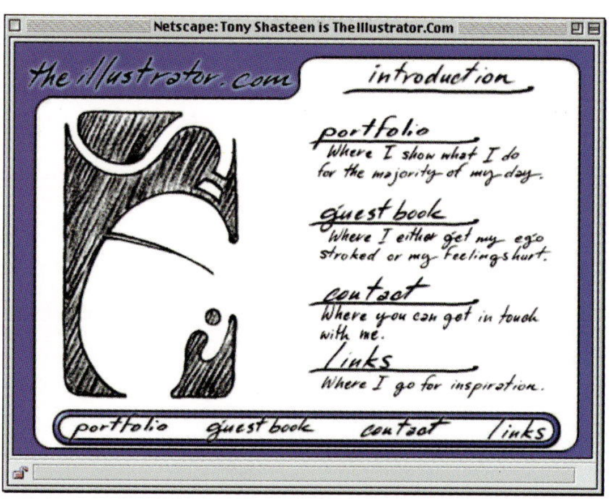

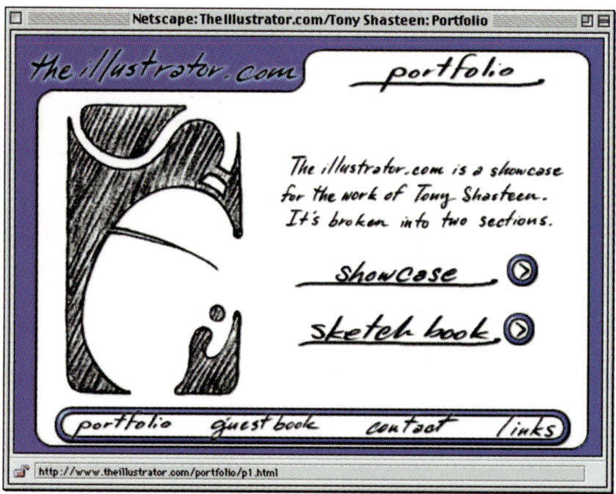

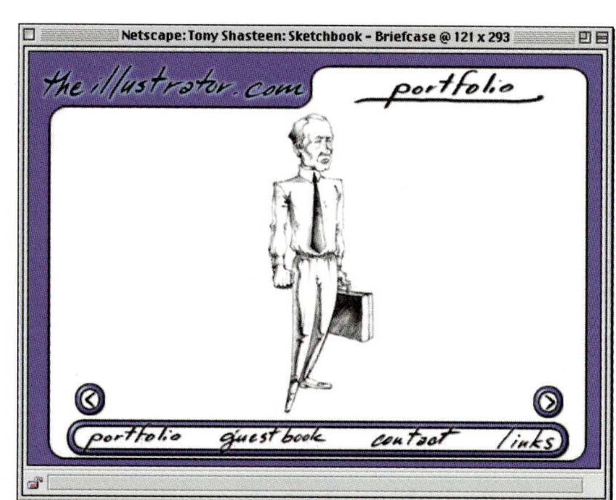

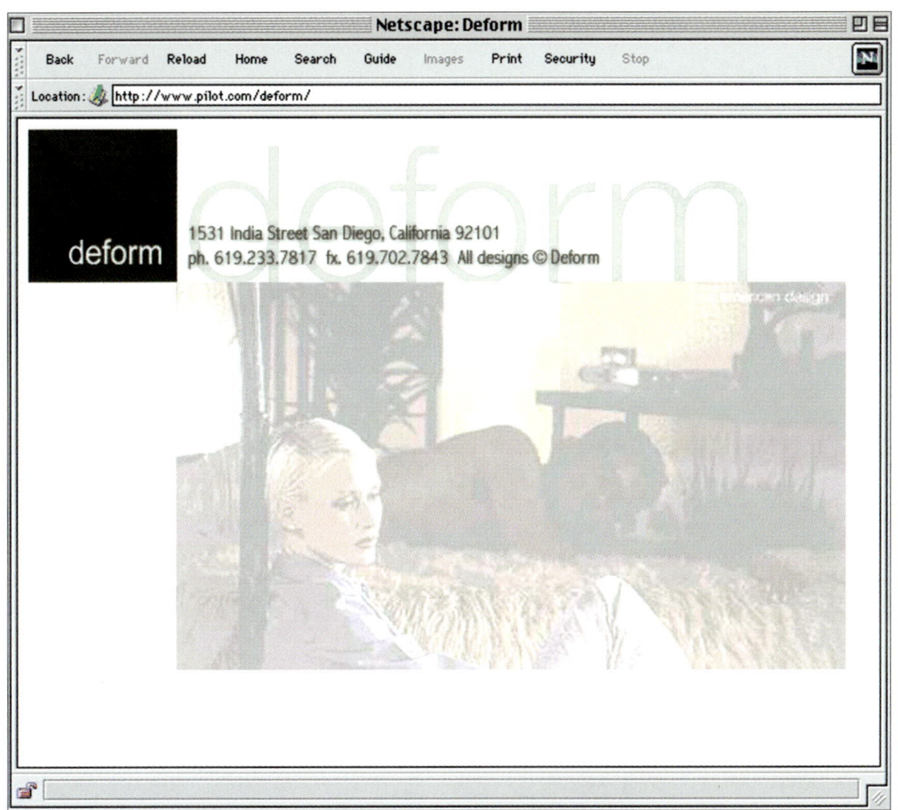

Title
deform

URL
http://www.pilot.com/deform

Design Firm
computer diversion

Designer/Illustrator/Programmer
Randal Antler

Photographer
David Harrison

Authoring Platform
pc

If you look into the area of text readability, you'll find that many experts believe that dark text placed on a light background (black on white, at the extreme) is easier to read. Here, however, you find white text on a white background, offset by a moderately dark drop shadow, along with pale green contact information and the word *deform* as further background texture.

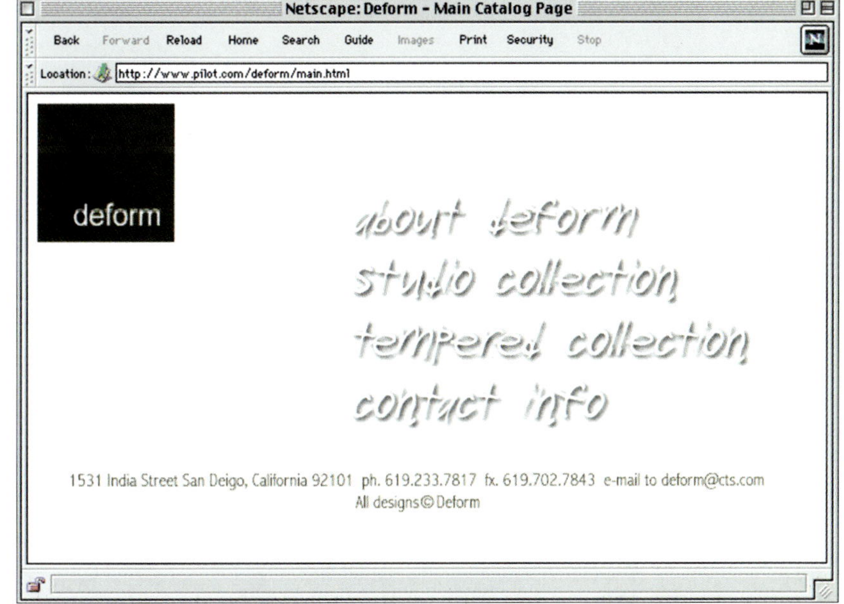

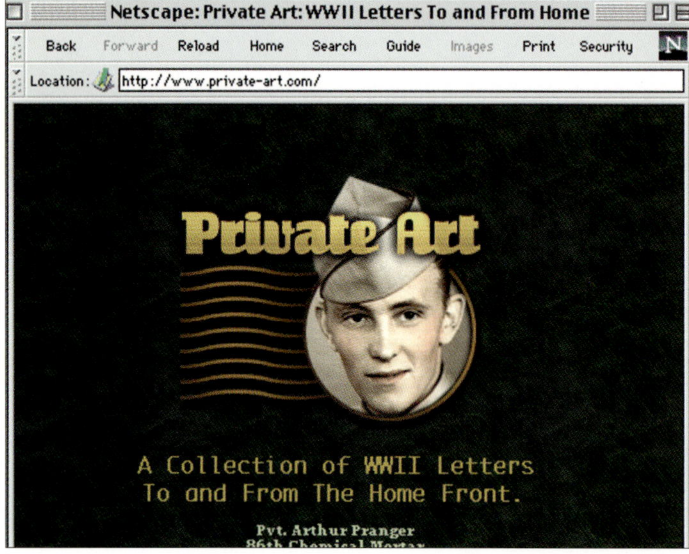

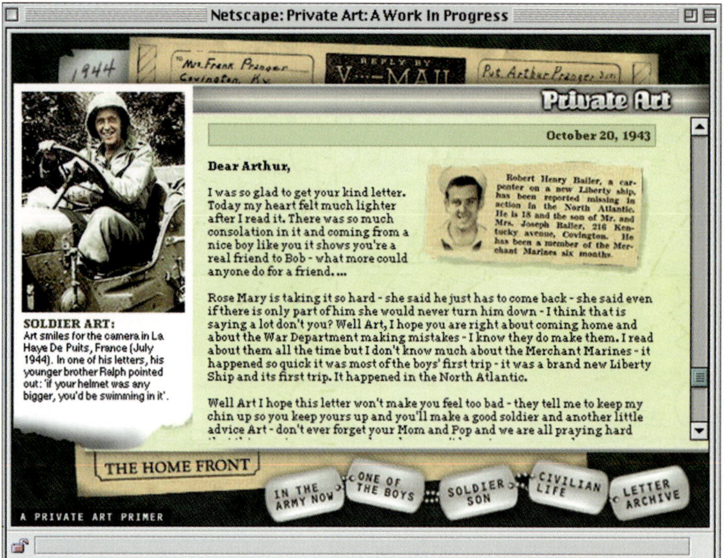

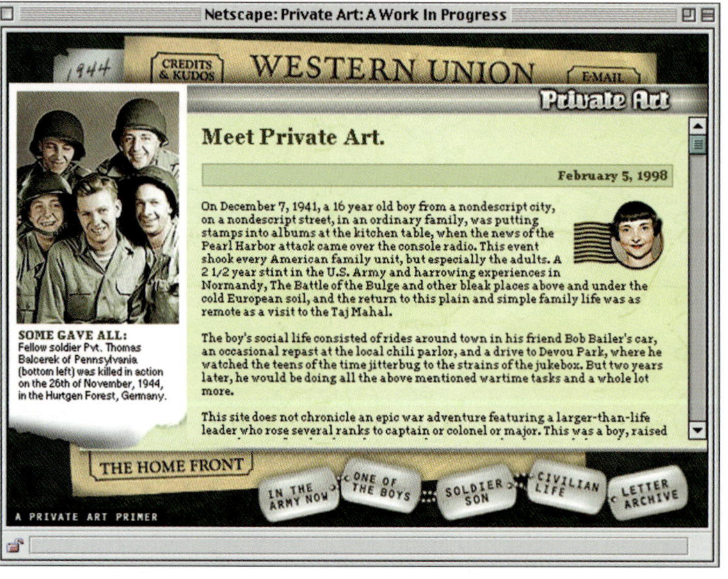

For the most part, the typography here isn't meant to suggest a certain mood, but rather to replicate the look of items in the United States during World War II—the combination of which serves to provide the site's atmosphere. For example, the equally spaced capital letters of dog tags rest near the rich serifs of Western Union stationery.

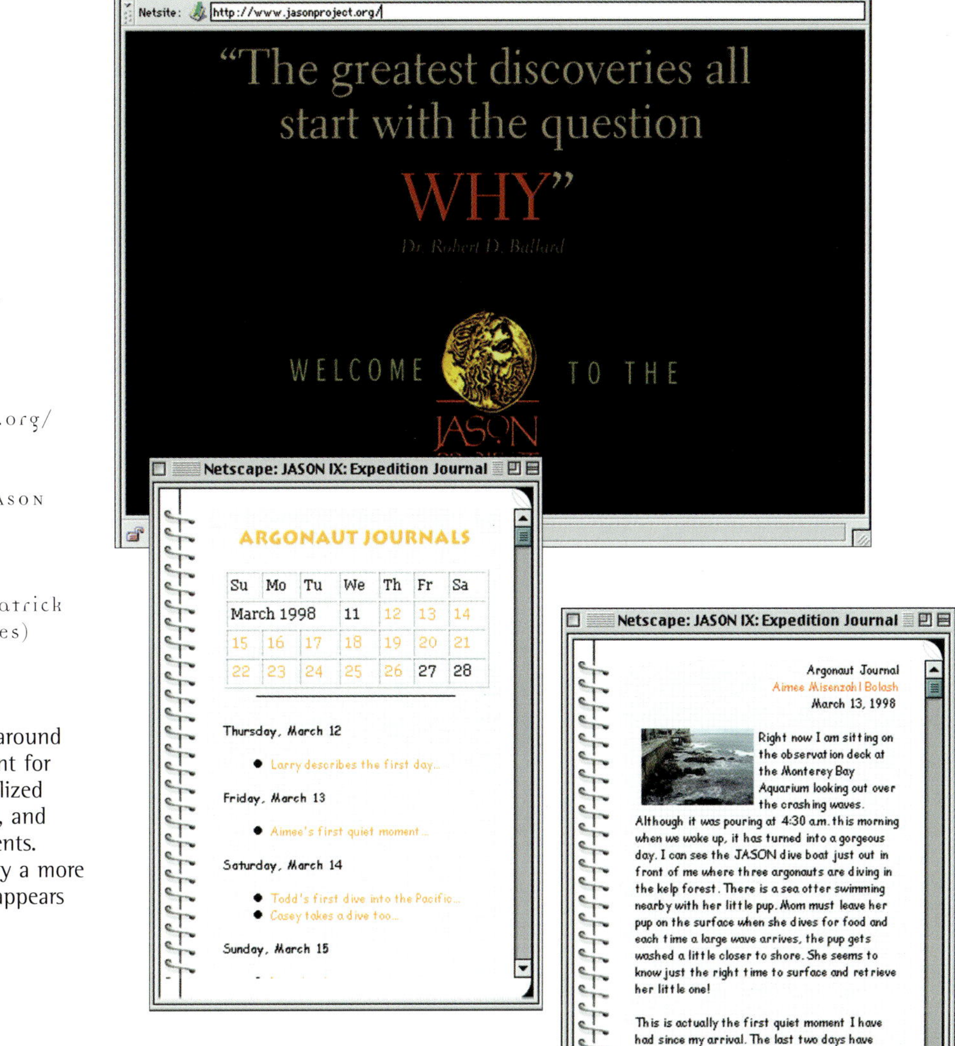

A research into history and the world around us, this site features a classical serif font for the quote adorning the front page, stylized capitals for the Jason Project logo text, and bolder sans-serif type for interior elements. The journal is coded in HTML to display a more informal typeface (Comic Sans, which appears if the user has it pre-installed) resembling handwriting.

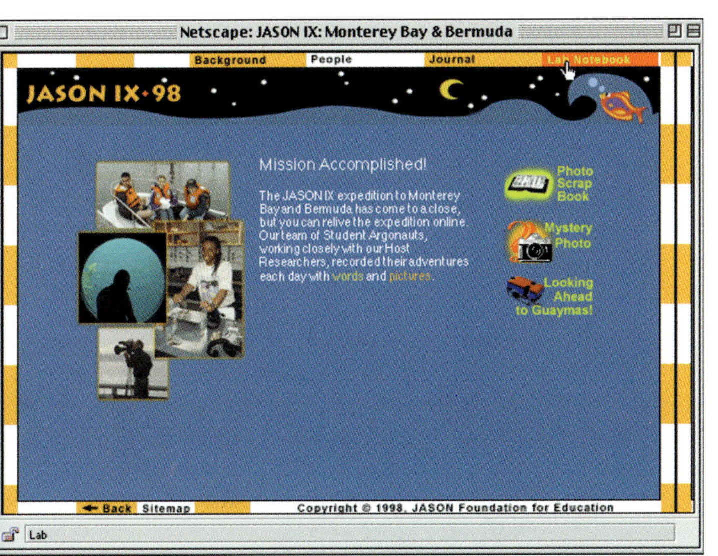

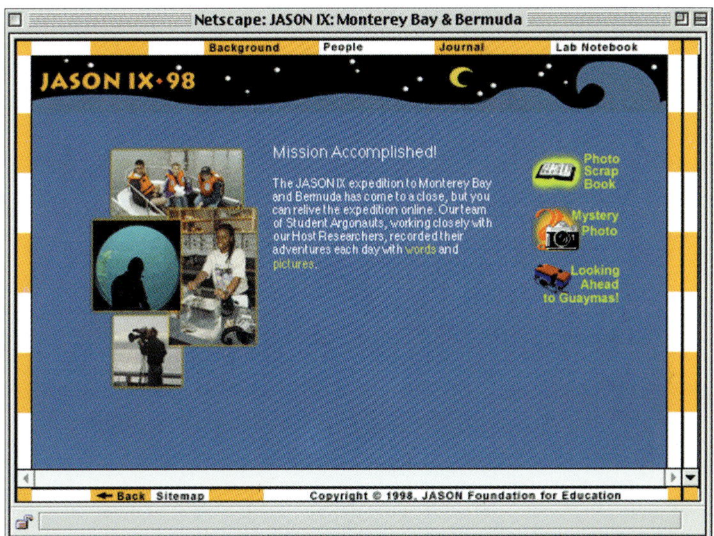

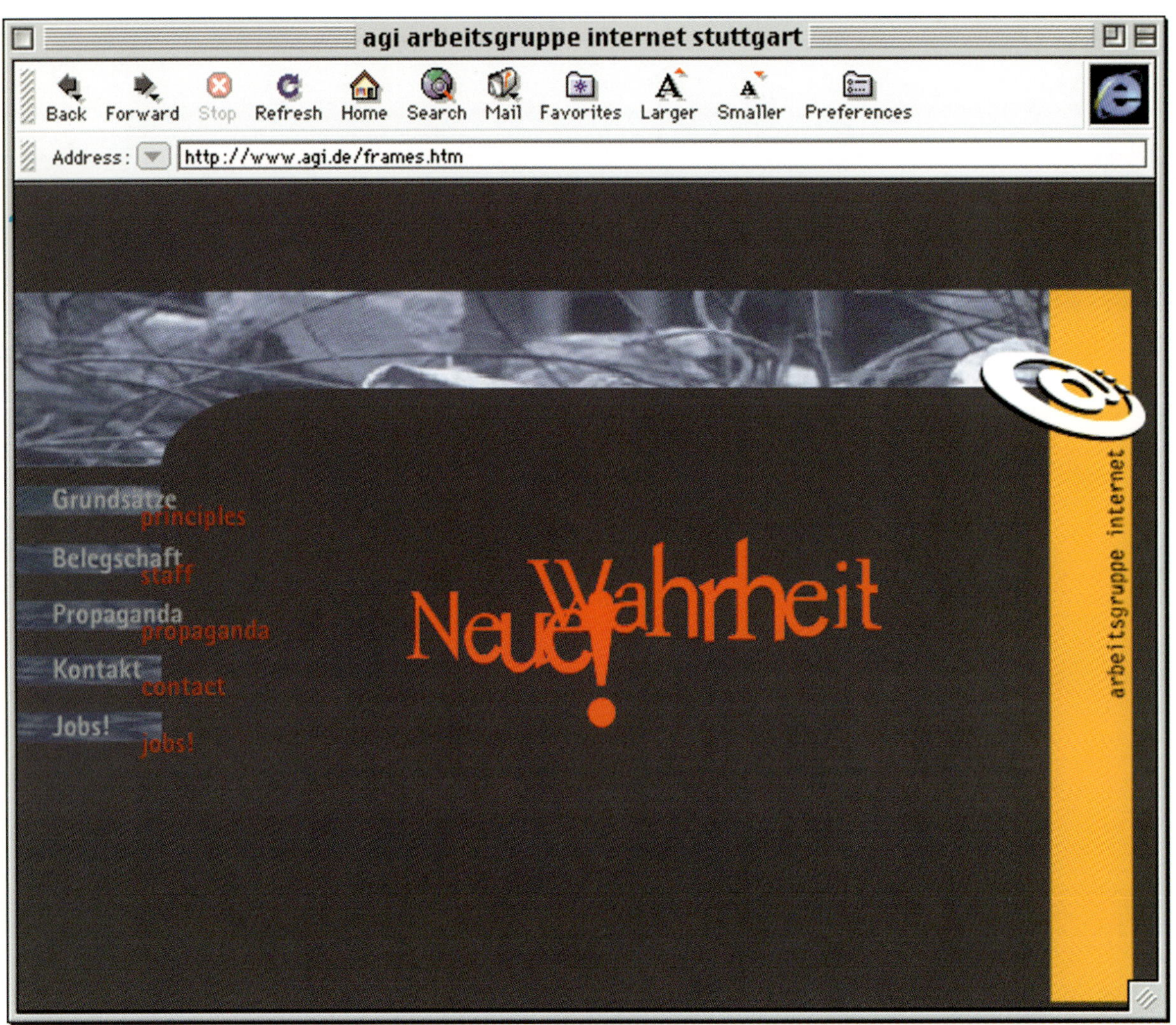

title
agi business media productions gmbh
url
http://www.agi.de/frames.htm
design firm
agi business media productions
designers
tim ruetz, bernd fessler, arwin
hambasic
photographer
thomas möller
programmers
agi technology—gaylord aulke,
oliver schmid, tim ruetz
authoring platform
mac, pc

The Arbeitsgruppe Internet (or Internet Workgroup) has an entirely bilingual site. They emphasize German slightly over English, making the German navigation elements and blocks of text in white; the navigation links are also capitalized. English text is slightly less legible, appearing in a dark red, smaller, and below the German. In each section, the section name appears on top of the list in a different, more irregular typeface.

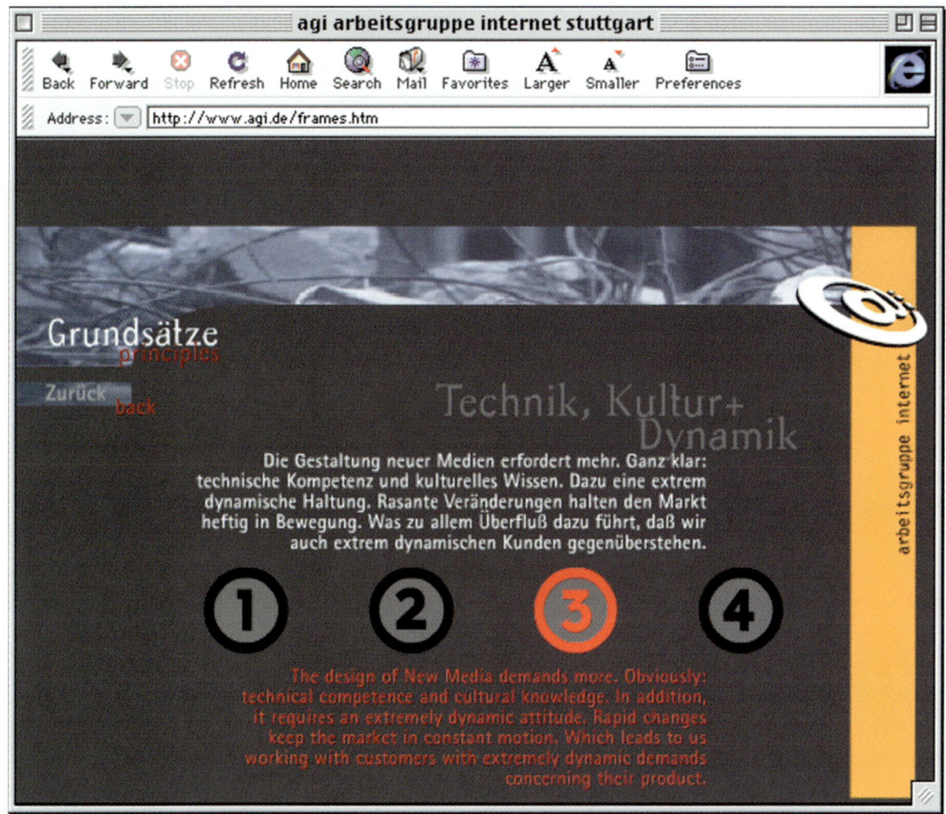

agi arbeitsgruppe internet stuttgart
Back Forward Stop Refresh Home Search Mail Favorites Larger Smaller Preferences
Address: http://www.agi.de/frames.htm
Grundsätze
principles
Zurück back
Technik, Kultur+ Dynamik
Die Gestaltung neuer Medien erfordert mehr. Ganz klar: technische Kompetenz und kulturelles Wissen. Dazu eine extrem dynamische Haltung. Rasante Veränderungen halten den Markt heftig in Bewegung. Was zu allem Überfluß dazu führt, daß wir auch extrem dynamischen Kunden gegenüberstehen.
1 2 3 4
The design of New Media demands more. Obviously: technical competence and cultural knowledge. In addition, it requires an extremely dynamic attitude. Rapid changes keep the market in constant motion. Which leads to us working with customers with extremely dynamic demands concerning their product.
arbeitsgruppe internet

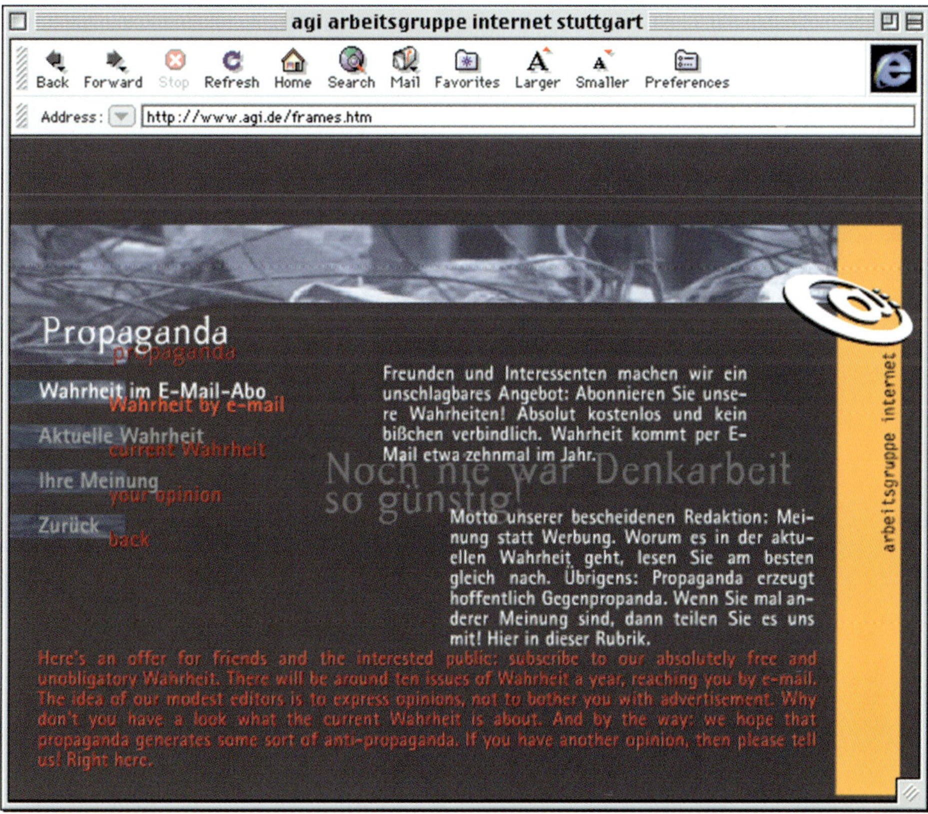

agi arbeitsgruppe internet stuttgart
Back Forward Stop Refresh Home Search Mail Favorites Larger Smaller Preferences
Address: http://www.agi.de/frames.htm
Propaganda
propaganda
Wahrheit im E-Mail-Abo
Wahrheit by e-mail
Aktuelle Wahrheit
current Wahrheit
Ihre Meinung
your opinion
Zurück
back
Freunden und Interessenten machen wir ein unschlagbares Angebot: Abonnieren Sie unsere Wahrheiten! Absolut kostenlos und kein bißchen verbindlich. Wahrheit kommt per E-Mail etwa zehnmal im Jahr.
Noch nie war Denkarbeit so günstig!
Motto unserer bescheidenen Redaktion: Meinung statt Werbung. Worum es in der aktuellen Wahrheit geht, lesen Sie am besten gleich nach. Übrigens: Propaganda erzeugt hoffentlich Gegenpropanda. Wenn Sie mal anderer Meinung sind, dann teilen Sie es uns mit! Hier in dieser Rubrik.
Here's an offer for friends and the interested public: subscribe to our absolutely free and unobligatory Wahrheit. There will be around ten issues of Wahrheit a year, reaching you by e-mail. The idea of our modest editors is to express opinions, not to bother you with advertisement. Why don't you have a look what the current Wahrheit is about. And by the way: we hope that propaganda generates some sort of anti-propaganda. If you have another opinion, then please tell us! Right here.
arbeitsgruppe internet

typography

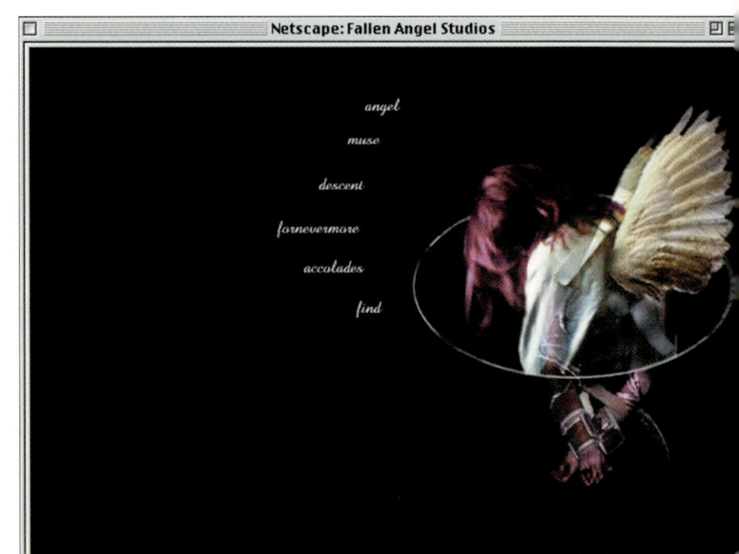

title
fallen angel studios
url
http://www.fallenangelstudio.com/
design firm
knight errant design
designer/illustrator/photographer
bob libby
authoring platform
pc

Darkness encroaches most of this site, with murky photos and dimly lit accents, like the tarnished-copper button marked *fin*. The typography appears equally in conflict with darkness: the white text looks almost overly anti-aliased, so the letters' edges drift into the surrounding black.

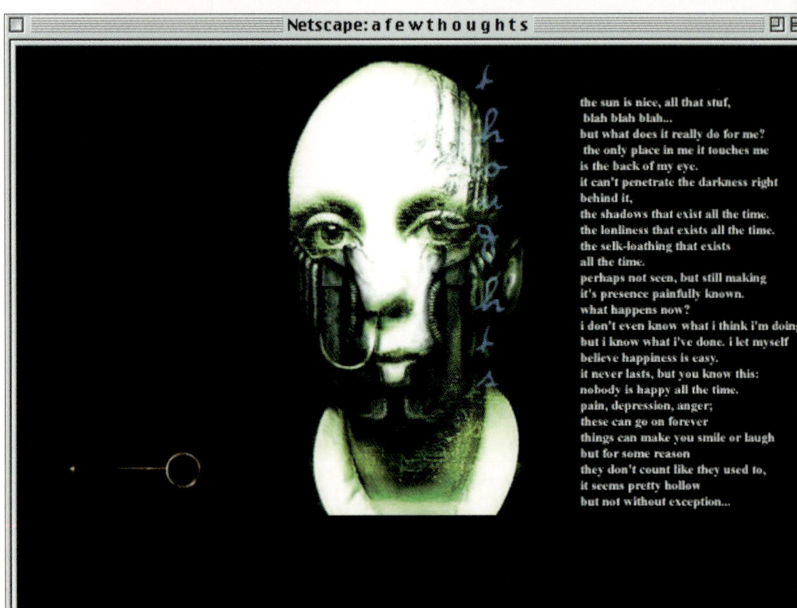

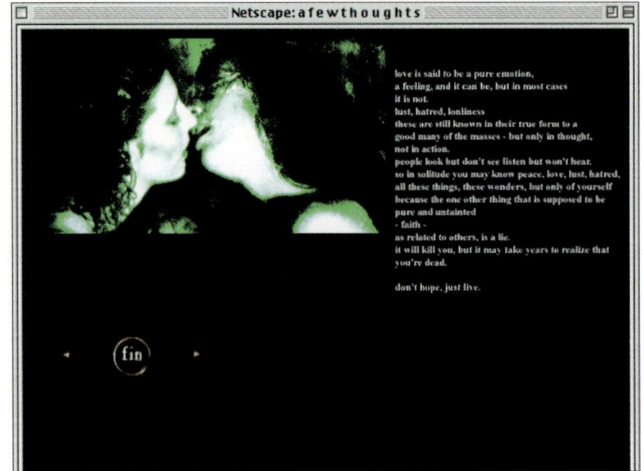

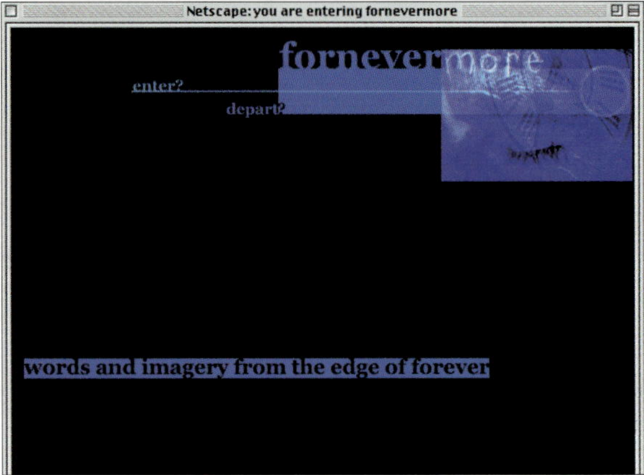

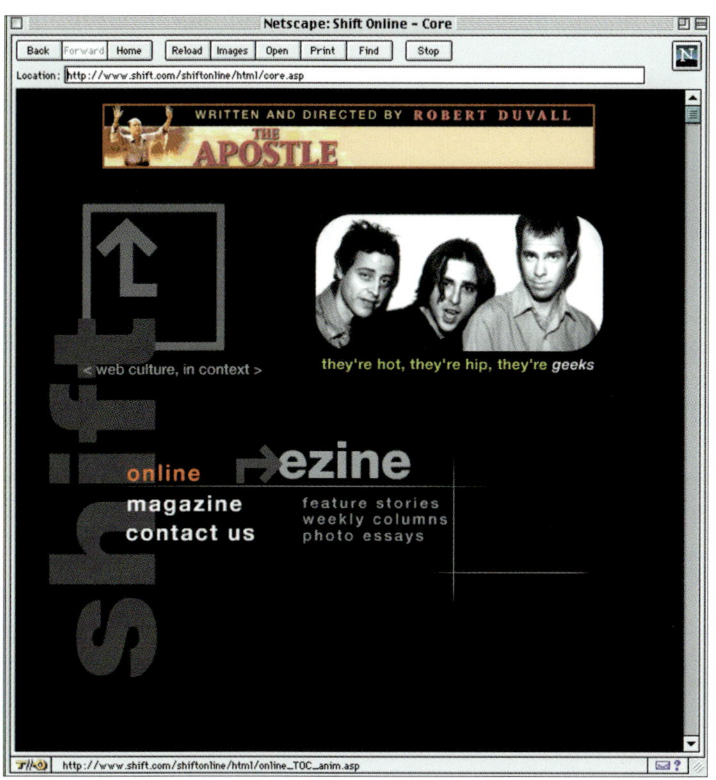

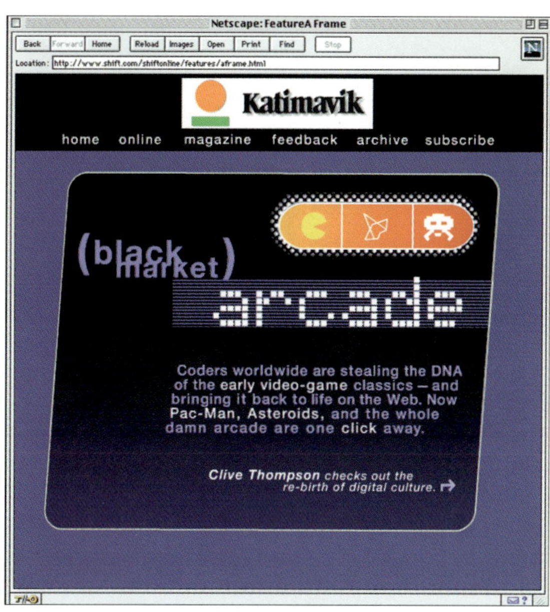

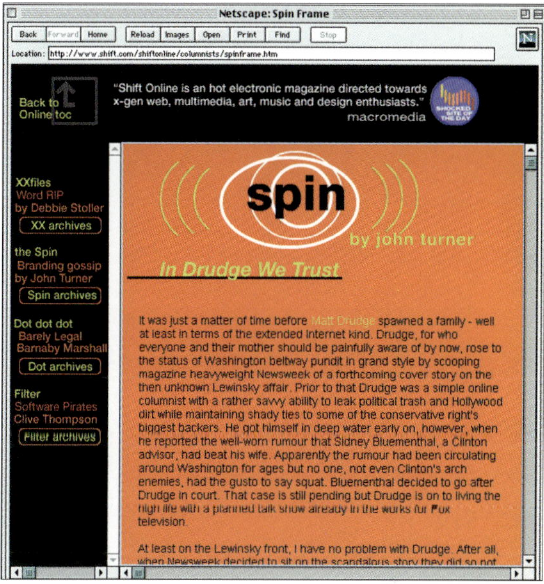

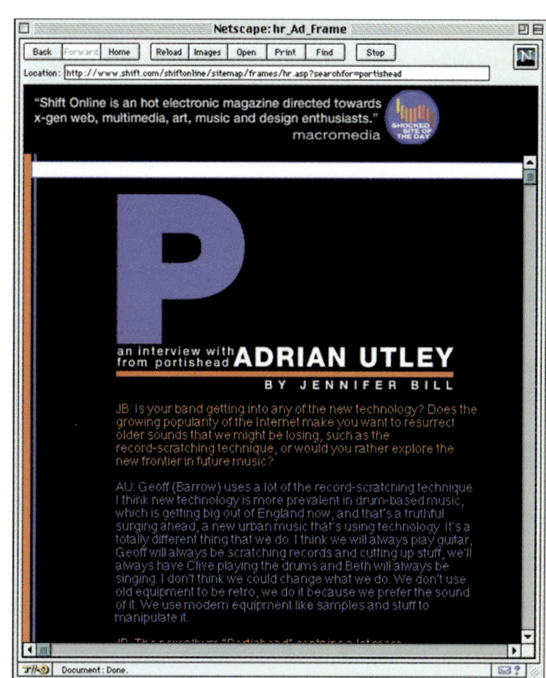

Another example of rendering type with Flash technology, the heavy sans-serifs of the title page do not try to be clever; the larger sizes and reserved color usage works to point you into the site. Once inside, animated titles are customized according to the articles' subject matter.

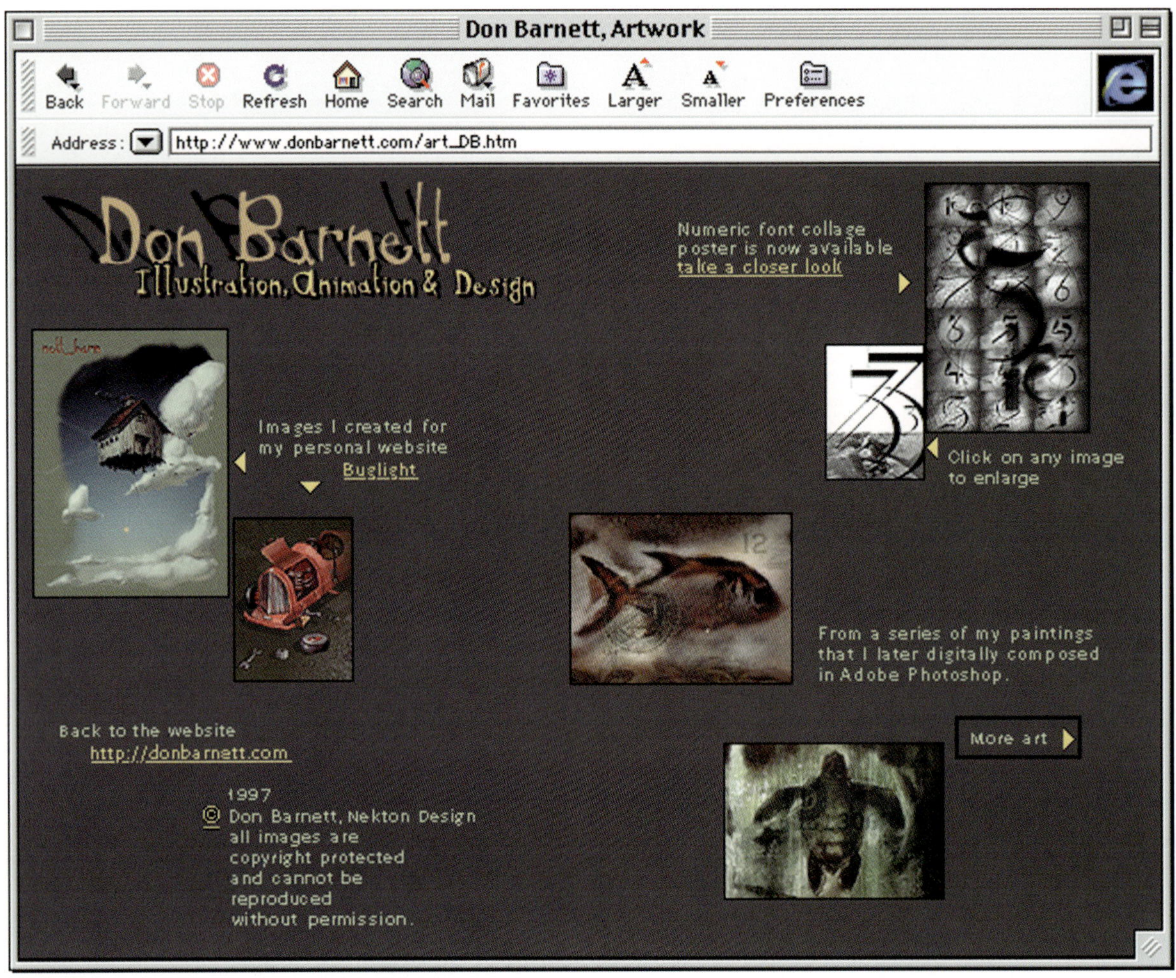

Title
Don Barnett
URL
http://www.donbarnett.com/
Design firm
Nekton Design
Designer/illustrator/programmer
Don Barnett
Authoring platform
Mac

Not everyone can design their own typefaces to use on a Web site, but you can draw a few lessons from how Don Barnett uses them. His site, Bug Light, plays with notions of light and shadow; there's usually an extra shading or extended shadow behind his name. He also plays with regular type to give it a quality of motion that matches his drawings and type as in the Gaudi tribute.

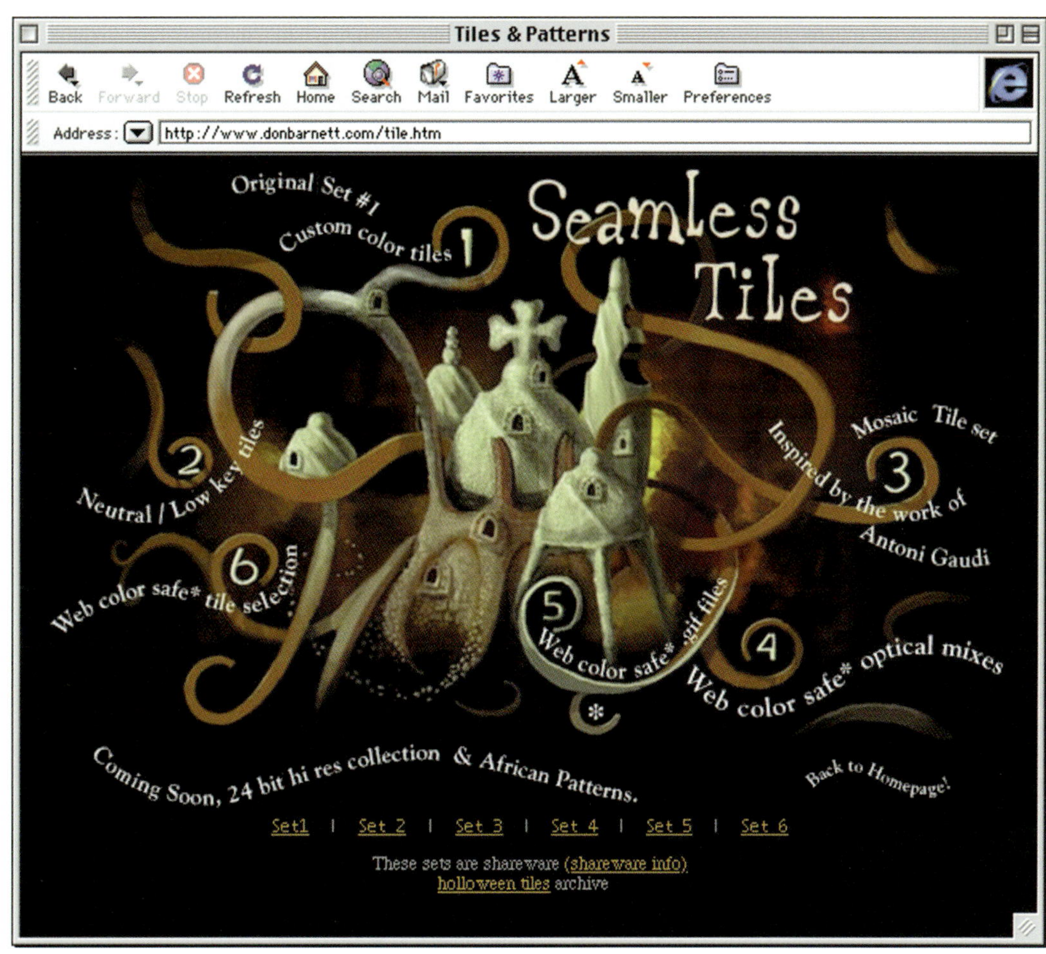

Tiles & Patterns
Back Forward Stop Refresh Home Search Mail Favorites Larger Smaller Preferences
Address: http://www.donbarnett.com/tile.htm
Original Set #1
Custom color tiles 1
Seamless Tiles
2
Neutral / Low key tiles
6
Web color safe* tile selection
Mosaic Tile set
Inspired by the work of
Antoni Gaudi
3
5
Web color safe* .gif files
4
Web color safe* optical mixes
*
Coming Soon, 24 bit hi res collection & African Patterns.
Back to Homepage!
Set1 | Set 2 | Set 3 | Set 4 | Set 5 | Set 6
These sets are shareware (shareware info)
holloween tiles archive

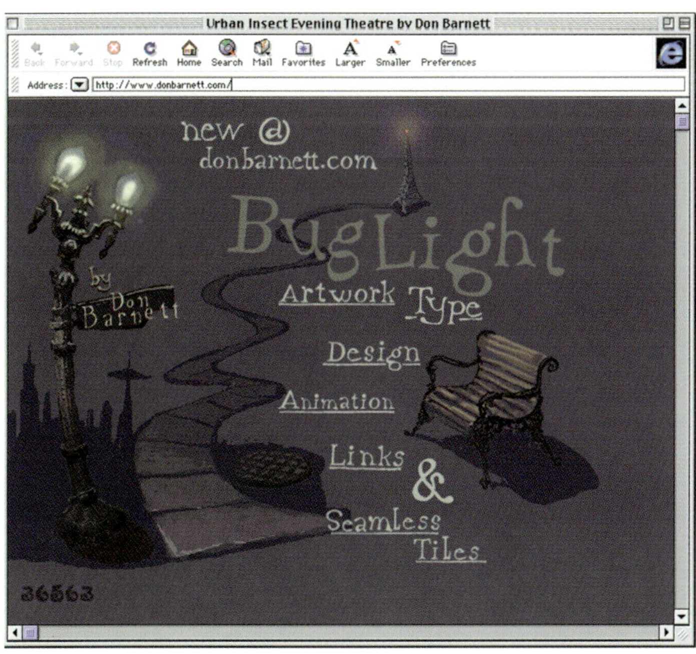

Urban Insect Evening Theatre by Don Barnett
Back Forward Stop Refresh Home Search Mail Favorites Larger Smaller Preferences
Address: http://www.donbarnett.com/
new @
donbarnett.com
BugLight
Artwork Type
Design
Animation
Links &
Seamless
Tiles
by
Don
Barnett
36563

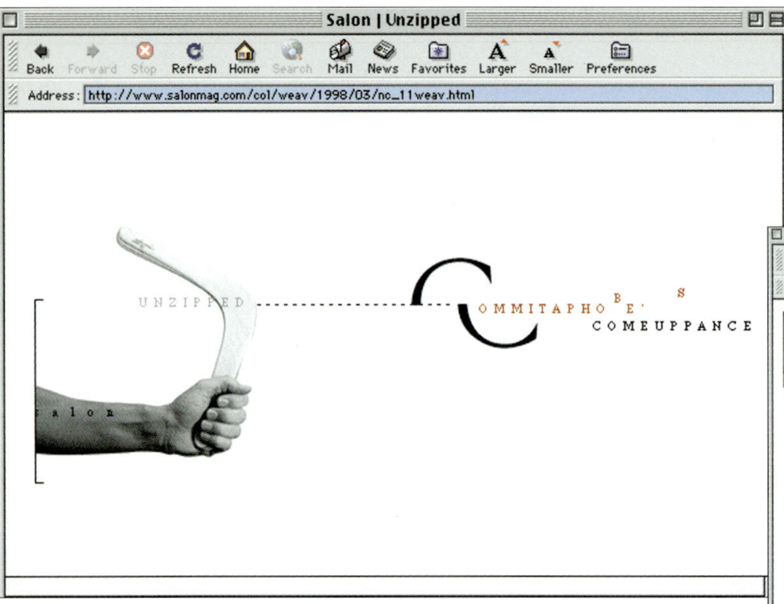

title
salon magazine

URL
http://www.salonmagazine.com/

design firm
salon magazine

designers
Mignon Khargie ("commitaphobe's comeuppance," "Girl in Landscape");

writer
Jonathan Lemen ("Girl in Landscape")

authoring platform
Mac

One of the strengths of Salon's design is the way it alters minor elements to achieve dramatic effects. Type plays heavily throughout the site; letters are often split, or positioned askew, or situated unusually. This creates a varied look that doesn't always have time for elaborate illustrations.

REVIEWS INTERVIEWS AUTHOR EVENTS BOOKCASE

A SALON REVIEWS
SECTION SPONSORED
BY BORDERS
BOOKS & MUSIC

[BOOKS ARCHIVE]

BOOKS
SALON

·g·i·r·l· IN LANDSCAPE

BY JONATHAN LETHEM

DOUBLEDAY

FICTION

272 PAGES

TO ORDER
Want to buy this book? All titles may not be immediately available.

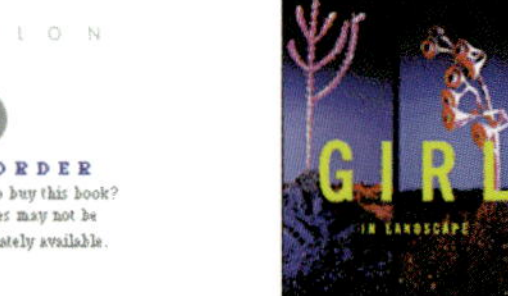

BY STEPHANIE ZACHAREK | When we were little kids and our parents and teachers urged us to flex our imagination, they thought they were doing us a favor -- and they were, under cover of daylight. But where were they after dark, when we'd lie stone awake and frozen with fear in our beds after we'd read one of Ray Bradbury's alien-spores-in-the-basement stories, under the covers with the flashlight, or taken a "Twilight Zone" episode much too close to heart? When we reached adulthood, we convinced ourselves those fears were just silly: The "Twilight Zone" sets were cheesy, and Bradbury turned out to be not nearly as scary as Richard Nixon.

But Jonathan Lethem is the kind of writer who reassures us that none of those nights were spent in vain: We had *plenty* to fear -- we just needed those stories because they gave us something to hook our terror onto. "Girl in Landscape" -- which could be called science fiction for those who like that sort of thing, although it shouldn't scare off those who don't -- uses the raw materials of those fears (mysterious viruses that change our perceptions; dry, spooky terrain that looks like nothing so much as nightmare territory; tiny, slimy creatures that grow inside of potatoes) as a way of exploring both the awe of female adolescent sexual awakening and the treachery of it.

Pella Marsh is 13 when her mother dies and her family -- including her ineffectual, failed-politician father, Clement, and her two younger brothers -- leave the apocalyptic wasteland of Brooklyn and strike out for a better life on the planet of the Archbuilders. The Archbuilders -- double-jointed creatures with bodies of fur, shell and leathery skin -- had once built a great civilization but have since fallen into a kind of lethargy. Their planet is a parched wonderland of crumbled towers and archways, a place where tiny giraffelike creatures called household deer skitter and scamper across the plains and in the corners of people's houses, like mice. Among the small group of settlers on the planet is Efram Nugent -- a loner, a bully and an enigmatic presence who acts as if he knows everything and sometimes really seems to. (The character clearly resembles Ethan Edwards, John Wayne's vengeful, nearly unhinged character in "The Searchers.") Pella is both attracted to and repelled by Efram. To her, he represents a jumble of conflicts: He's an arbiter of order in this strange new world, an idiot grown-up who doesn't know as much as he thinks he does and a lightning rod for both her sexual bewilderment and her half-conscious sense of her own allure.

Lethem tells Pella's story with the same lucidity and unaffected elegance he brought to his 1997 novel "As She Climbed Across the Table." And if he's unflinching about probing the dark side of Pella's transformation, he's also almost painfully sympathetic to her, capturing the awkwardness a young woman feels when she's getting ready to fold up her girl self forever: "She moved toward her father, slowly, giving him time to catch the hint. He sat just in time, and she climbed into his lap. She didn't really fit there, but she drew up her knees and pretended. It was strange how Efram had mistaken her for a grown woman even as he towered over her, made her feel small. Whereas Clement, with whom she was still unquestionably a child, was nearly her same size." And even when Lethem uses the language of science fiction to shape his story, he doesn't have to stretch to make his fantastic metaphors work. He knows adolescence is its own kind of weird tale, and if the fear of it wasn't exactly what kept us awake all those childhood nights -- well, maybe it should have been.
SALON | March 17, 1998

Stephanie Zacharek lives in Boston. She is a regular contributor to Salon.

TABLE TALK

What favorite writers of yours are missing in action? Fear their retirement; hope for their return in the Books area of Table Talk

RECENTLY

One Nation, After All
By Alan Wolfe
Nonfiction
(03/16/98)

The Blonde on the Streetcorner
By David Goodis
Fiction
(03/13/98)

Jackie After Jack
By Christopher Andersen
Nonfiction
(03/12/98)

Singing in the Comeback Choir
By Bebe Moore Campbell
Fiction
(03/11/98)

Confederates in the Attic
By Tony Horwitz
Nonfiction
(03/10/98)

SEARCH REVIEWS BY:
title of book
author
publisher
reviewer

INTERVIEW

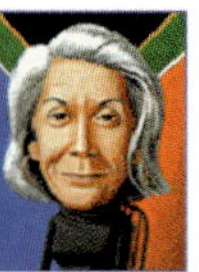

African queen
Nadine Gordimer on her country's dangerous passage to freedom
(03/09/98)

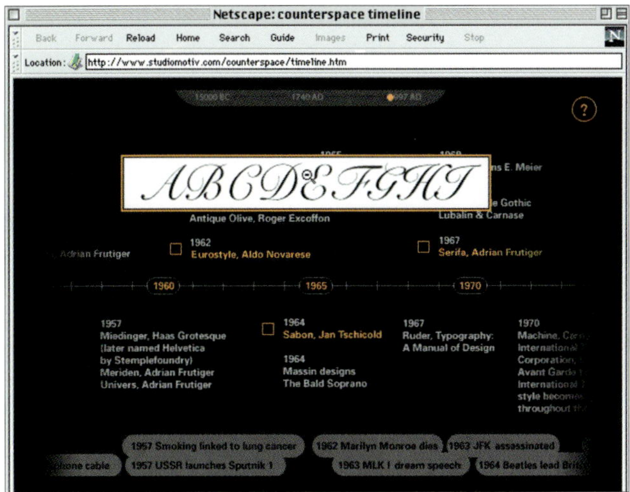

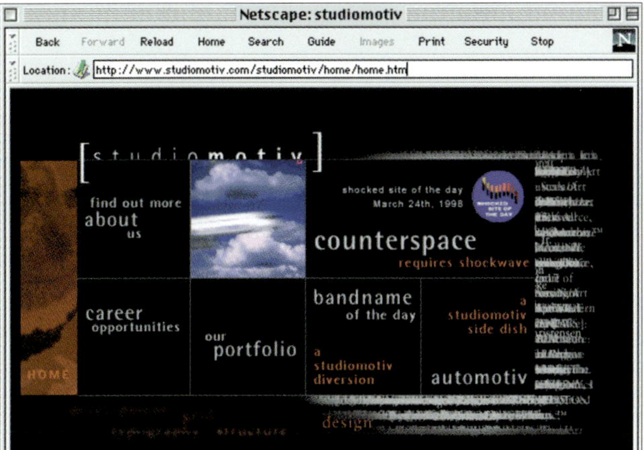

This site, rooted in typography, employs a number of techniques that make it stand apart from the crowd. The title on the main page, for example, shows only the upper parts of the letters but remains legible; the word *space* in *counter space* shares letters to write the word twice; and using Macromedia Flash, titles and navigation blend into the screen, rather than appearing immediately.

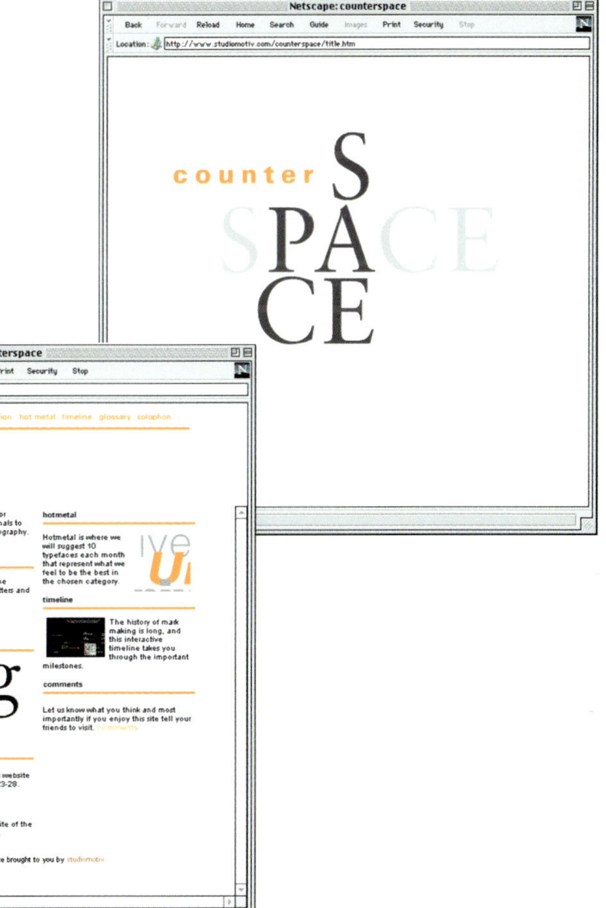

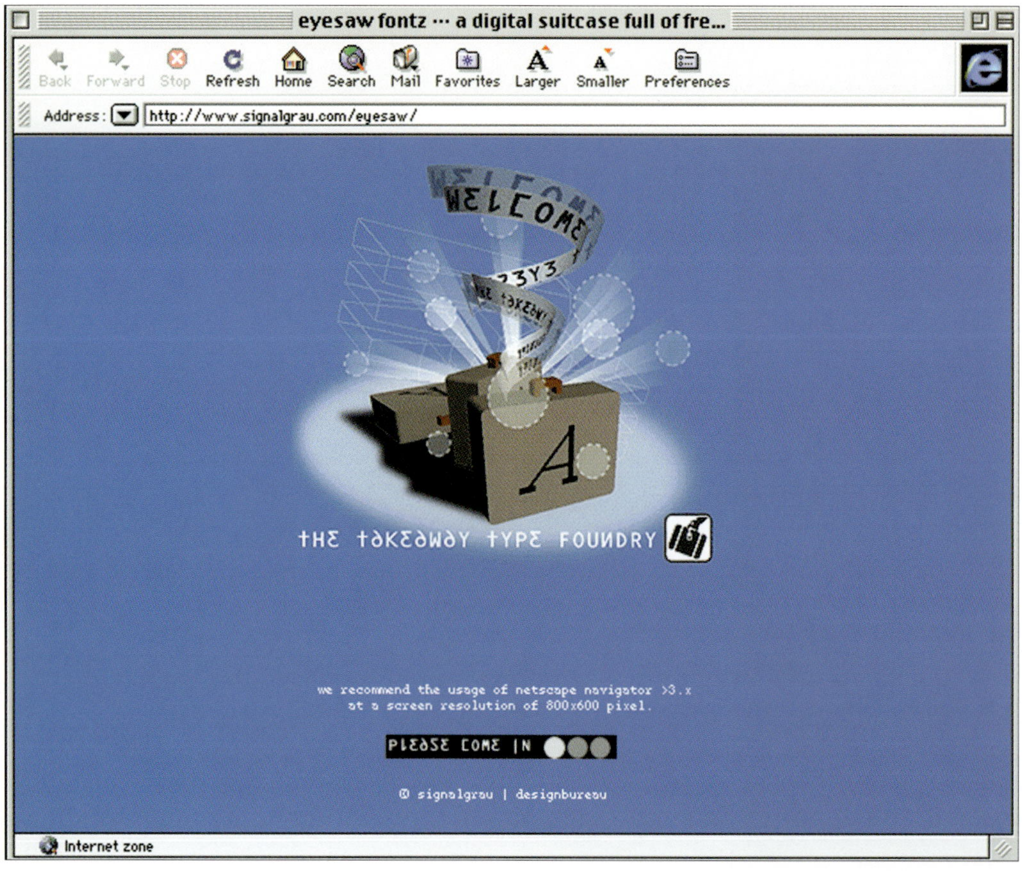

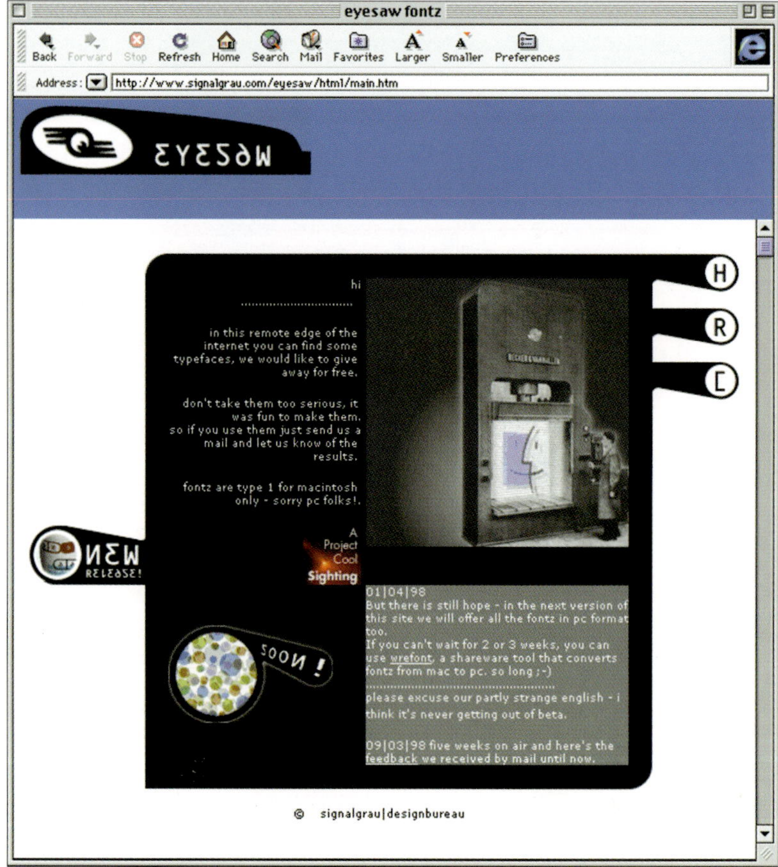

title

eyesaw fontz

URL

http://www.signalgrau.com/eyesaw/

design firm

signalgrau design bureau

designer/illustrator/
photographer/programmer

dirk uhlenbrock

authoring platform

mac

Like many sites devoted to type, Eyesaw takes a minimal approach to type on the site, using a total of three faces in about four sizes: the standard Courier (used for navigation), a small sans serif (used for body copy), and their display font for rendered heads. The main display face turns typographic conventions on their head—literally. Every character in the font is a transposed, reversed, upside down, or rotated version of a real letter; many letters are made up of numerals that have been flipped.

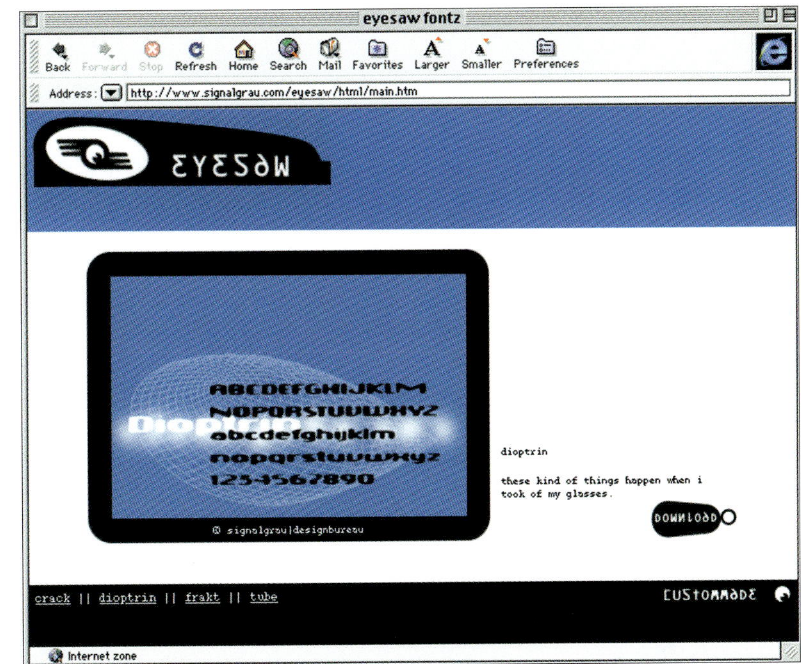

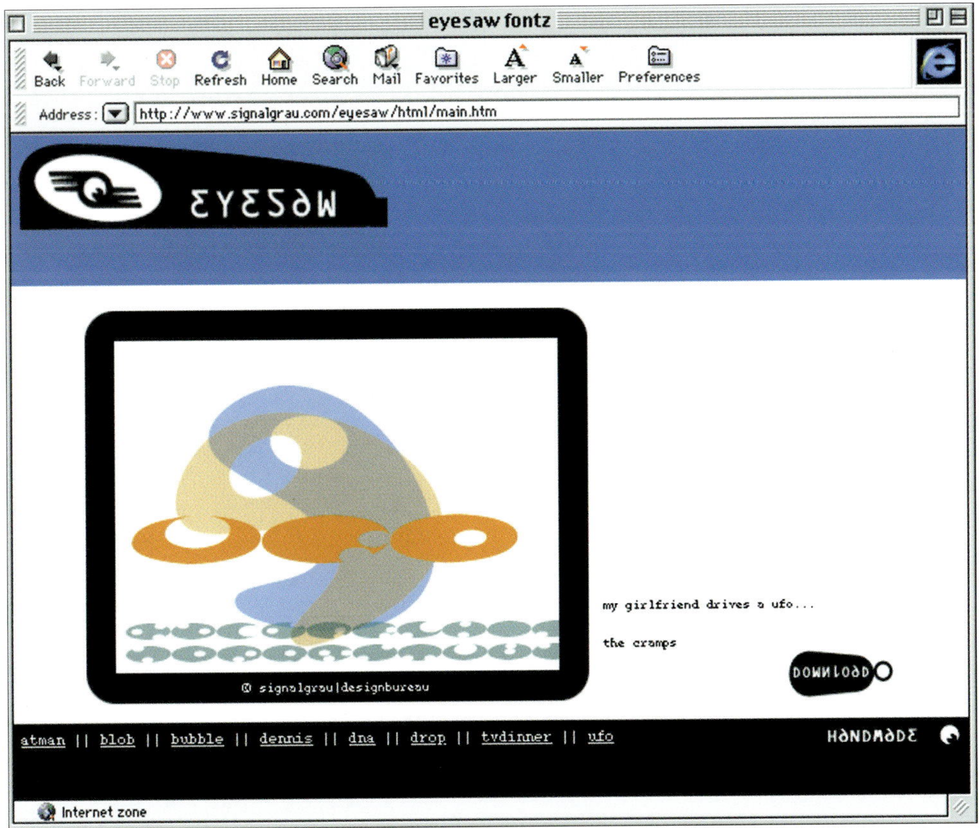

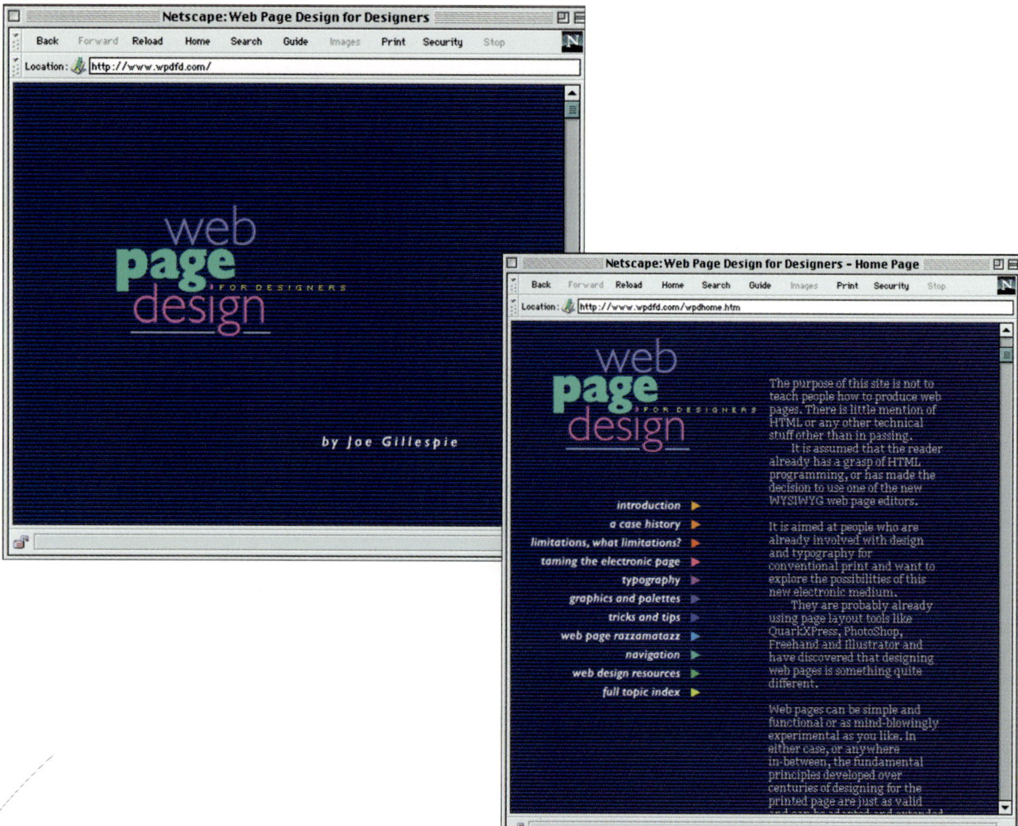

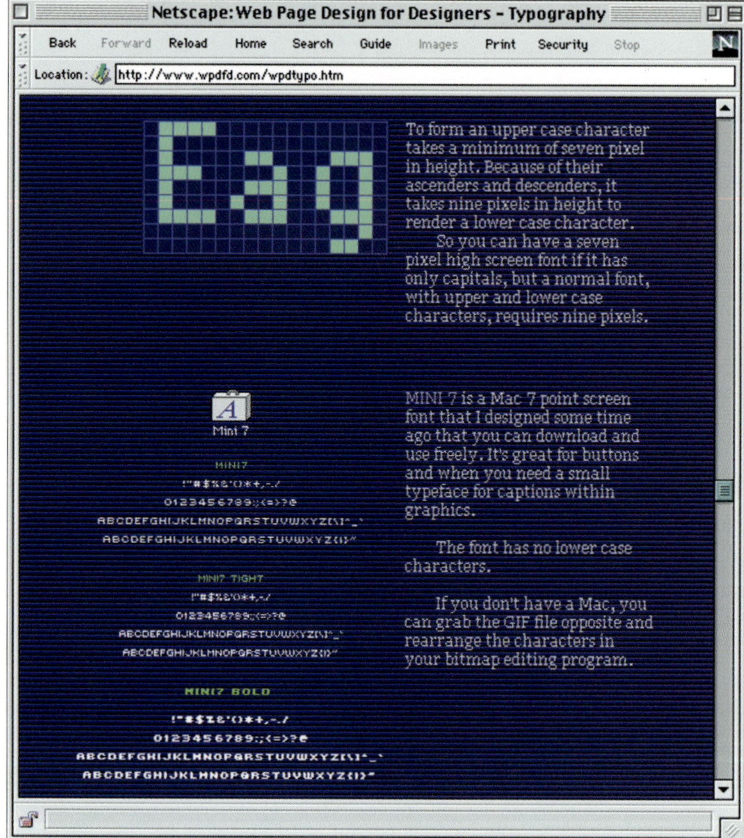

Title
web page Design for Designers

URL
http://www.wpdfd.com/

Design Firm
pixel productions UK

**Designer/Illustrator/
photographer/programmer**
Joe Gillespie

Authoring platform
Mac

It is fair to say that most good
design is built upon simplicity, and
this is a site that thrives on simplicity.
Except for the patterned background,
the typography here is the design.
Using extreme light and heavy widths
of the same font, and positioning
the words so they naturally rest
upon one another, the title works
as a single, coherent element. Adding
for designers in an aliased Web-friendly
typeface emphasizes the techniques
to be found inside the site.

With the large number of visual elements packed onto these pages, there's not much room for tossing a bunch of different typefaces into the mix. The navigation and most of the titles are variations of the same minimally serifed condensed font. On a few pages, the titles are rendered appropriate to the page's content, such as *Technique*, shown here.

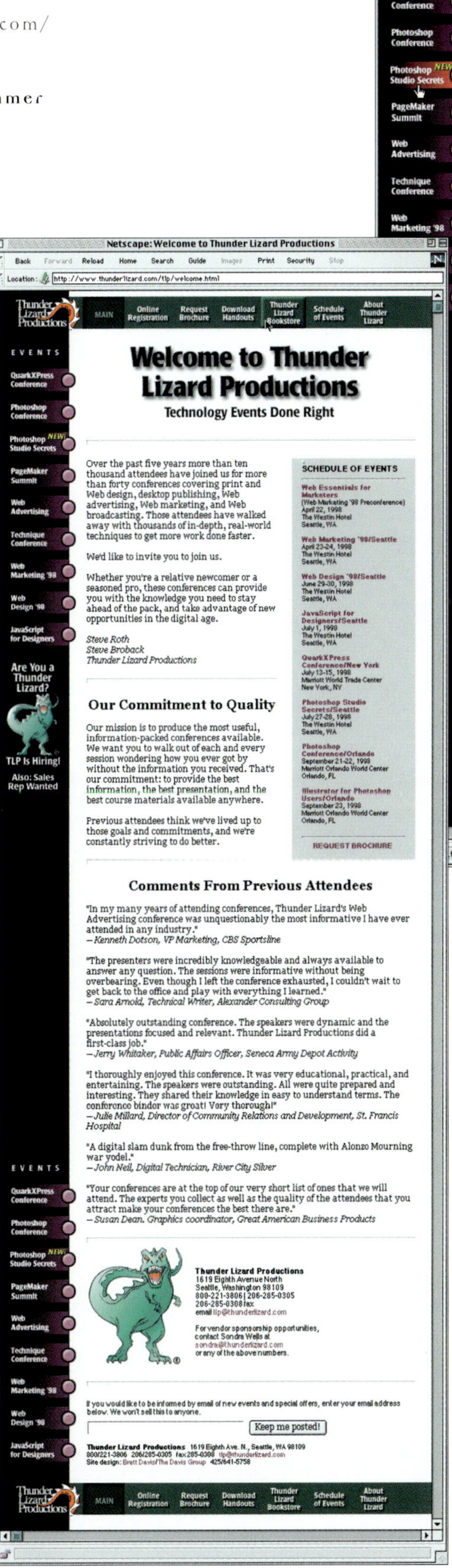

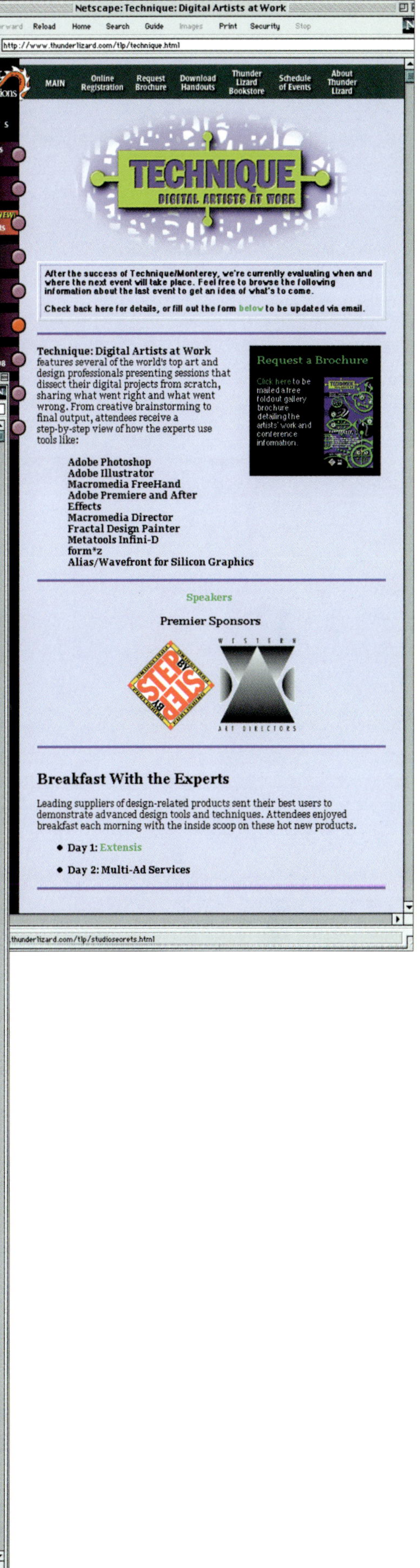

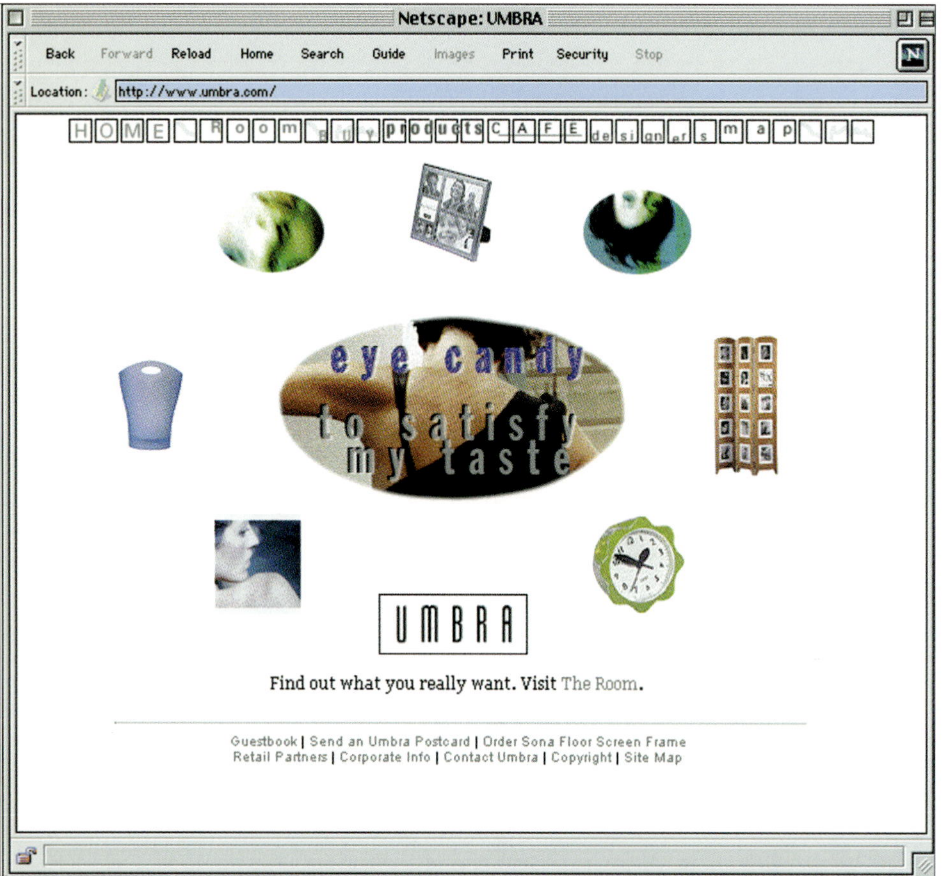

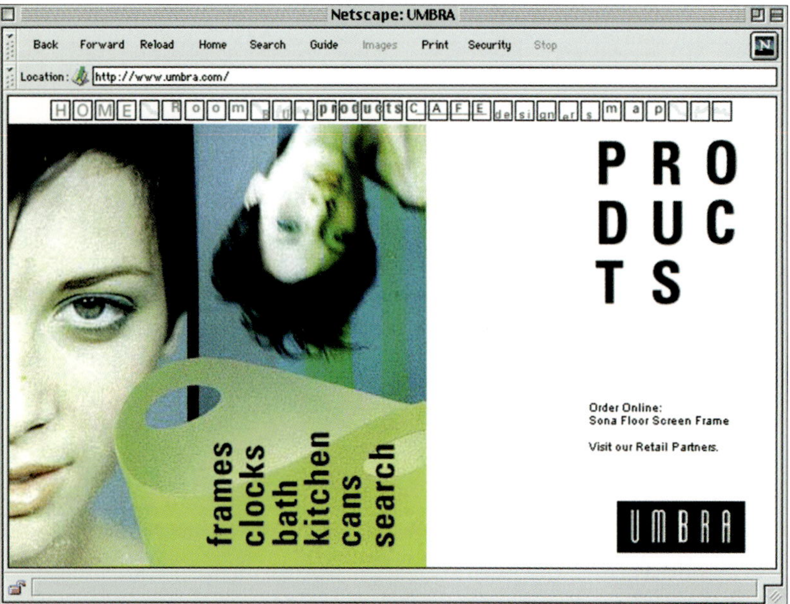

TITLE
umbra

URL
http://www.umbra.com/

DESIGN FIRM
The James Gang

DESIGNERS
Bill James, Franke James

ILLUSTRATOR/PHOTOGRAPHER
Franke James

PROGRAMMER
Bill James

AUTHORING PLATFORM
Mac

Discussions of typography invariably revolve around fonts, but that doesn't cover the field. Equally important, in some cases, is the placement of the type. Here, a horizontal navigation bar stands apart because the text labels for each link vary in size, don't share a common baseline, and occasionally get truncated or spaced unusually.

title
urban desires

URL
http://www.desires.com/

design firm
agency.com

designers/illustrators
Jean Esquivel (Gateway and
TOC/1st & 2nd screen);
Chris Alegra (Korean food)

programmers
Mike Parker (Gateway and TOC/1st &
2nd screen); Chris Alegra (Korean food)

authoring platform
Mac

This online magazine's title is a good example of using typefaces that clearly communicate the words' meanings: *Urban* is sparsely serifed and condensed like an imaginary sprawl of skyscrapers; *Desires*, on the other hand, is a traditional romantic script. Reversing the latter makes it stand out more, while also keeping the thinner aspects of each letter from getting lost amid the background pattern.

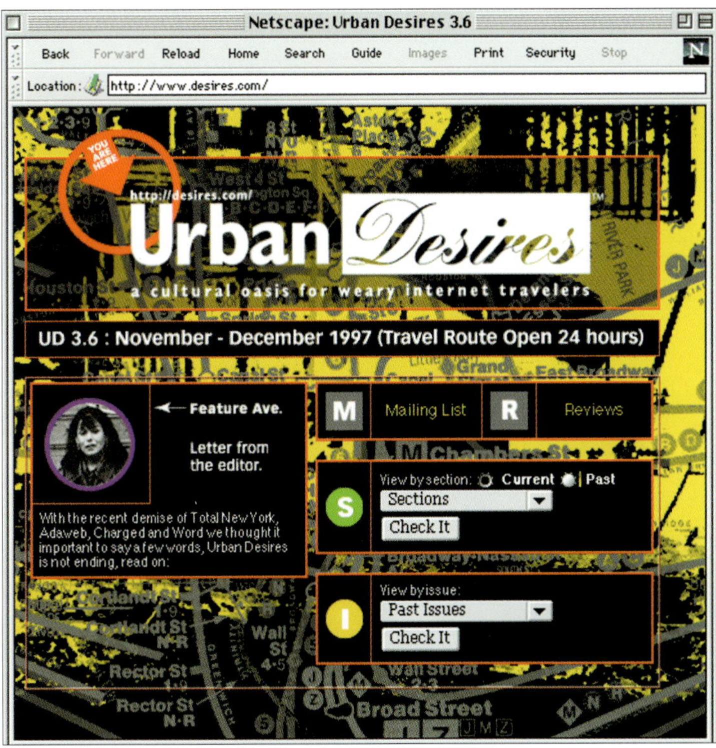

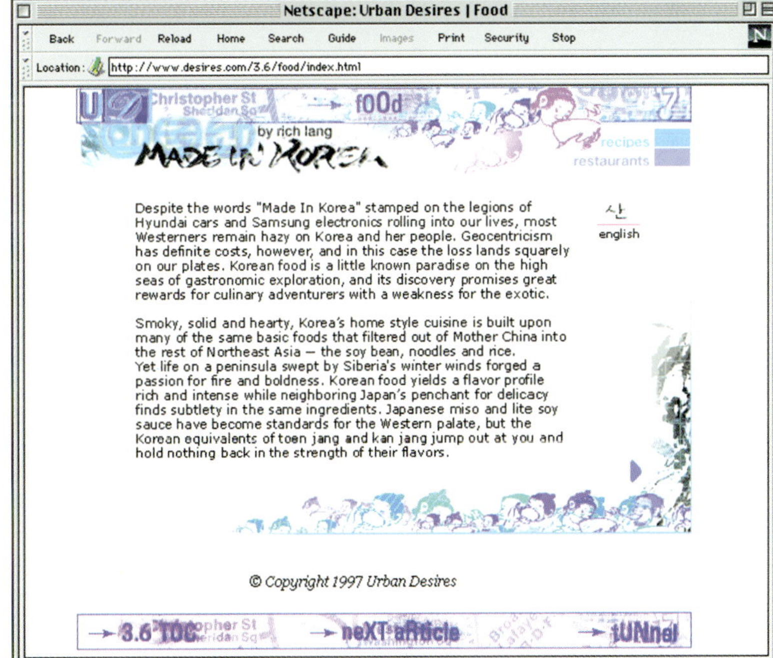

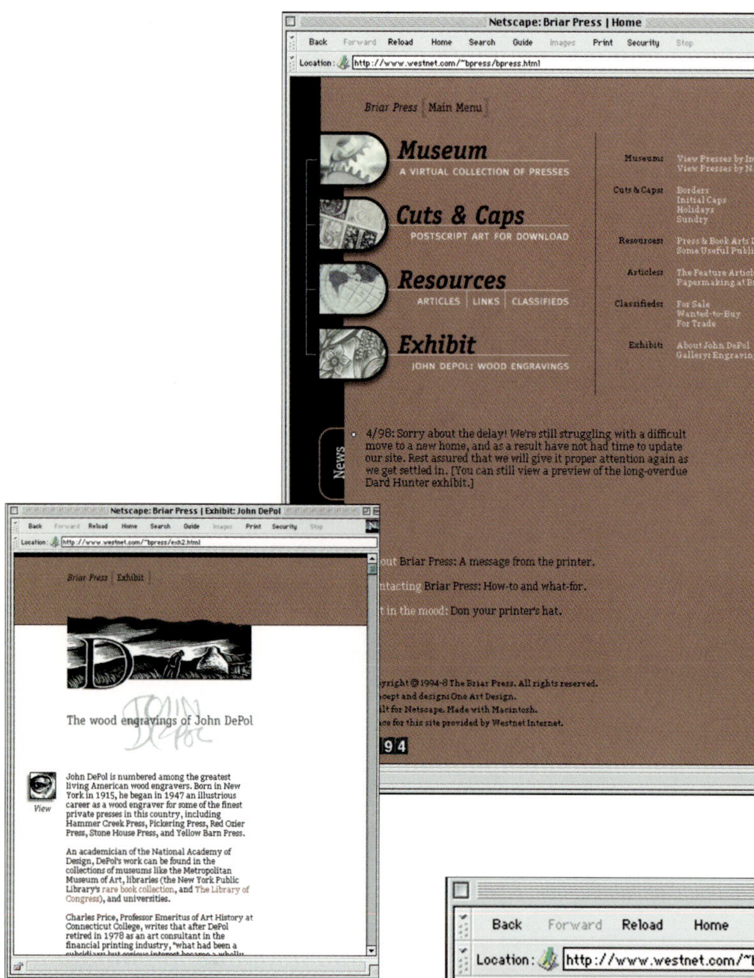

The typography used here is pleasantly muted, drawing only enough attention to the titles as to interest the reader in their context, rather than assaulting one's eye with unnecessary flash. The subtle partial outline around the opening page's letters gives the type a rich dimensional effect of being pressed into heavy material.

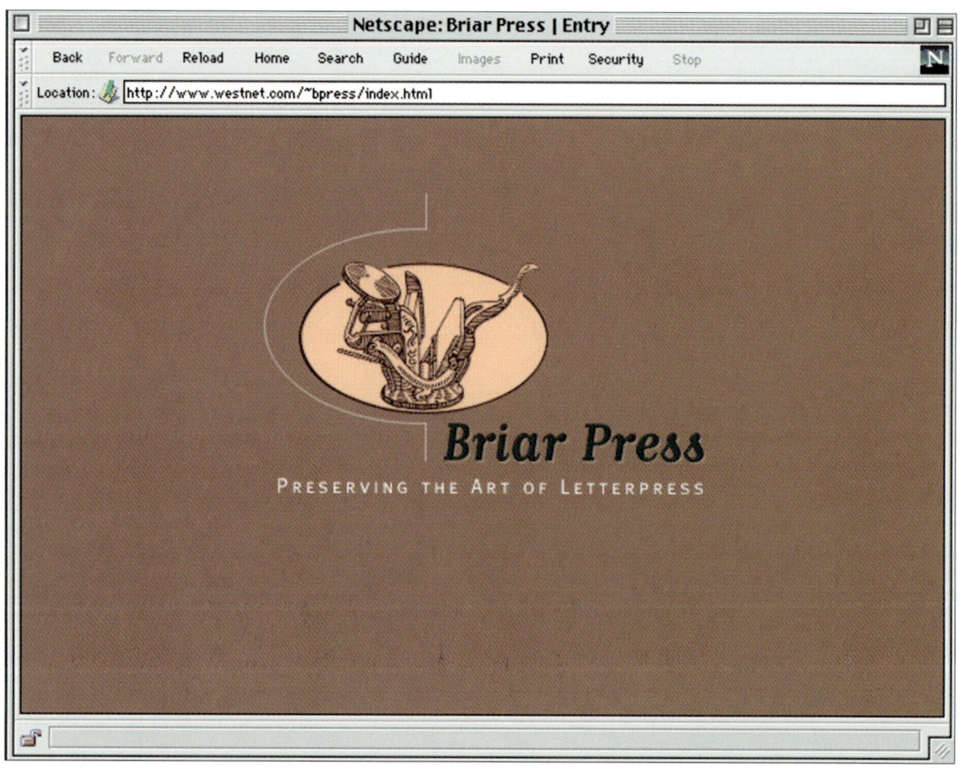

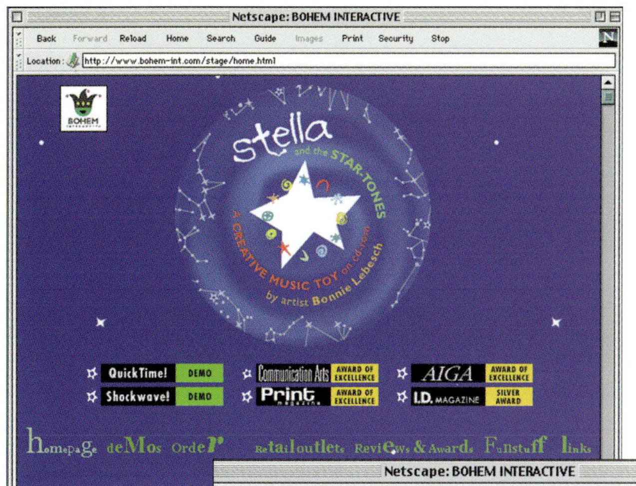

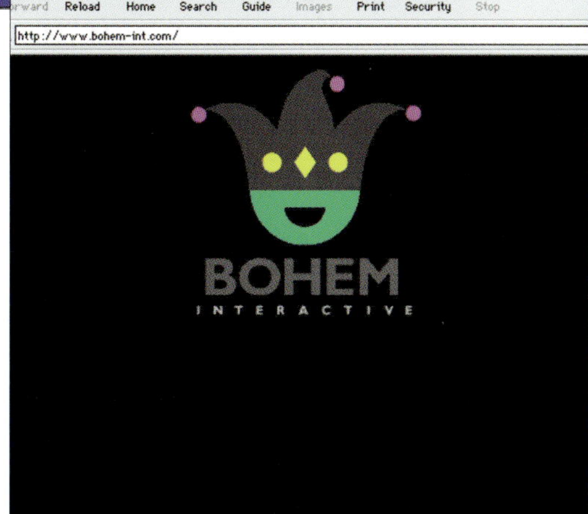

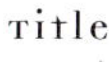

title
  bohem interactive
  URL
    http://www.bohem-int.com/
      design firm
      bohem interactive
        designer/photographer
        bonnie lebesch
          illustrators/programmers
          bonnie lebesch, Don Barnett
          authoring platform
          mac

A site containing child-like typography, it is not until the second viewing that you realize that there really are not any child-like typefaces here at all. Although "stella" includes the random edges associated with such faces, its globular serifs suggest a deliberate hand wielding an overfilled rounded pen. The pages' navigational elements are strictly HTML-formatted text, mixing serif and sans-serif fonts in a variety of sizes and styles.

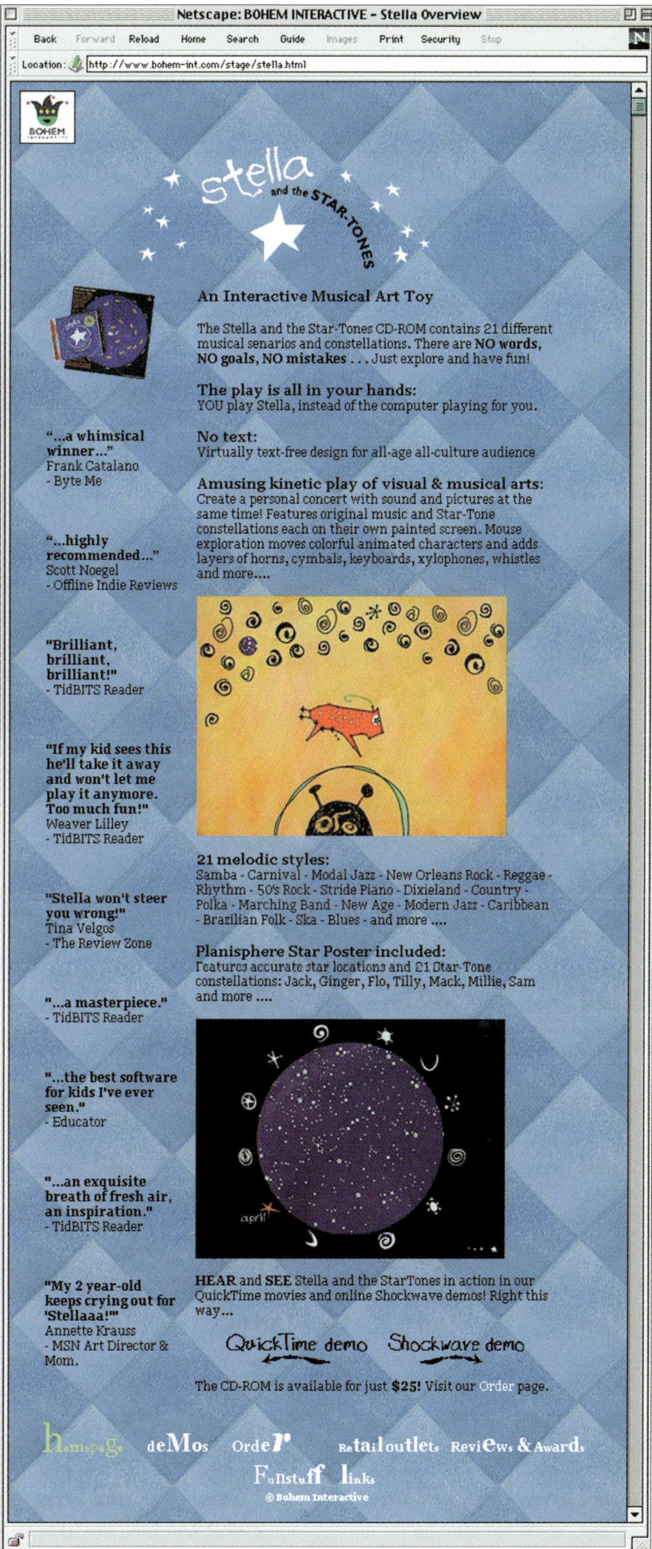

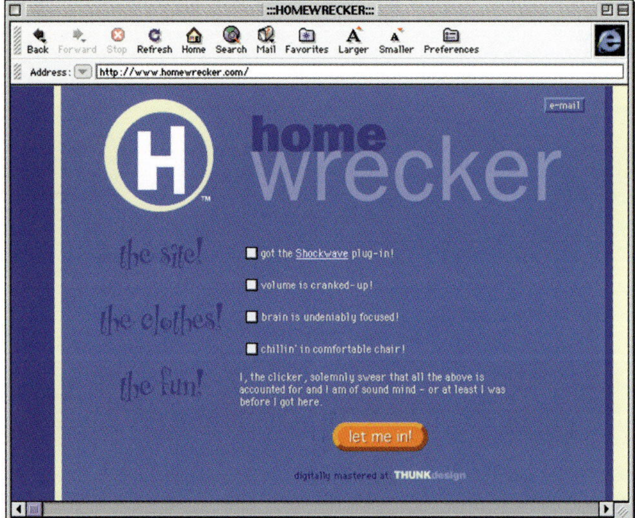

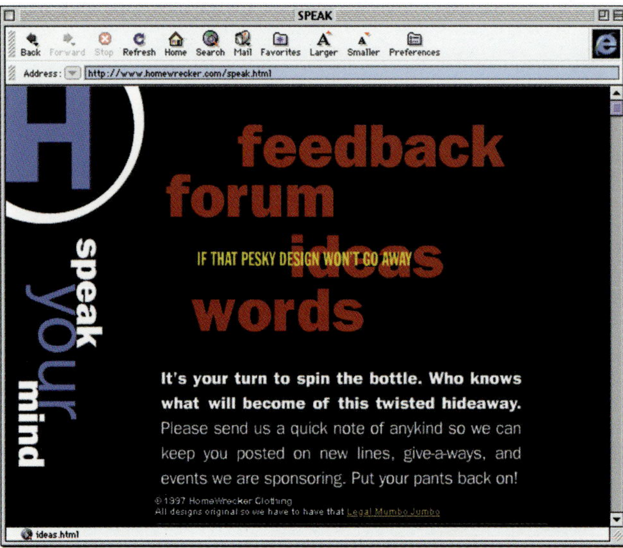

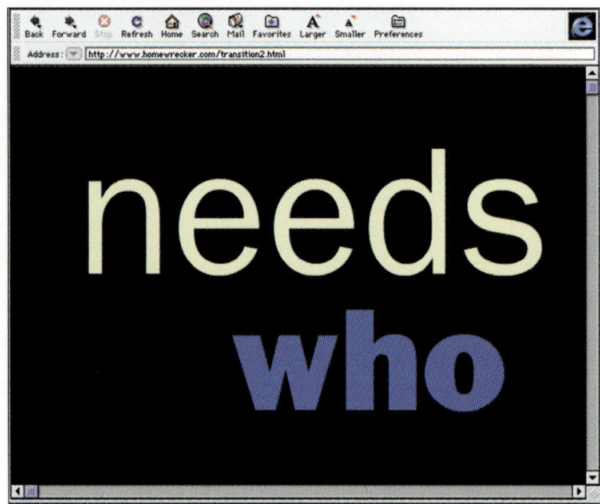

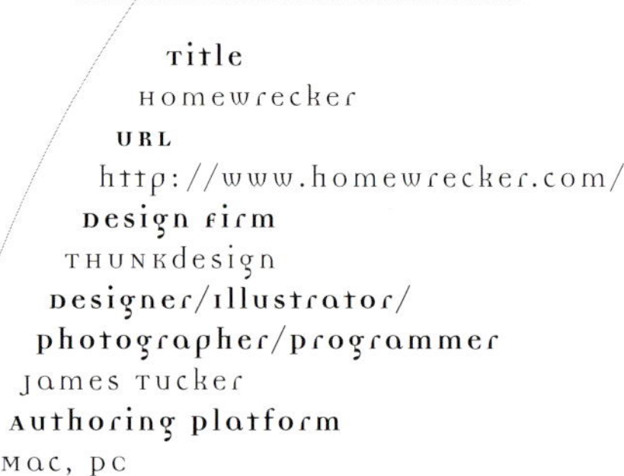

Homewrecker echoes earlier Microsoft
advertising campaigns in type and color,
ricocheting off a world-domination
theme by playing with the typographic
elements. A small Shockwave movie
uses only Helvetica to get the point
across. Nice touches permeate the site;
there's not a page that doesn't create
some visual interest by overlapping,
coloring, or rotating type.

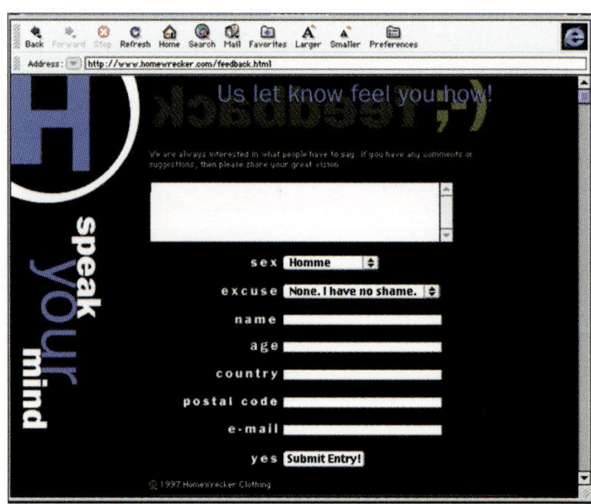

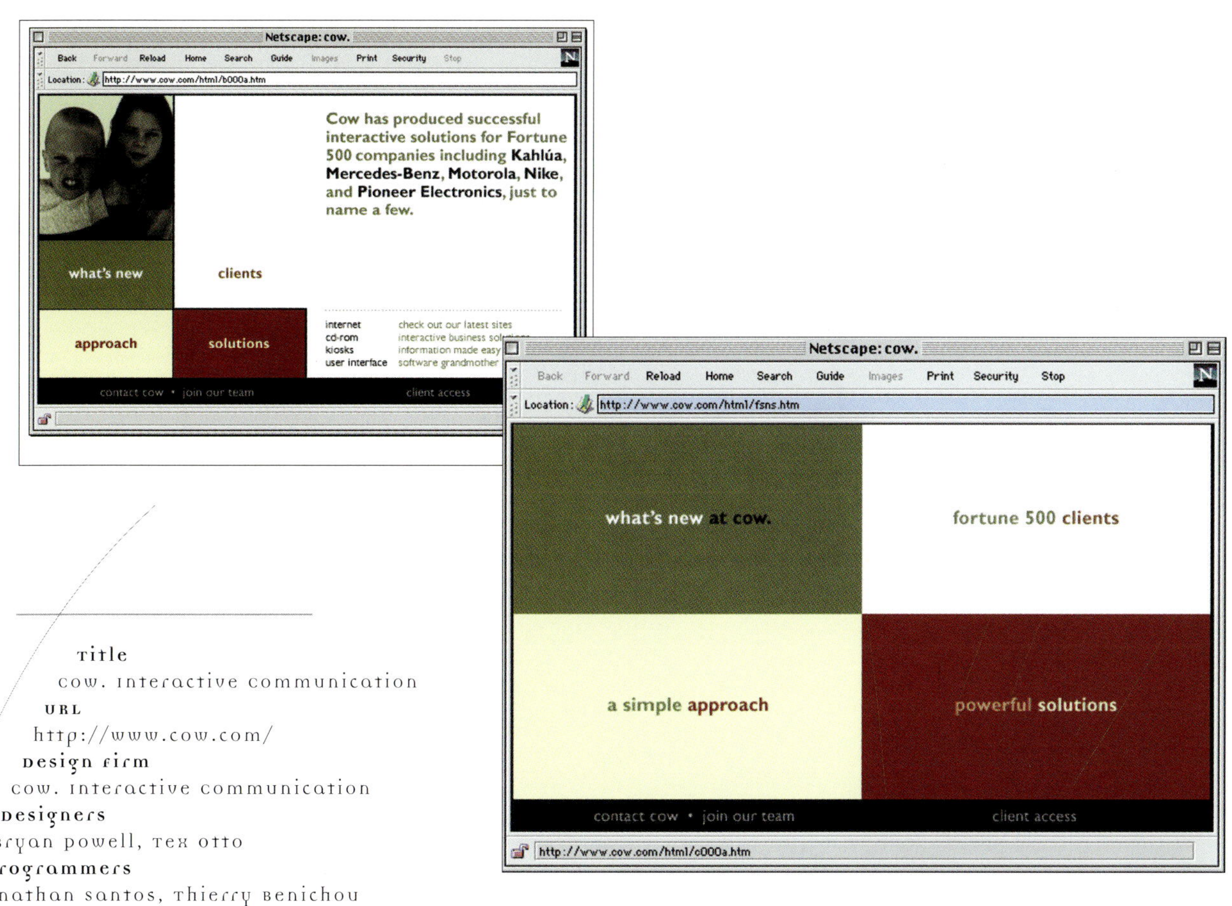

TITLE
cow. interactive communication
URL
http://www.cow.com/
DESIGN FIRM
cow. interactive communication
DESIGNERS
bryan powell, tex otto
PROGRAMMERS
jonathan santos, thierry benichou
ACCOUNT DIRECTOR
drew sievers
CREATIVE DIRECTORS
bryan dorsey, mateo neri
TECHNICAL DIRECTOR
jonathan santos
CONTENT MANAGER
steven lovy
BACKEND ENGINEER
tammy mckean
COPYWRITERS
bryan dorsey, steven lovy,
tom pope, brian higa

These pages excel at demonstrating that you do not always need new typefaces fresh from the foundry in order to make typography work wonders. This site appears to use only one font in various weights and colors, a rounded sans serif that conveys a comfortable mixture of professionalism and creativity.

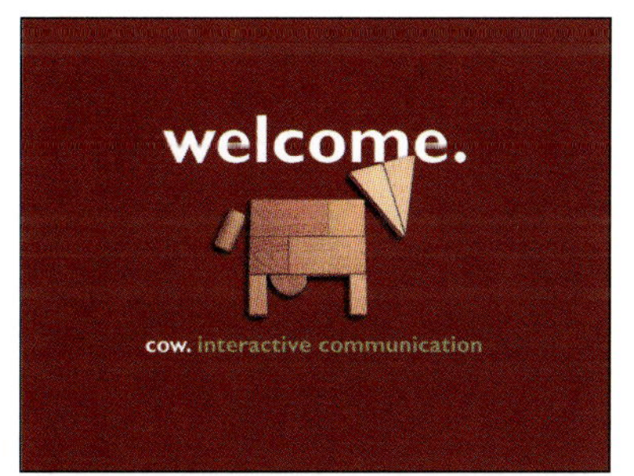

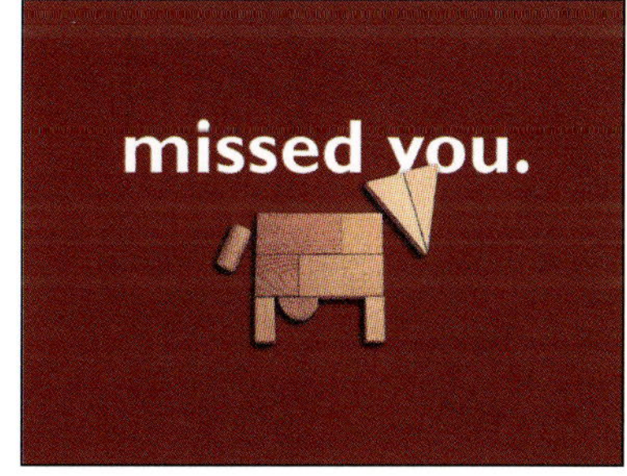

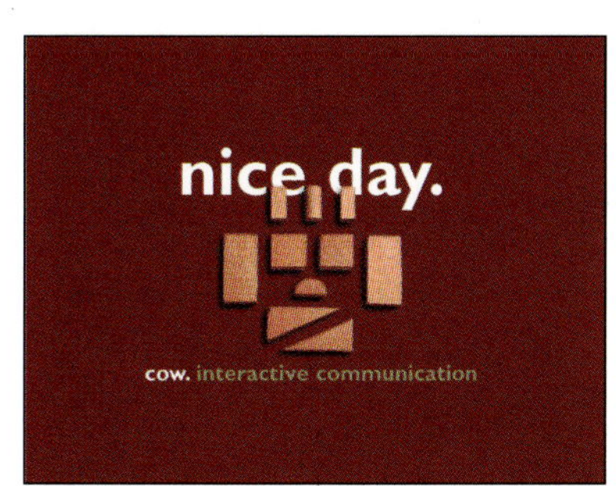

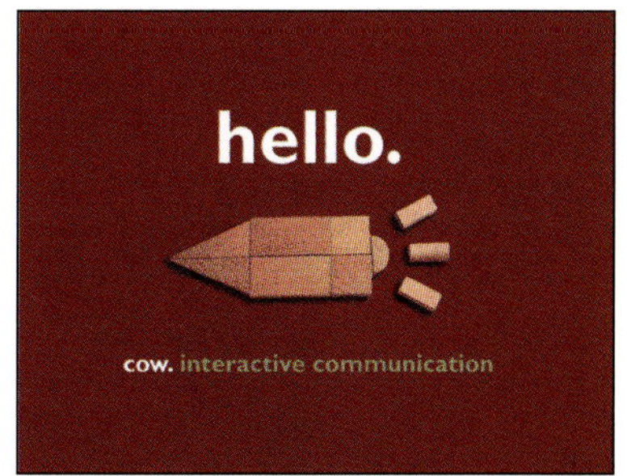

typography

Title
souldanse: Art for the soul
URL
http://www.souldanse.com/melanie/
Designer
Melanie A. Ceraso
Illustrator
Paul Pearson
Photographer
Dave Siekaniec
Programmers
John M. Carlin, Melanie A. Ceraso
Authoring platform
PC

Here's an example of hand-brushed lettering that's been turned into a digital typeface. The designer accents the seemingly spontaneous writing by layering gray over white in the title, and alternating muted colors in the main quote.

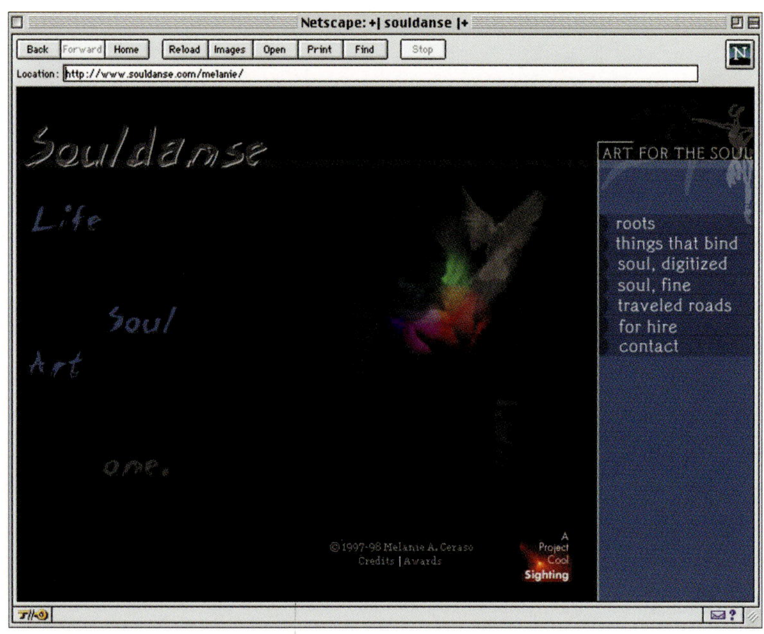

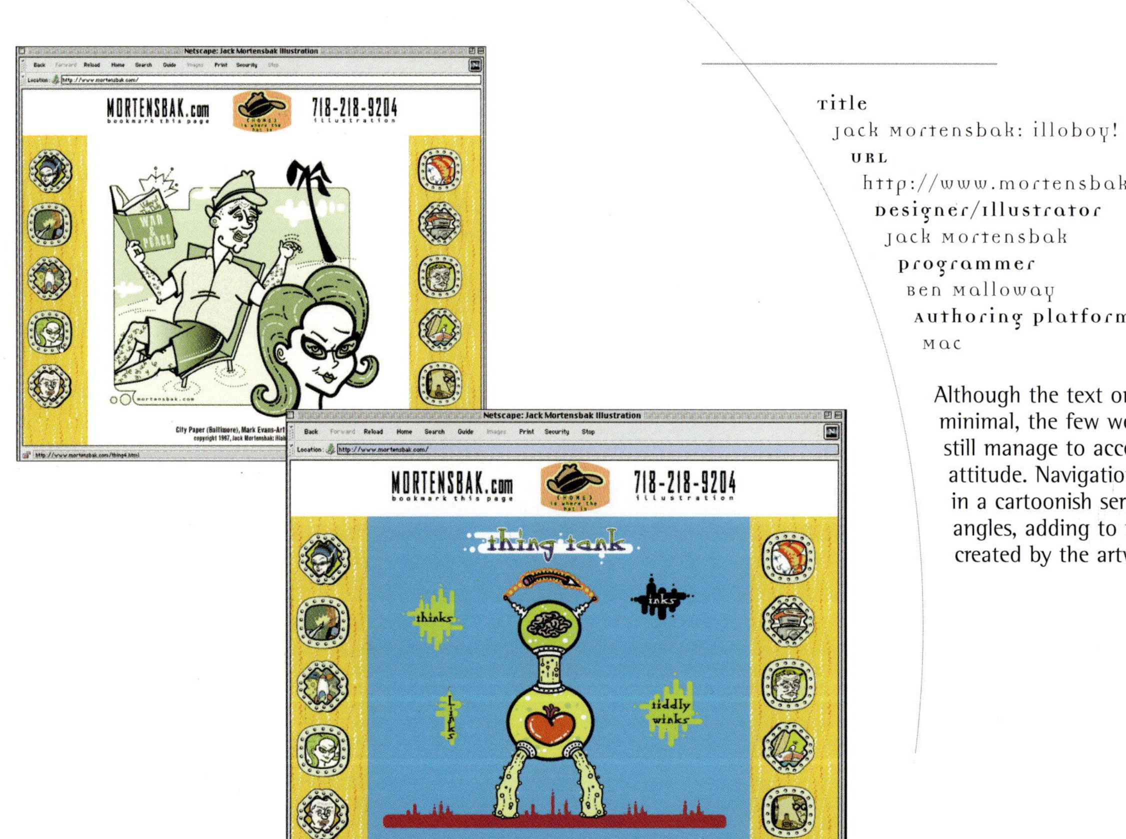

Title
Jack Mortensbak: illoboy!
URL
http://www.mortensbak.com/
Designer/Illustrator
Jack Mortensbak
Programmer
Ben Malloway
Authoring platform
Mac

Although the text on this site is minimal, the few words rendered still manage to accentuate the pages' attitude. Navigational links are set in a cartoonish serif with odd sharp angles, adding to the eccentric feeling created by the artwork.

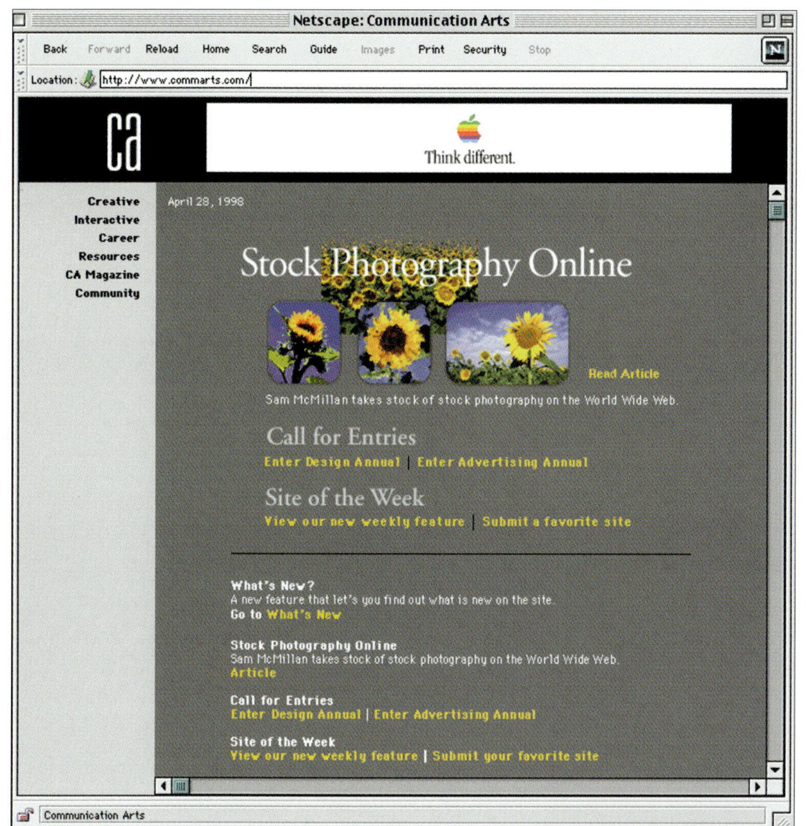

title
communication Arts
URL
http://www.commarts.com/
interactive media Designer
bonnie smetts
interactive media Developer
gary wium
technology Director
jeff stafford
stock photography
photoDisc, inc.
Editors/creative Directors
patrick coyne, jeff stafford
Authoring platform
mac, pc

At first glance, the type on these pages looks bland and featureless, especially if you are used to viewing text on a computer monitor. Closer inspection reveals a deliberate use of fonts designed for onscreen readability, such as the bold Geneva used for the left-hand navigation (note that the words are rendered as graphics, not HTML-based text, for compatibility among various operating systems).

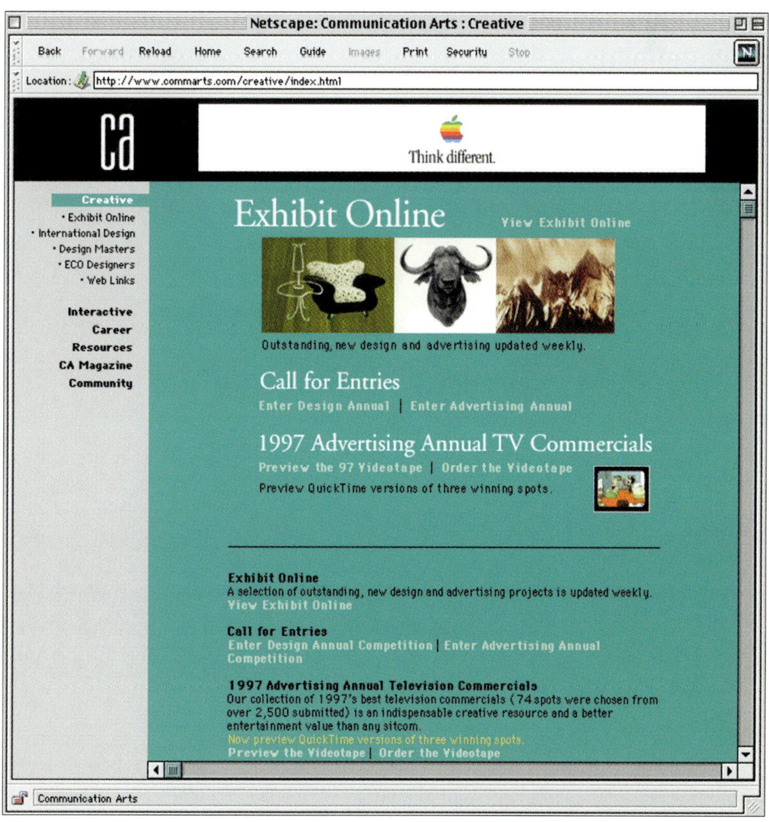

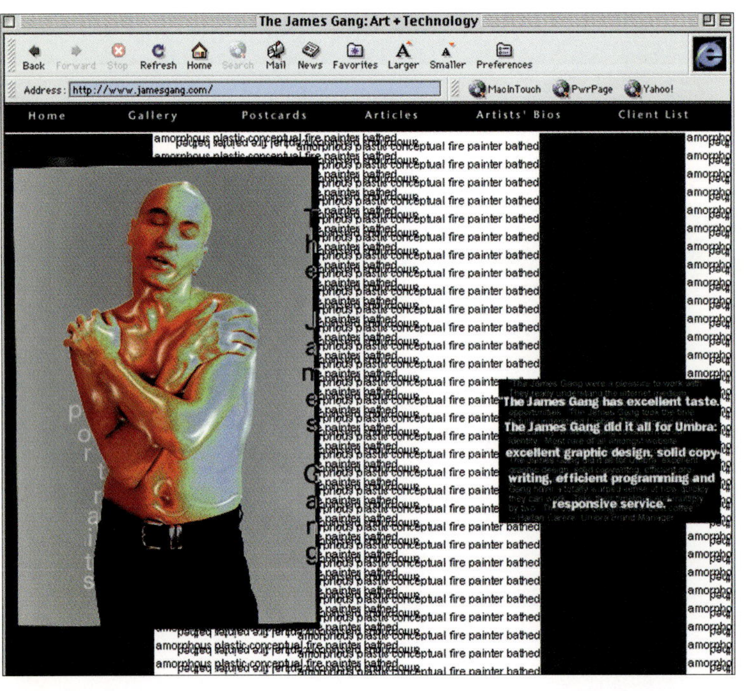

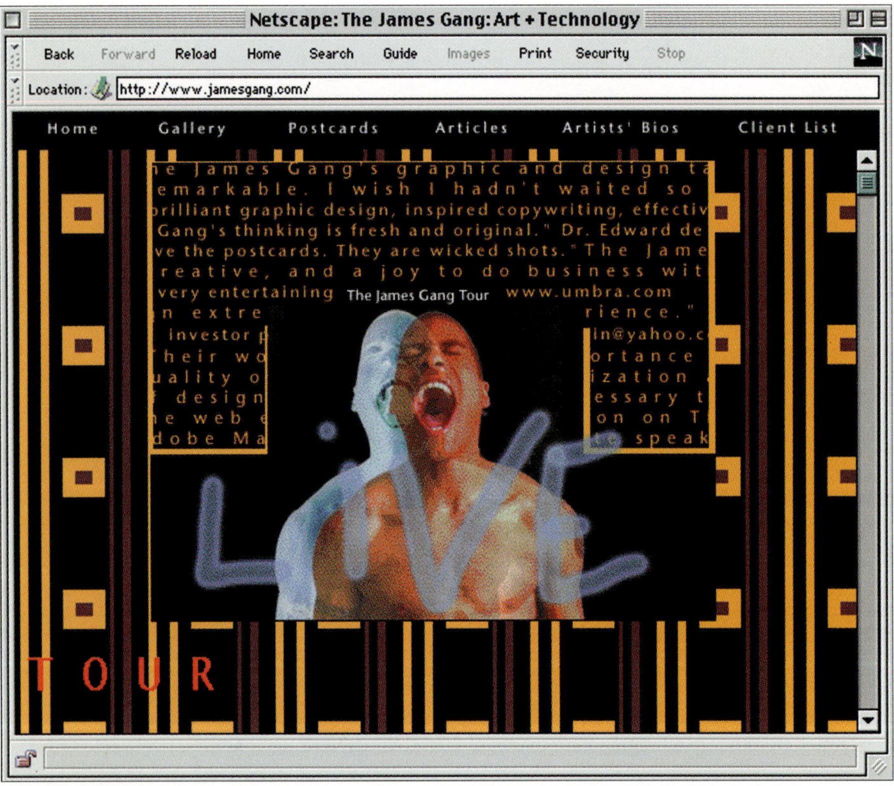

TITLE
The James Gang

URL
http://www.jamesgang.com/

DESIGN FIRM
The James Gang: Art + Technology

DESIGNERS
Franke James, MFA; Bill James

ILLUSTRATOR/PHOTOGRAPHER
Franke James, MFA

PROGRAMMER
Bill James

MODEL
Bonnae (Ford Models)

AUTHORING PLATFORM
Mac

Type works here both as texture and as a highlight to the diversity of styles this design firm offers. From the overlaid repetition of the main page's background, to the liberally letterspaced quotes adorning the tour page, you get the idea that you're not likely to find minor variations of just one single vision.

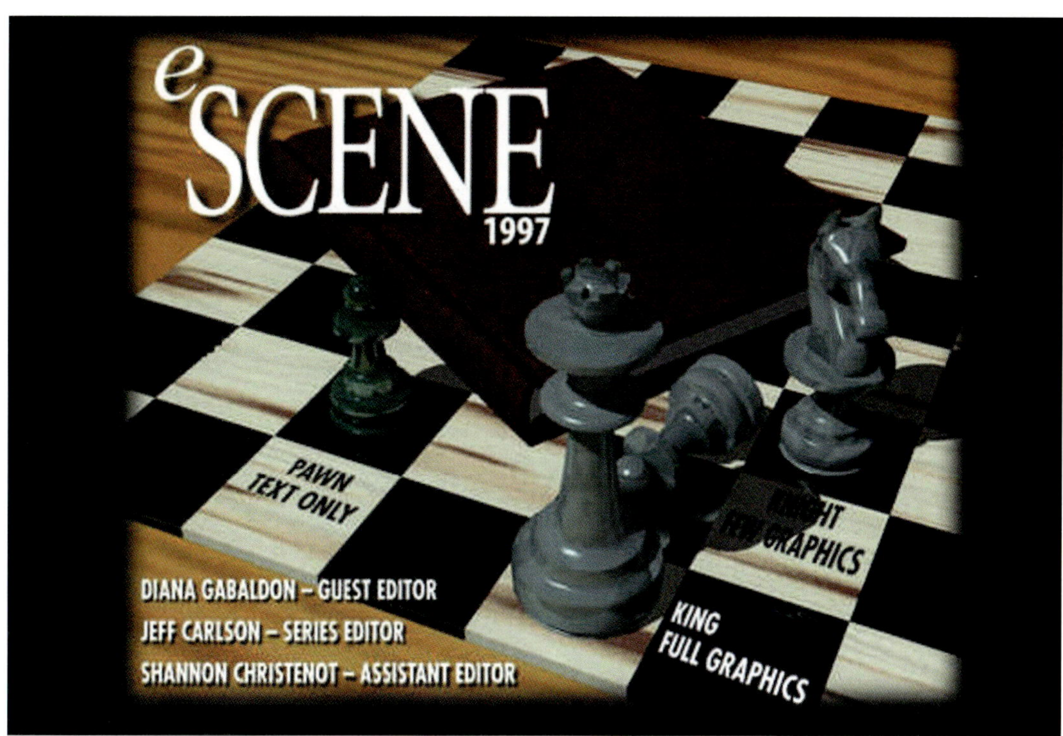

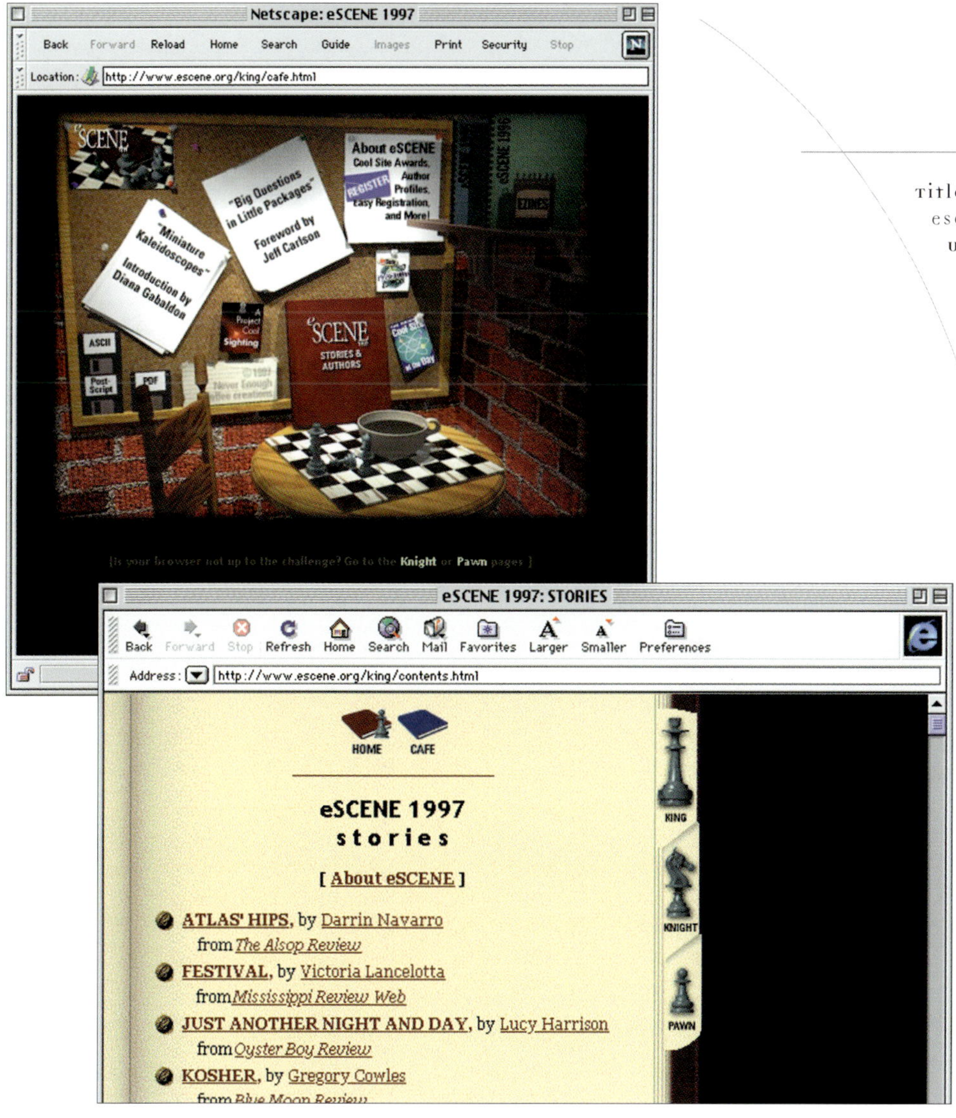

Title
eSCENE

URL
http://www.escene.org/

Design firm
Never Enough Coffee Creations

Designer/Illustrator/Programmer
Jeff Carlson

Authoring platform
Mac

Most type is rendered, but eSCENE suggests something for the rest of its look that few sites dare: It notes that you can download special fonts (for free) that will make the site look better. Using special fonts, but not requiring them, is a strategy that works for an audience that's going to be involved with the work, either reading or printing the short stories featured on the site. To improve readability, Cascading Stylesheets are used on story pages to increase leading.

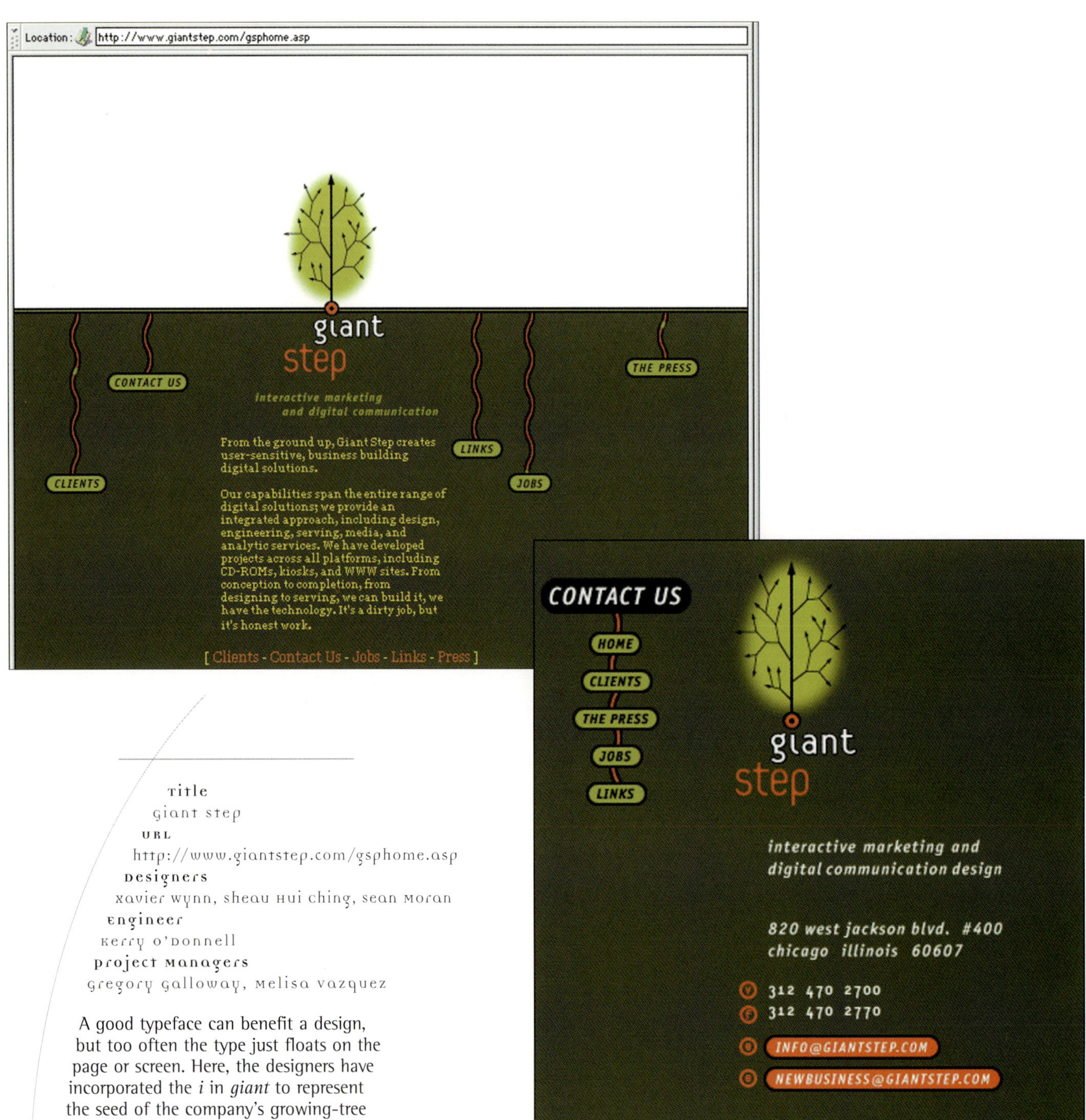

Title
Giant Step

URL
http://www.giantstep.com/gsphome.asp

Designers
Xavier Wynn, Sheau Hui Ching, Sean Moran

Engineer
Kerry O'Donnell

Project Managers
Gregory Galloway, Melisa Vazquez

A good typeface can benefit a design, but too often the type just floats on the page or screen. Here, the designers have incorporated the *i* in *giant* to represent the seed of the company's growing-tree logo. Note also that *giant* isn't very giant at all, though its size and placement suggest larger things for the future.

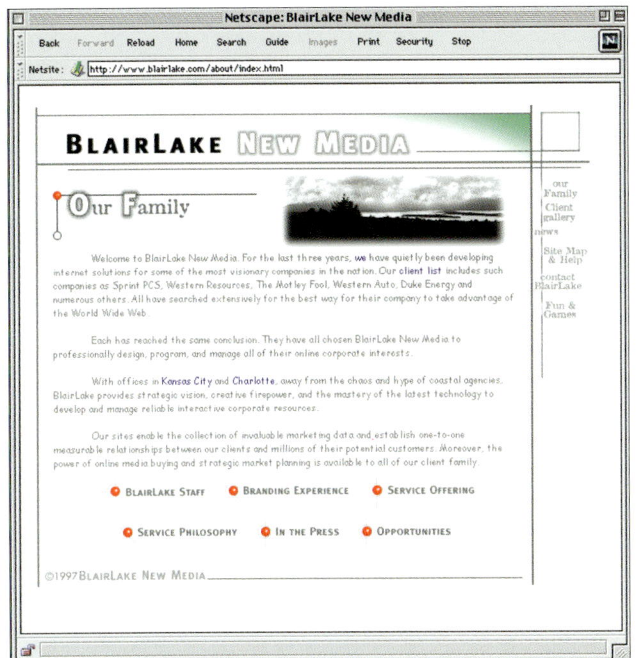

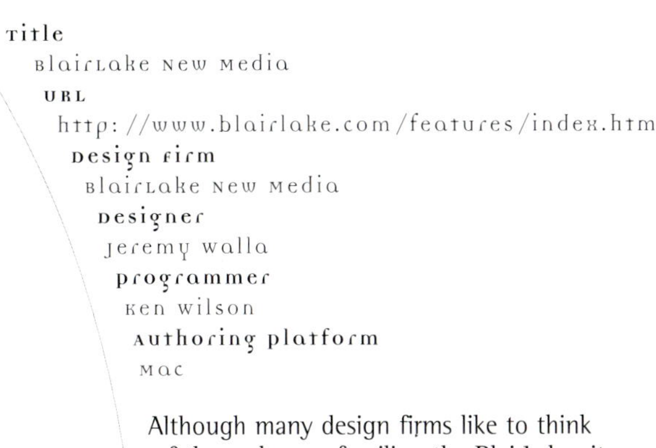

Although many design firms like to think of themselves as families, the BlairLake site tries to extend the concept of a small, friendly design house throughout their site. One method of reinforcing that idea is by using the Web-friendly font Comic Sans for body text; while remaining legible, it also carries a slightly informal attitude with it.

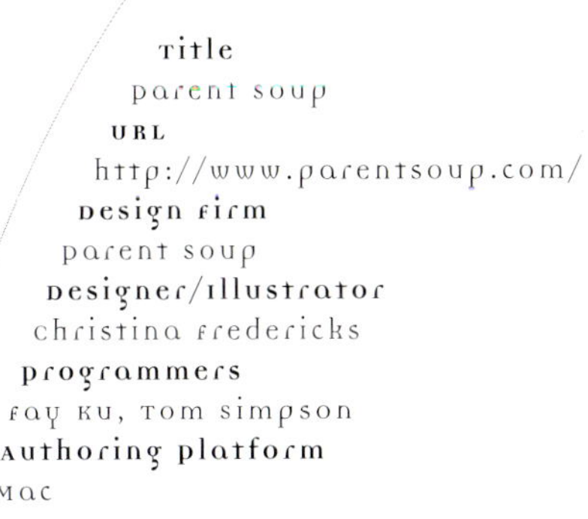

Parent Soup makes Poster Bodoni seem like an exclamation. Instead of using one typeface for much of the navigation, Parent Soup stirs in a simple, light sans serif with the world's most circus-like typeface. They have avoided the common trap of having to name categories with single words by putting the differentiating word (*expecting* in *expecting parents*) in the Bodoni, and putting the explanatory word or words (*parents*) in the plainer type.

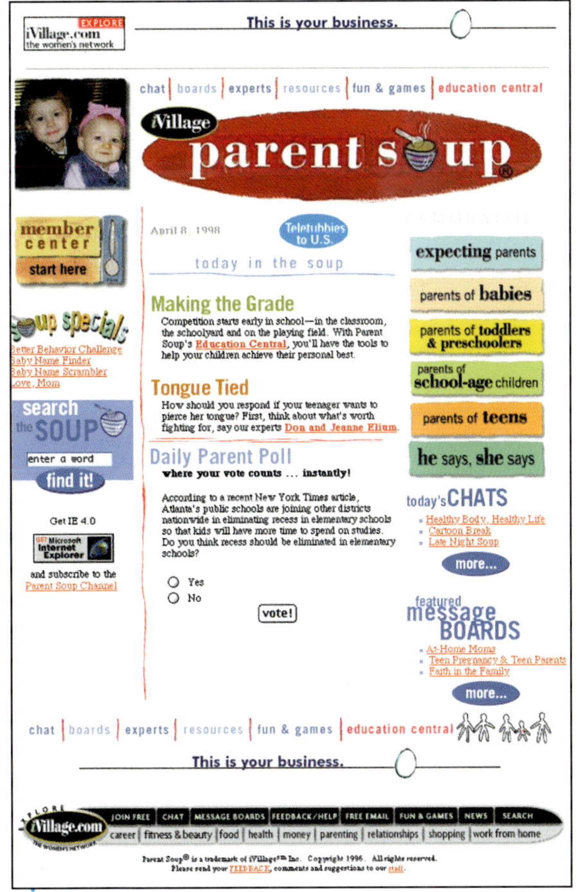

title
boxtop software, inc.

url
http://www.boxtopsoft.com/

design firm
mwb interactive/invisible, ink

designer
ed sultan, invisible, ink

illustrators
daniel thomas, mwb interactive;
ed sultan, invisible, ink;
travis anton, boxtop software, inc.

photographer
travis anton, boxtop software, inc.

programmers
html—ed sultan, invisible, ink;
travis anton, boxtop software, inc.;
cgi—danny lowe, boxtop software, inc;
travis anton, boxtop software, inc.;
java—open cube technologies

producer/writer
travis anton, boxtop software, inc.

authoring platform
mac

Because of the use of intercaps (capital letters in the middle of words) and intermittent capitalization, the large headline type used for each product becomes almost a logotype: a typographic element that serves as a graphical one, too.

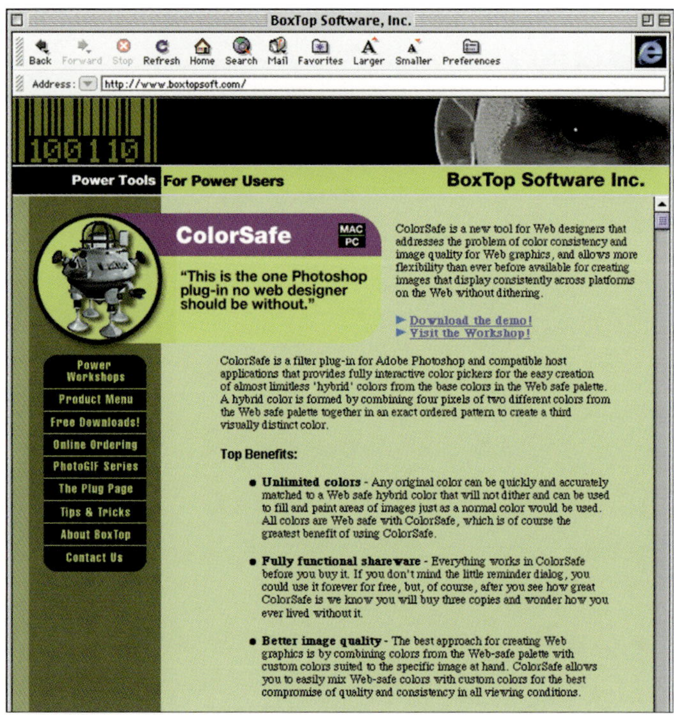

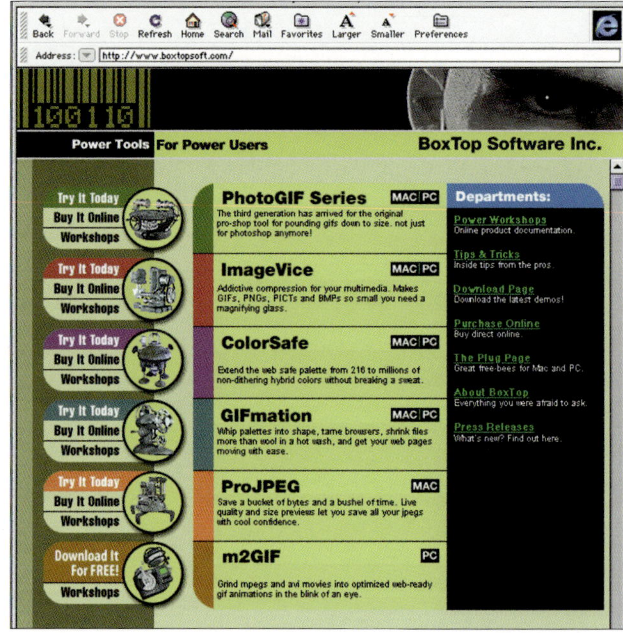

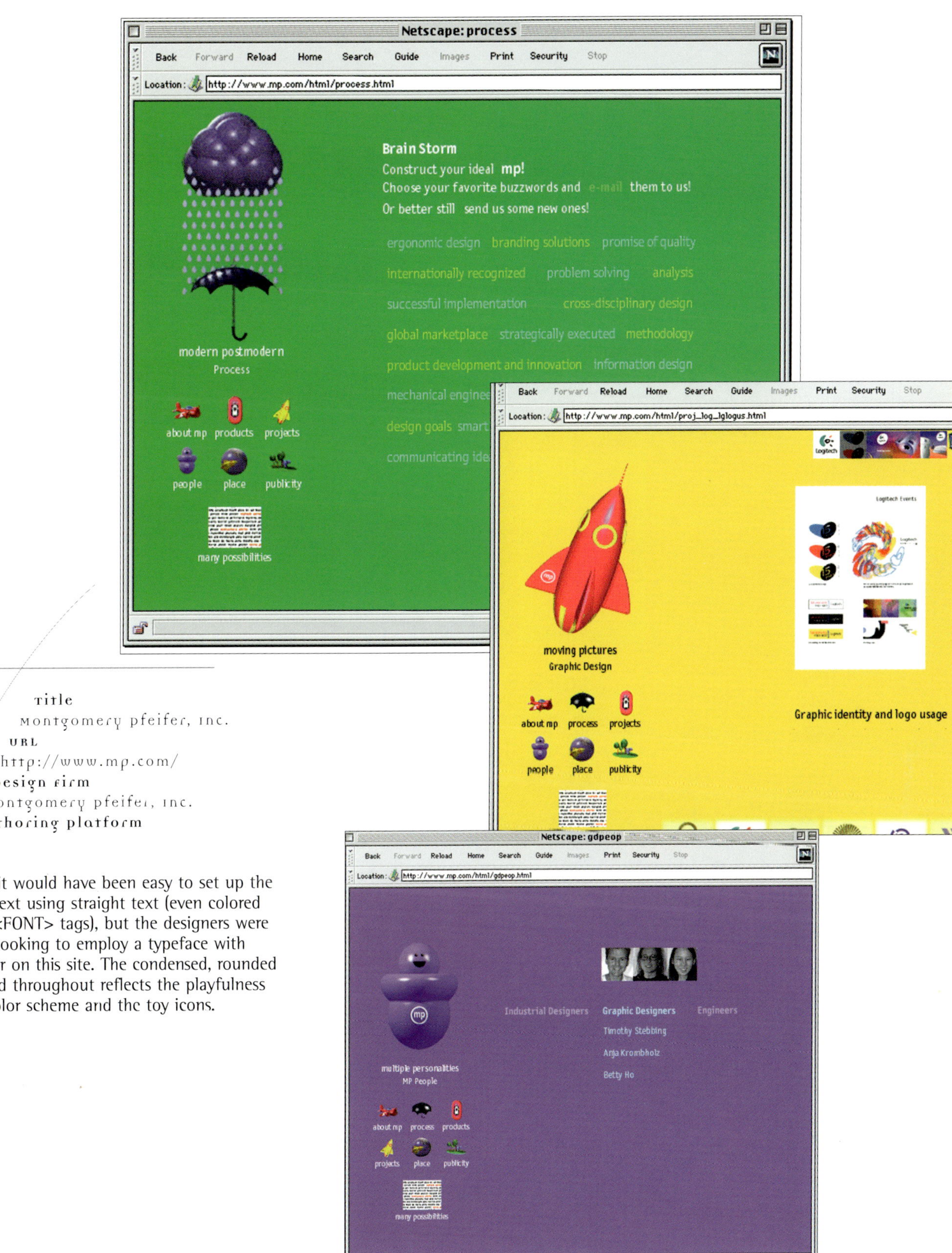

title
Montgomery Pfeifer, Inc.
URL
http://www.mp.com/
Design Firm
Montgomery Pfeifer, Inc.
Authoring Platform
Mac

Sure, it would have been easy to set up the body text using straight text (even colored using <FONT> tags), but the designers were clearly looking to employ a typeface with character on this site. The condensed, rounded font used throughout reflects the playfulness of the color scheme and the toy icons.

title
yale-new haven medical center
url
http://info.med.yale.edu/index.html
design firm
center for advanced instructional media,
yale university
designer/illustrator
patrick j. lynch
photographer
yale university biomedical communications
programmer
sean jackson
authoring platform
mac

This site uses type that varies little in size, is
sufficiently differentiated through placements
and color to avoid having to use lots of emphasis
(bold, italic, etc.), sizes, and heading styles.
Headings are typically in the same gray used
for the top navigation bar. A sans serif and
serif face are used for slightly different purposes.
Main headings are gray and sans serif as
are the navigation elements and noteworthy
items on the left.

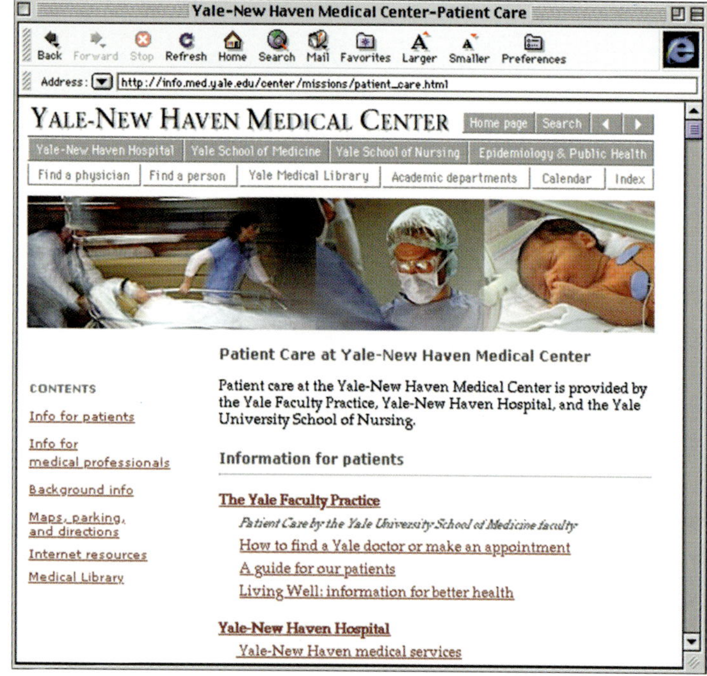

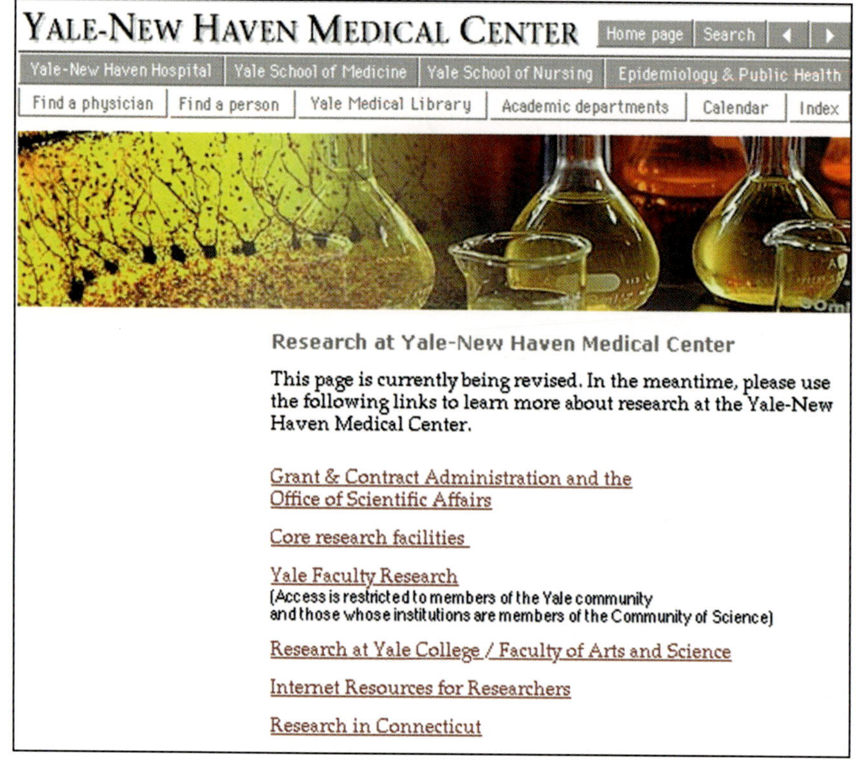

Title
typographic.com
URL
http://www.typographic.com/
Design firm
typographic.com
Designer/illustrator/programmer
Jimmy Chen
Authoring platform
Mac

Approaching illegibility, typographic.com pushes against the limits of what acceptable typography can be. Some elements are just perverse, such as the bottom navigation bar, where the labels for the sections aren't where the links are. Instead, they're jumbled on top of each in dim colors at the far left. A client list has the type flipped horizontally, while the client names themselves are overscored with black lines and surrounded by fuzz—a repeated theme.

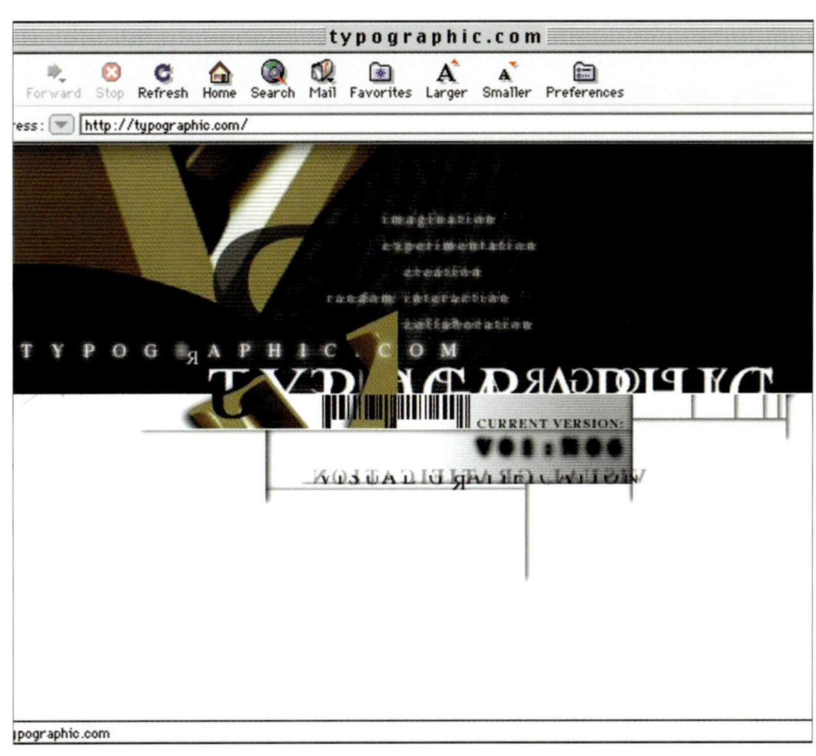

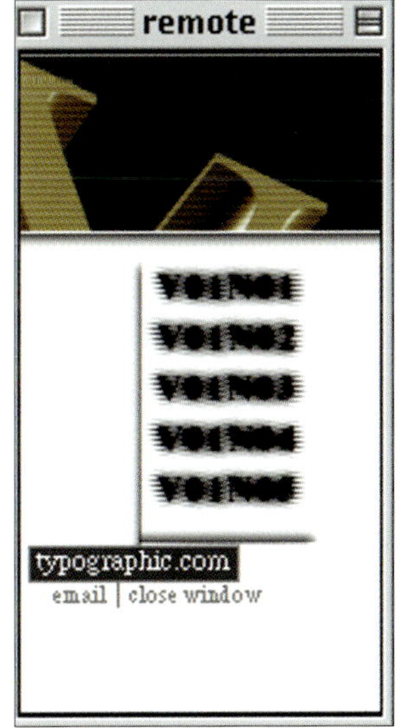

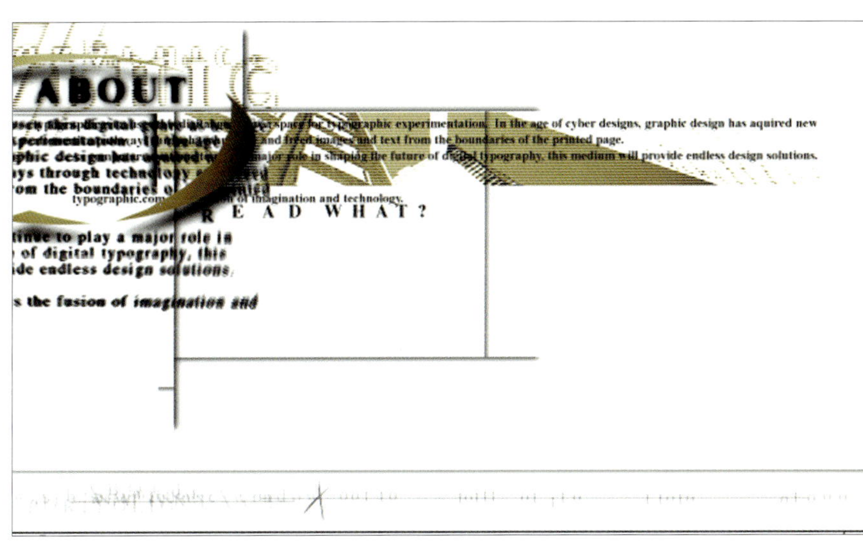

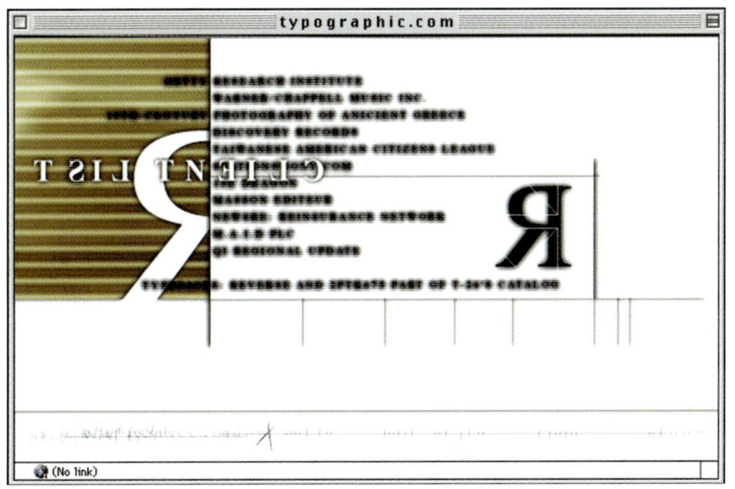

About the Authors

Jeff Carlson

Jeff spent several years doing desktop publishing before jumping into the Web publishing arena by founding and editing *eSCENE*, the Internet's only yearly anthology of the best short fiction appearing on the Web. A stint as Managing Editor at a small Seattle-based book publisher convinced Adam and Tonya Engst that they should tap him for the same position at the widely-read newsletter *TidBITS*. Jeff has published articles in *HOW Magazine, Macworld,* and *Adobe Magazine,* and was a contributing editor and columnist for Adobe's online venture, *adobe.mag.* He is also the author of *The Palm III/PalmPilot Visual QuickStart Guide.* In addition to writing and editing, he's an accomplished Web designer and consultant through his company Never Enough Coffee creations. People around him seem to possess strong urges to constantly ask him questions. <http://www.necoffee.com>.

Toby Malina

In 1995 Toby joined Thunder Lizard Productions, a Seattle-based conference production company, as Editorial/Technical Director. At Thunder Lizard, she worked in collaboration with the editorial staff and outside experts in the desktop publishing and Web design fields to develop editorial content for The Photoshop Conference, The Adobe Internet Conferences, and Web Design: HTML and Beyond, amongst many others. In addition, Toby was responsible for the coordination and execution of all conference audio visual including computer systems, lighting, sound, and projection. If it broke, she fixed it. In 1997 she served as product manager for Technique: Digital Artists at Work and The PageMaker Summit.

For the past ten years, Toby has also worked independently as a graphic designer and Macintosh consultant. Her multi-faceted roles have included art director, production artist, MIS manager, software/systems trainer, and mental health professional. Her greatest triumph: wrenching a motherboard from the jaws of a client's basset hound and successfully reseating it.

Glenn Fleishman

Glenn Fleishman has written about technology and its use in several publications, including *InfoWorld* and *NetGuide.* He was a founding contributing editor and columnist at the print edition of *Web Developer* (now only found on the Web), and is a contributing editor and columnist for *Adobe Magazine,* where he writes the Web Watcher column. Glenn was course manager at the legendary Kodak Center for Creative Imaging in Camden, Maine, and later worked doing scanning and color correction at a showcase imaging center nearby, High Resolution Inc. Glenn later worked as a managing editor for Open House, where he technical- and copy-edited several books for Peachpit. He founded one of the first web development companies, Point of Presence Company (POPCO), offering firms Web site programming and hosting. While at POPCO, he helped broadcast the first feature film over the Internet. Glenn worked briefly as a senior manager at Amazon.com Books; while there as catalog manager, he was responsible for increasing the catalog from 1 million to 2.5 million titles. He now works as a consultant, conference chair, writer, and itinerant perl programmer, and recently co-authored the second edition of *Real World Scanning and Halftones.* <http://www. glenns.org>

AdEra Digital Media AB
Ostra Hamngatan 41-43
41110 Gotenburg
Sweden

agi business media
productions GmbH
Falkertstrasse 71/2
70176 Stuttgart
Germany

Atlas Web Design
1201 B Howard Street
San Francisco, CA 94103

Barclay Web
16, rue des Fosses
St.-Jacques
75005 Paris, France

Bau-Da Design Lab, Inc.
480 Canal Street #11024
New York, NY 10013

beyondexpress.com
19 Delaware Avenue
Delhi, NY 13753

Bianca Troll Productions
P. O. Box 78097
San Francisco, CA 94107

BlairLake New Media
104 West 42nd Street
Kansas City, MO 64111

Blind Visual Propaganda
2020 North Main Street
#235
Los Angeles, CA 90031

Blue Marlin
540 Florida Street
San Francisco, CA 94110

Bohem Interactive
2226 Eastlake Avenue
Suite 61
Seattle, WA 98102

Boxtop Software, Inc.
101 North Lafayette Street
Starkville, MS 39759

Center for Advanced
Instructional Media, Yale
University
47 College Street
New Haven, CT 06510

Circumstance Design
164 Townsend, #4
San Francisco, CA 94107

Citrus 21
49 Cromwell Road
Great Glen, Leicester
LE8 9GU United Kingdom

Communications Arts
410 Sherman Avenue
Palo Alto, CA 94306

Construct Internet
Design
448 Bryant Street
San Francisco, CA 94107

Contempt Productions
144 West 23rd Street
#11C
New York, NY 10011

Core77
561 Broadway
6th Floor
New York, NY 10012

cow.Interactive
Communications
1522 Cloverfield
Boulevard
Suite E
Santa Monica, CA 90404

DDB Interactive
3500 Maple Avenue
Suite 250
Dallas, TX 75219

DeForm
1531 India Street
San Diego, CA 92101

Dreamless Studios
1 Keystone Avenue #36
Cherry Hill, NJ 08003

Electric Ocean
53 Wale Street
8001 Cape Town
South Africa

Elliott/Dickens
97 South Second Street
Suite 220
San Jose, CA 95113

eLogic Communications
1608 Pacific Avenue
Suite 203
Venice, CA 90291

Emergent Media, Inc.
1809 7th Avenue
Suite 908
Seattle, WA 98101

enviromedia, Inc.
617 Vine Street
Suite 1336
Cincinnati, OH 45202

Fabric8 Productions
P. O. Box 420794
San Francisco, CA 94142

52mm
12 John Street
10th Floor
New York, NY 10038

Fractal Cow Studio
2 Achilles Street
Acropolis, Libia
Quezon City, Metro
Manila
Philippines, 1100

Funny Garbage
73 Spring Street
Suite 605
New York, NY 10012

Giant Robot
811 Traction Avenue #1C
Los Angeles, CA 90013

Giant Step
820 West Jackson
Suite 400
Chicago, IL 60607

Goblin Design
Josef-Reiertstrasse 4
69190 Walldorf
Germany

Gr8
2400 Boston Street
3rd Floor
Baltimore, MD 21224

Kha Hoang
305 Franklin Street #21
San Francisco, CA 94102

HyperHead New Media
P. O. Box 367
Dana Point, CA 92609

The Iconfactory
1 Moss Cove Court
Greensboro, NC 27407

Jack Mortensbak
P. O. Box 2510
New York, NY 10009

The James Gang
3080 Yonge Street
Suite 5044
Toronto, Ontario
M4N 3N3 Canada

JASON Foundation
395 Totten Pond Road
Waltham, MA 02154

Jessica Helfand/William
Drenttel
P. O. Box 159
Falls Village, CT 06031

Jetset Design
Gerardus Gullaan 4
1217 LN Hilversam
The Netherlands

Kjetil Vatne Graphics +
Design
Langarinden 407
N-5090, Nyborg
Norway

KMTT-FM
1100 Olive Way #1650
Seattle, WA 98101

Knight Errant Design
8948 SW Barbur
Boulevard
Suite 168
Portland, OR 97219

MCO Digital Productions
2226 York Avenue,
Suite 3
Vancouver, British
Columbia
M5K 1K4 Canada

Montgomery Pfeifer, Inc.
461 Bush Street
San Francisco, CA 94108

Mike Motz
Anythyme Web Design
60 MacEwan Meadow
Way NW
Alberta, Canada

N2K Entertainment
55 Broad Street
New York, NY 10004

Never Enough Coffee
Creations
1619 Eighth Avenue
North
Seattle, WA 98109

One Art Design
P. O. Box 490
Briarcliff, NY 10510

Parent Soup
170 Fifth Avenue
New York, NY 10010

Phinney/Bischoff Design
House, Inc.
614 Boylstone
Seattle, WA 98102

Pittard Sullivan
3535 Hayden Avenue
Culver City, CA 90232

Pixel Productions UK
39 Ripley Gardens
London SW14 8HF
United Kingdom

Planet Interactive, Inc.
36 Drydock Avenue
Boston, MA

Prophet Communications
355 Bryant Street #109
San Francisco, CA 94107

pulse.interactive
Roemer Visscherstraat 42
1054 EZ Amsterdam
The Netherlands

Qaswa Communications
423 Washington Street
Floor 5
San Francisco, CA 84111

Saksi, Miika
P. O. Box 262
Helsinki FIN-00171
Finland

Salon Magazine
706 Mission Street
2nd Floor
San Francisco, CA 94040

sfstation
3528 17th Street
San Francisco, CA 94110

signalgrau design bureau
Vadenspelderstrasse 42
45142 Essen
Germany

Souldanse Digital Design
33 Braxton Lane
Aurora, IL 60504

Stagebill
144 East 44
7th Floor
New York, NY 10017

Studiomotiv
300 Marconi Boulevard
Columbus, OH 43215

Sub Pop Records
1932 1st Avenue
Suite 1103
Seattle, WA 98101

Syndetic Design
1302 White Dove Cove
Cedar Park, TX 78613

Teknoland
Almirante, 16 1st Floor
28004 Madrid
Spain

That's Interactive
7th Floor
206 Prince Edward Road
West
Kowloon, Hong Kong

The James Gang
3080 Yonge Street
Suige 5044
Toronto, Ontario
M4N 3N3 Canada

THUNKdesign
293 Missouri Street
San Francisco, CA 94107

Tony Shasteen
Illustration & Design
1079 Megan Court
Sugar Hill, GA 30518

Tim Trompeter
28 East 10th Street, 9B
New York, NY 10003

Typographic.com
557 Dolores Street
San Francisco, CA 94110

Joshua Ulm
525 Brannan Street
Ground Floor
San Francisco, CA 94107

Urban Desires
665 Broadway
Suite 504
New York, NY 10012

US Web
139 Richmond Street
El Segundo, CA 90245

Will-Harris House
Box 1235
Pt. Reyes, CA 94956